GOLDEN JAGUAR OF THE SUN

BY

OLIVER EADE

FIRST BOOK OF THE
BEAST TO GOD TRILOGY

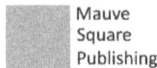

Mauve
Square
Publishing

www.mauvesquare.com

For Yvonne Wei-Lun

'And the beast which I saw was like a leopard with feet like the feet of a bear and it had the mouth of a lion...'

Book of Revelation 13:1

Tezcatlipoca ('Smoking Mirror') The first of the Aztec gods to assume the sun on earth, he was also the deity of night sky, hurricanes, conflict and his *nagual* (animal spirit) was the jaguar.

Quetzalcóatl ('Plumed Serpent') The brother of Tezcatlipoca, both sons of the Creator Gods. He was usually associated with goodness and positive attributes.

Nahuatl The language of the Aztecs, now spoken, together with other Nahua languages, by the indigenous Nahua people of Mexico.

Tenochtitlan Aztec Island City State on Lake Texcoco, capital of the Aztec Empire prior to the Spanish conquest.

Tlaxcala Pre-Hispanic city at war with the Aztecs. The Tlaxcalans allied themselves with the Spanish who granted them concessions during colonial rule.

Xibalba The afterlife 'Place of Fear' in Mayan Mythology ruled over by the Death Gods, One Death (*'Hun-Came'*) and Seven Death (*'Vucub-Came'*).

Quinceañera Coming of age celebration of a girl's fifteenth birthday in some Latin American communities.

Mexican Drug Cartels Powerful rival criminal organisations involved in promoting and controlling drug trafficking, also at 'war' with the Mexican Government.

DEA US Government's Drug Enforcement Agency.

Membrane or M-Theory An attempt to unify forces of nature involved in versions of the superstring theory of physics by postulating eleven dimensions of supergravity.

Zapatistas Leftist revolutionary movement of liberation based in the Chiapas State of Mexico.

Chapters

Chapter 1: The First Bracelet

The Forest Without Time stretches endlessly in all directions in a dimension that knows no passing of hours, no limitation of space. Its lush trees and colourful flowers give the impression of paradise but this is illusion. Creatures terrifying beyond our wildest nightmares lurk behind that beauty, the most feared being the Golden Jaguar of the Sun.

This beast, once the scourge of hapless captives of the ancient Aztecs, would ensure none escaped ritual sacrifice to its master, the Great Sun God, when called to that other dimension by warrior-priests. But in this world of Man lived a mysterious power unknown to the dark-cloaked priest as he stood beside the stone altar, his raised brown hands firm around the razor-sharp obsidian blade, poised for the moment when the golden fingers of the ancient Sun God would touch the temple platform. Only then could he plunge the blade into the bared chest of the young native princess dressed in a green jade skirt and held down across the altar. Only then could her beating heart be ripped out so that, when still, the release of her warm blood into the lake might bring rain to the parched land.

Or was this merely Tezcatlipoca's excuse to destroy that other power, having banished Quetzalcóatl by trickery?

***

"Close your eyes!"

The pretty Mexican girl sitting beside Adam Winters on the Boeing 767 bound for New York grinned as she reached for her bag under the seat in front.

"Sure!" He screwed up his eyes.

1

Adam couldn't believe his luck. Ten days in New York with María López whilst she recorded her first album. How could he not have fallen for the loveliest girl in his junior high school in Houston, Texas, when she got up on that stage and sang like an angel for the school singing contest? But she was Spike's girl. Spike, the handsome hulk of a quarterback with a brain small enough to balance on a pinhead; the guy all the girls were crazy about and who had made the shy, studious Adam's life hell:

"Hi, Snowflake! Pretty warm today, huh? Folks like you might jus' melt away!"

The jerk particularly enjoyed teasing him in front of María. His overfed side-kick, Carlos, would wobble like a jelly in an earthquake as he shook with fake laughter in response to Spike's razor-sharp remarks.

One day Spike went too far. Beat Adam up in front of María for calling him 'Santa' in retaliation. How that boy hated his real name: Klaus. María's Latin temper exploded when she saw him hammer Adam with his gut-bursting fists. Gave Spike one hell of a slap across the face and told him he'd "blown it". Adam, who had never dared tell María how much he loved her, thought he was in heaven when the tearful girl came up and hugged him. That evening was even better than heaven. In the privacy of his room at home, he and María had their first kiss. After that they became inseparable.

But Adam feared it could never last and the fear of this gnawed at his brain like cockroach. The boy's self-esteem had been beaten down by years of bullying from the likes of Spike. Perhaps he was too hurt to understand that the girl loved him for reasons no one could explain; no one in their dimension. Also, she had faith in the boy who was so very different from Spike and the others. After all, it was he who'd persuaded her to enter the talent show in San Antonio

Golden Jaguar of the Sun

where a scout for a New York label had heard her sing and organized the contract for her first album.

Adam refused to believe his luck.

"Happy birthday!" the girl said.

The boy opened his eyes. He stared in amazement at the object on his lap.

"Wow, thanks, María! Cool! Ancient Mexican, right? Man – it looks kinda – well, genuine like!"

María frowned.

Offended! What did you say that for, you goddamn bird-brain? But genuine? A girl like María genuine about me? Sorry – no way.

The girl's frown vanished. She grinned: "Oh, it's genuine all right! Been in our family hundreds of years. The Mexican, not the Spanish side. There's another one hidden somewhere in Mexico. And a story about them. Any guy wearing the two together used to be protected from the scary Golden Jaguar of the Sun that prowled round the base of the ancient Aztec Sun Temple during human sacrifices. The beast killed people who tried to rescue their loved ones. But whoever wore the bracelets became its master. They were safe."

"María, it's – it's awesome! Priceless! I can't possibly–"

"Adam, you *must* have it! My Mama's daddy gave it to me. Said something before he died. Can't say what, but–"

Can't say? Huh! Heard that one before!

María peered out at the airplane shadow surfing the clouds below.

"What he said means I've gotta give it to you. No one else. Your birthday seemed the best time. Anyway, it frightens me!" She chuckled, turning to face him. "Fifteen, ay? For the Aztecs that meant you're a man now!"

A man? Half the size of Spike? God, she's making fun of me – but why? Pities the weakling who dared to face up to that flathead boyfriend of hers? But – why this ancient gold bracelet?

He stared at the bracelet's primitive, chunky design of a symbolised sun face entrapping the head of a large cat with dagger teeth and a lolling tongue. The eyes of the cat seemed to be – no – couldn't be. Just his imagination. Gold can't catch fire. He slipped the precious artifact over his wrist.

"Will it protect me from the beautiful creature sitting next to me?" he joked.

"I told you," María replied, laughing, "you've gotta have *two* if you're needing protection!"

Needing protection? From the likes of Spike? Taunting me?

"Sure!" Adam smiled feebly. Perhaps coming to New York with the girl wasn't such a great idea. "Still – better keep it on in the Big Apple. Could meet a mugger the size of Spike, huh?" he added, looking for a reaction. There was none.

Has she already slept with Spike, the boy wondered?

"You may need this, too," added Ann Winters handing her son a new Smart phone

She sat the other side of him. Adam's mother, now a close friend of the López family, had been asked to accompany the girl to New York. No way could Mrs López take time off from looking after a large family to go with her daughter. Ann agreed if Adam were to join them. Not María's idea. Was the girl just trying to be polite?

"Happy Birthday!" Ann Winters added, kissing her son.

So why doesn't María kiss me?

It was María's first visit to the great metropolis and she adored every minute. The recording went perfectly and the record label company arranged a party for the girl, convinced her album, *A Gentle Loving,* would be a hit. Adam had never been one for parties but bubbly María was in her element. Whilst she cheerfully chatted away to designer-stubbled media guys, bursting into fits of giggles at their wit, Adam sank into the background as that deeply-ingrained insecurity re-surfaced – a thousand times worse because of María. He couldn't take his eyes of the girl but it seemed he no longer existed for her. Boy, the pain of jealousy hurt like a firebrand from hell!

"Can't trust those Hispanic girls!"

Adam turned to see who'd spoken.

"Hi! I'm Chrissy. My Daddy, he owns the company."

"Oh!" exclaimed Adam, confused. His eyes widened. Chrissy was a stunner. Fifteen – possibly sixteen. Long golden curls down to below her shoulders and a mini-skirt that revealed ninety-nine percent of her shapely legs.

"Party tonight? Brooklyn? Do come. Bring Miss Taco Shell if you must. Bound to be some hunk there who can keep her happy. Satisfy her needs, if you get my meaning! (She winked.) Then you and me, we'll have *real* fun!"

Adam glanced again at María smiling coyly at those handsome hunks.

Can't trust Hispanic girls? Satisfy her?

Just as Chrissy, without warning, kissed Adam on the cheek and pressed a piece of paper into his hand, María looked back at him and frowned. Adam avoided her for the rest of the party.

"I saw that white girl kiss you," she said frostily in the taxi back to the hotel. "What was that about?"

"Chrissy's the boss's daughter. Asked us to a party tonight. Anyway—"

He was attempting to muster courage to accuse her of throwing herself at lecherous media guys when María interrupted his muddled thoughts:

"Asked you! Right?"

She turned away and stared glumly at the bustle of New York from the cab window.

We'll talk about it later. Of course I won't phone the number on that piece of paper. I love María! No one else! And perhaps, in her own way, she kinda cares about me? Just a teeny bit?

In his room at the hotel, Adam vowed they'd kiss, make up and forget the whole goddamn business but it didn't turn out like that. Adam's mom knocked on his door then entered. She appeared embarrassed.

María's gone and told her how she hates me and wants me to return to Houston on my own?

"Dinner tonight, Adam – with – erm – Spike. Spike and his sister. See—"

Adam exploded.

"Spike? Spike here in New York? How could you, Mom? Are you crazy? You've no bloody idea!"

"Honey, his mommy and I, we were real good friends at work in the beauty salon before she died from cancer. I kept up with his big sister, Rachel. She and her husband live here. Spike's had a hard time, you know. He's staying with Rachel over the summer vacation and wants to apologise. To *you*. That's all. Give him that chance, Adam. María says it's okay!"

"Okay? For her, maybe! Give her back to him then! Go on – and tell her to goddamn sleep with the dude if that's what she wants. Like she did before – I guess. See if I care! I'm staying right here!"

Ann Winters' eyes flashed anger.

"Adam! Don't be so childish! *Trust* her. She's not like that. For Heaven's sake, what's come over you?"

Too tired to argue, and upset by the return of the moody Adam she thought had become history after the boy took up with María, she stood in the doorway gripping the door handle. She'd grown so very fond of María. Chloe, Adam's extraordinary little sister, adored the girl.

"What do I tell her, then?" she finally asked.

6

"Can't trust Hispanic girls and that's a fact!" was all Adam said, looking the other way.

Ann Winters sighed.

"I'll tell her you're not well," she decided.

Adam remained silent. His mother left the room, quietly closing the door behind her.

"Say what you like!" he said to the door before cursing himself.

What the heck have I done?

Then he remembered the girl laughing with those hunks at the party, wearing the red dress her mother had made for the talent show in San Antonio. When he first saw her in it, revealing her Mexican curves in a way that would delight any male, he felt pride for she was no longer Spike's girl but his. Plus the matching red shoes, her "first high heels" she told him, somehow made her stunning legs even more so. But at that party it seemed the owner of those legs, shoes and dress now belonged to others. He imagined the girl sitting beside Spike; imagined the bastard placing a filthy paw on her thigh and saw María respond with a pretty smile. Next thing, they were in bed together – in his mind. He pulled out that piece of paper and called the number:

"Hi, Adam! Yeah, sure I'll fetch you. Be round in twenty minutes. On your own, then? Miss Taco Shell found her own bit of beef, huh?"

Beef? Spike? María wrapped in his quarterback arms? His legs around hers? Chrissy's legs? Oh man, those legs!

In the taxi on the way to Brooklyn, Adam's eyes were drawn to Chrissy's legs to which they remained stuck for the entire duration of the ride. They worked their magic. He forgot about María and Spike – until they arrived at that apartment in Brooklyn.

A tsunami of sound blasted out as soon as the door opened, almost punching the boy backwards. Adam loved pop music but this was something else and he could think only of María's gentle voice as he followed Chrissy into a vision of hell: dim red lights, the smell of sweat and booze plus snogging bodies on the floor and, of course, deafening music. It became apparent that Chrissy's idea of 'real fun' did not involve Adam when she flung her arms around a long, lanky guy with pimples and a flashing gold tooth. Obviously she, like María, just wished to humiliate him.

Or was he wrong about María? Had he misread her signals in the taxi? He'd never seen her look so miserable but had assumed that was because she found herself with a weakling like himself rather than in the arms of one of those hunky media men on her way to the guy's apartment for—

For that?

He tried, unsuccessfully, to avoid staring at a writhing couple, the short-skirted girl's limbs wrapped around the man, her pink panties on public display. Again, he saw María in Spike's arms.

No – I cannot think of María lowering herself to mating in full view of others!

Adam grabbed a beer bottle and slumped to the floor, his back to the wall. He took out his cell phone and keyed in María's number, trying to work out what to text – how to apologise.

Chrissy's electrifying legs appeared barely (yes, barely!) one foot away. Briefly, he forgot María. Chrissy used the freeze-frame moment to reach down and grab the phone. She stooped and kissed the boy as she held this at arm's length, photographing herself, including cleavage, and Adam. Before he could retrieve the phone, she'd sent the picture to María. Adam jumped up, angrily snatching it back.

"What the—?" he began.

"Calm down, my little Texan cutie. Just letting Miss Taco Shell know what fun you're having!"

Little Texan cutie? Miss Taco Shell? Jesus, man!

Golden Jaguar of the Sun

Adam felt fist-thumping furious. He had to find somewhere quiet to speak with María. Stepping over intertwined bodies, he pushed his way out of the room, along the corridor, opened the first door he came to, then...

"HELP ME, ADAM! STOP THEM!"

It was Lee, kid brother of Bruno, the friendly African-American guy in charge of recording María's album at the studio. He was being held down on the edge of a bed by two heavy dudes whilst a third attempted to push something into his arm. *A syringe with a needle?*

Adam saw terror in the boy's eyes. Without a second thought, he sprang forward and hit the man holding the syringe over the head with his bottle. The rest was like Hollywood movie footage. Stunned, the drug pusher dropped the syringe. The other guys released their hold on Lee who broke free and ran to stand behind Adam.

"Man, you're goosed!" threatened a bull-sized bruiser, reaching for something. It glistened in the dim light.

"Run, Adam," cried Lee before fleeing.

But Adam froze. He would never willingly hurt anyone and wondered whether he should simply say 'sorry' and walk away. If only he had time to phone María – ask her what he should do. Dropping the bottle, he stroked the Golden Jaguar bracelet around his wrist. Why he did this, he had no idea. Immediately something snapped into his mind. It felt like a part of him that had been missing all his life. *Courage? Strength?* Two eyes of crimson fire flashed infront of him. He held his hand up to shield his face then turned to leave – too late.

At first he felt only a thump on the back. He stopped. Pain arrived moments later. Soon he was crouching as pain transformed into agony. It seemed to tear open his chest, forcing him forwards. His face hit the floor and he tasted the dirt of the carpet. There were screams. Whose, he had no idea.

9

"HE'S BEEN STABBED!"

Lee's voice? Why so far off – as if it had nothing to do with that curled-up body clawing at the floor? *His* body. Then María's voice—

Oh my God!

Singing so clearly, it overwhelmed the background clamour. Made no sense that he could hear her, but, Sweet Jesus, it was beautiful. It seemed as if he was afloat on the liquid sound of her voice as he reached out for the girl's hand. She had to be there if she was singing to him. *Him...* and no one else. He called her name, but nothing emerged from his mouth.

Everything went blank.

Chapter 2: The Other Bracelet

*"**Don't** fail me!" Tezcatlipoca sounded angry. "You know where the girl is. And remember, this one's mine. Nothing to do with the Water Deity. The girl's blood might keep the Deity happy but her soul is mine!"*

The high priest bowed before the image of the god then sent his warriors to the city by the lake.

After opening his eyes Adam blinked but what he saw failed to change. Nothing made sense. María's gold bracelet encircled his wrist but where was María? He couldn't understand why she wasn't with him? He vaguely remembered a party somewhere, but that was all – apart from a lingering feeling he'd wronged the girl. But how?

Standing up, he glanced anxiously at the strange surroundings.

"MARÍA!" he shouted.

No reply.

Before him was a vast lake and on the lake, in the distance, an island covered with squat buildings above which towered an ominous, grey and red stepped pyramid. Close by, ripples lapped at the reed-fringed shore of the lake and a sturdy canoe, moored to a post, bobbed lazily on the brown water.

"MARÍA!" he called again.

Voices...

Adam turned. A line of men stood on a dusty track staring in silence. Behind them was a town of mud and reed huts. Young children played happily in the streets as women worked away outside the huts. They wore colourful, cotton tunics and the men and boys also had long hair although not as long as the women's. The faces of these sturdy people were like those of immigrant Mexican workers in Houston.

One of the men stepped forward and spoke. A weird language, yet Adam understood it.

"Who are you?"

Adam glanced nervously at the stone-studded club that hung from the man's waist. There was also a quiver full of arrows and the guy had a bow slung over one shoulder.

"I'm Adam Winters from Houston, Texas. Looking for a girl called María."

Curiously, he could also speak their language. The man approached, his hand gripped around the handle of the club.

"Where's Houston, Texas?" he asked.

"USA."

The man shrugged his shoulders.

"Aztec spy?"

What a peculiar question!

"No, of course I'm not an Aztec. They were all dead and buried hundreds of years ago."

The man studied Adam with interest but there was kindness in his eyes. He spoke again:

"Then we're friends, Adam Winters. But if only it was true what you say about those Aztecs. Did you come from the sea to the east with the bearded white men?"

"Bearded?" Adam shook his head. "Dunno why I'm here – but I've a feeling it's something to do with a girl called María. She's my girlfriend. I hope. Maybe she's here. Mexican, see. Very pretty."

"All our women are beautiful," chuckled the man. He caught sight of Adam's Golden Jaguar bracelet. His eyes betrayed alarm. "The Golden Jaguar of the Sun?"

How come he knows about María's bracelet?

"Yeah," answered Adam. "María gave it to me." The boy turned to face the sinister island city perched on its reflection. "Erm... Tenochtitlan?" he asked uneasily.

Keen on Mesoamerican history since dating María, he knew Tenochtitlan to be the ancient Aztec capital. The man appeared puzzled.

"Of course," he replied.

"And the language we're speaking?"

The man laughed again.

"Why, Nahuatl! What else?"

"Oh my God!" exclaimed Adam. "Look, I'm only a school-kid from Houston. I've gotta find María. Tell her I really do love her."

The man addressed the others:

"Leave us! He's no threat." He glanced at Adam's bracelet. "Maybe he can help." He smiled. "I'm Atalotl," he added looking up at Adam.

"Just call me Adam."

The other men departed, leaving Adam and Atalotl standing side-by-side on the shore of that alien lake. Adam remembered María telling him her native ancestors lived in a city called Tlaxcala.

"This girl, María – her people came from Tlaxcala way back," he continued. "Perhaps—"

"Tlaxcala?" interrupted Atalotl. "The Tlaxcalans are our friends. But María? Never heard the name. Come with me, Adam. You must meet our unhappy chief, Mixihuetl. His wife is Tlaxcalan. He might know of this María. Whilst we walk to the palace I'll tell you about the terrible things that have befallen our people."

"There was a great battle," Atalotl began as they made their way through the narrow streets of the noisy town. "Our warriors fought bravely but their numbers couldn't match those of the Aztec warriors. The demons entered our city, captured many women and children then smashed down our temple sanctuary. We knew then we'd be forever enslaved by them. Of course, there was a reason for the attack. It wasn't just to destroy our temple. You see, it all started with the great famine. The Water Deity was angry. Three wet seasons passed and she gave up hardly a drop of rain. Without rain the cycle of life is broken and there's no food. The Aztecs need so much food for their large cities and greedy nobles! When the food ran out they attacked us to find a *Chalchiuhtlicue* maiden. A beautiful young girl who'll be dressed in a jade skirt, sacrificed on the Temple of the Sun and her still-beating heart cut out as an offering to the deities. Her blood'll be mixed with the ground water of the lake after the planting of the *Tota* tree, the tree of life."

"Yuk!" exclaimed Adam. Atalotl glanced at the boy then continued:

"It's the Aztec way of appeasing the deities during a period of drought. They chose our city because of the beauty of our women. Mixihuetl hid his own daughter, the lovely Princess Arima, in a secret cave. The Aztec warrior-priests searched the city. They knew of her legendary beauty and sweet nature. Failing to find her they chose one of the palace servant girls. They took the terrified child to their camp. Arima was devastated when she found out for this girl was like a friend to the princess. Then Arima herself vanished. A short while later, the servant girl returned. She'd been released and at first was too upset to speak."

Atalotl paused before skirting round an old man who lay stiff and still in the dust. Adam wondered how he could be so callous as to ignore a dead body, but said nothing. To find María was his priority.

"Soon we heard the awful news. Arima had gone to the Aztec camp by herself. She'd persuaded the warrior-priests to take her instead. Seeing the beauty of our chieftain's daughter they released the servant girl. They took Arima to Tenochtitlan this morning and tomorrow she'll be cruelly sacrificed. Mixihuetl is beside himself with grief."

That poor girl – to have her living heart ripped from her! Adam felt sickened.

14

Golden Jaguar of the Sun

"The servant said more," continued the ancient Mexican. "Arima had lost her heart to a boy who gave his own to another. She told the servant girl that since hers was already broken she might as well give it to the Aztecs. If the boy she loved didn't want her heart they could use it for the sacrifice that'll help all our peoples. Not only is the chieftain's daughter beautiful, she's gentle and kind, but – oh, she can be so headstrong!"

Adam thought it such a sad story even though it had nothing to do with him. They soon reached a large square with stone buildings at all four corners. Atalotl halted and pointed to charred, wooden remains on top of a squat, tiered rectangular pyramid in the centre.

"Our temple! Destroyed!" he explained. "Wait here. I'll return soon."

He vanished into the largest of the buildings only to reappear almost immediately with another man. Adam got the shock of his life. The figure accompanying Atalotl was Miguel López, María's father. He wore an elaborate headdress of exotic feathers with a colourful cloak covering his tunic, but the face was unmistakable. Adam rubbed his eyes to see whether the apparition would go away. It didn't. When the man stood in front of him there was no doubt.

"Mr López?" he asked weakly.

Miguel López – or Mixihuetl – turned to Atalotl, puzzled, then back to face Adam. He obviously didn't recognise the boy, so, Adam reckoned, probably no more than an uncanny likeness.

"Your bracelet, Adam! Atalotl told me about this. May I see it?"

Adam removed the Golden Jaguar bracelet and handed it to the chieftain who carefully examined the object.

"This surely must be the omen Pedrocoatl foretold, Atalotl. Right now Arima will be lying bound and hidden near the Temple of the Sun God, guarded by the Golden

15

Jaguar. There'll be no warriors allowed near her for fear of upsetting the female Water Deity. They'll all be up on *Tlaloc* Hill preparing for—"

Returning the bracelet, Mixihuetl closed his eyes. Tears streaked his cheeks. He couldn't bring himself to speak of the terrifying ordeal his daughter, the *Chalchiuhtlicue* maiden, would be forced to endure.

"This girl you call María who gave you the bracelet – tell me more. I too want to find her. Perhaps she's our only hope for Arima."

Adam remembered the photograph of María in his wallet in the back pocket of his jeans. Atalotl and Mixihuetl looked on with curiosity as the boy removed this and, fingers fumbling, extracted loose cards, notes and three US ten dollar bills. Finally he found María's photograph. Seeing her beautiful face again he knew he had wronged her and wished he could remember how.

"María!" Adam proudly announced, handing the photograph to Mixihuetl. Mixihuetl stared in stunned silence before letting out a heart-rending shriek:

"ARIMA!"

He sank to the ground, clutching the photograph of María to his breast, and sobbed. Adam, overcome with panic, yelled:

"NO! YOU'RE WRONG. DON'T SAY THAT! IT'S MARÍA. I LOVE HER."

But Mixihuetl only wept, repeating "Arima" over and over. Atalotl put his arm around the chieftain's shoulders and took the photograph. He, too, appeared stunned when he saw the image of the smiling young girl in a red dress. He touched her hair.

"This *is* Arima. But – but I don't understand how she looks so real. What artist could do this?"

"Photograph," Adam replied. He just wanted out of this nightmare. He wished María was there with him and he couldn't bear the thought of her being dragged away by the Aztecs for—

"No! This cannot be happening," he whispered as he took back the photograph. "Is this really A—?"

"Arima? Yes. See that dark spot there."

Atalotl pointed to a tiny mole on the girl's forehead, the one he'd kissed so many times, but Adam's only thought now was to rescue his girlfriend whatever they called her here. If it meant sacrificing his own life he didn't care. Mixihuetl was grieving too much to talk, so the boy spoke to Atalotl.

Neither could understand how the girl in the photograph could possibly be María and Mixihuetl's daughter, Arima, at the same time. Both agreed, however, that Arima, whether or not she was also María, must be rescued. And quickly, for Atalotl explained that when the men had finished their ceremonies on the hill prior to dawn they would come down to the lake to plant the *Tota* tree before the blood from Arima's torn-out heart could be mixed with the water of the lake to bring life back to the land. The girl would be sacrificed on the altar of the Temple of the Sun God when the rays from the dawning sun touched the top of the pyramid temple. Priests would hold her down whilst the terrifying Golden Jaguar prowled at the foot of the temple. With the deed done, a runner would rush the girl's still beating heart to the lakeside harbour for the ghoulish ceremony to proceed.

"This bracelet—" Adam began, "María told me there's another one and whoever wears the two might overcome the Golden Jaguar. Atalotl, we've gotta find the other bracelet. María said it was hidden. Maybe by someone escaping from the Aztec priests? In Tenochtitlan?"

Atalotl appeared pensive.

"Well – there is an old woman with strange powers who lives in the hills. Some say she's crazy but she definitely knows and sees things others don't." He pointed to the bracelet around Adam's wrist. "Perhaps if she were to hold that bracelet she might be able to speak across the wall of death to the man who hid the other one."

"What the heck are we waiting for?" Adam asked impatiently. "I must get the other bracelet! I'll wear it and free María – Arima – whatever! No one bloody harms my girlfriend!"

"Adam, this is dangerous. If the Golden Jaguar doesn't kill you the warrior-priests surely will."

"Without María my life's worth nothing!"

Mixihuetl looked up then pulled out an obsidian knife from his belt. It was surprisingly sharp.

"Take this," he said, handing it to Adam. "You could use it against the priests if not the beast. And should you return without Arima please bring back the knife so I can end my own miserable life with it."

"Quick," urged Atalotl. "We'll have to run like the flight of an arrow!"

Adam soon found out what Atalotl meant. He had difficulty keeping up with the man as they sped along narrow streets dodging laughing, playing children, merchants selling meagre wares and women carrying jars of water on their shoulders. Puffing and panting behind the tireless Latino of the past, he wished he'd taken up his father's suggestion of baseball coaching.

At least you have to run fast in baseball even though girls don't idolise baseball players as they do hunky football quarterbacks!

They left the city and took a well-marked path, running up and over steeper and steeper hills until, as the sun sank below the dark cut-out outline of the wild, shaggy mountains, they located the old woman's cave on a cliff face high above them, reached by a narrow zig-zagging trail.

Golden Jaguar of the Sun

When Adam first met the wizened woman crouched over a gnarled walking stick, he did wonder whether she wasn't totally mad. She took his bracelet, muttered gibberish half-sentences then disappeared into her cave. With the sun gone, it was rapidly turning dark. Atalotl remained annoyingly calm as he sat motionless on a rock at the cave entrance. Adam tried to follow his example but all he could think about was María's life ebbing like sand in an hourglass, convinced this was all because of him. Irritation forced him to pace up and down like a kid outside the principal's office, anger giving way to fury.

Just as his patience became stretched to the limit, the old woman reappeared clutching a folded parchment. Adam peered at this in the dim moonlight. A map? She whispered something to Atalotl who explained to the boy that she'd made contact. The bracelet's previous owner was only too happy to see the other put to use against the murdering Aztecs and she indicated precisely where the second bracelet had been buried:

"Under the floor of an abandonned building where the wounded ground touches the wall," she informed them, stabbing at the map with a bony finger.

Wounded ground? Daft as a demented bat!

Twilight slipped inexorably into night time. Hope drained from Adam as life would soon drain from his girlfriend in a gush of warm blood. How on earth could they reach the Temple of the Sun God and find the second bracelet before dawn? But Atalotl, composed and confident, said he knew what she meant and reassured the boy that darkness would be in their favour. Under its cover, they could cross the lake to Tenochtitlan and locate that ruin without arousing suspicion. The old lady wished them luck and they left the mountain cave, Adam again struggling to keep up with his newly-found friend.

Golden Jaguar of the Sun

Back at the lakeside, Atalotl pulled the canoe to the shore. They climbed in, each grabbed an oar and together they paddled the boat quietly and swiftly over the liquorice-black water towards the gloomy sprawl of the Aztec island city.

They paddled without stopping for almost an hour before reaching the island. Adam should have felt shattered, but his mind refused to abandon María to her inescapable fate in the hands of those Aztec dudes. Something beyond his control and understanding urged him on.

As Atalotl predicted, the city appeared deserted apart from small bands of Aztec warriors. They beached the craft beneath a canal bridge and Adam followed Atalotl into the silent streets of Tenochtitlan, the two hiding in open doorways whenever they spotted warriors.

Atalotl stopped and held up his hand. Before them was a sizeable square. At the far end of this, a stone building. One of its side walls had partly caved in and a crack scarred the wall facing them.

The wounded ground – left by an earthquake?

This had to be the building, but Adam's heart dropped like a brick thrown from a sky-scraper, for two warriors sat in animated conversation on either side of the doorway. The boy remained statue-still as he watched Atalotl with cat-like stealth pull back an arrow against the string of his bow until the flint tip was snug against the tautened edge of the bow. The arrow whistled. One of the warriors clutched at his neck, jerked and slumped to the ground. Before his companion had a chance to lift his own weapon, a second arrow shot from Atalotl's bow and hit him in the chest. The man staggered to his feet before dropping lifeless beside his stricken comrade. Atalotl glanced at Adam. The boy knew what to do. They ran across the square and each dragged a dead warrior backwards into the ruined building.

"What luck!" whispered Atalotl, and Adam soon realised what the man meant. They removed the dead warriors' animal skin uniforms and feather-covered helmets and hurriedly changed into them. A perfect disguise. Adam and Atalotl searched the building. There were low tables and stools in one of the rooms and a makeshift roof. The two warriors had been using the place as a temporary billet.

Atalotl located the spot where a rift in the ground joined the crack in the wall. He scraped away at the dirt and the rubble until his fingers touched something. Adam's heart leapt when the man lifted out a small leather pouch. Inside they found a second bracelet identical to the one around Adam's left wrist. After slipping it over his right wrist, Adam sensed a strength way beyond that of a fifteen year-old boy – indeed, of any man and perhaps greater than that of the Golden Jaguar of the Sun. He felt invincible.

"Now get some sleep," whispered Atalotl. "We'll sit outside against the wall just as our late friends did. Anything else will arouse suspicion. I'll stay awake and keep guard. Remember, I do the talking if we're approached. I can imitate the dreadful Aztec accent. I'll awaken you whilst it's still dark and take you to the square of the Temple of the Sun God. Then you're on your own. If I were to approach whilst the Golden Jaguar is guarding the temple I'd be killed straightaway. This would be useless against the magical beast." He held up his bow. "I'll wait by the canoe under the bridge. Meanwhile let's hope your gods will protect Arima."

My gods? If only!

Back outside, against the wall, the boy closed his eyes and slipped into a deep and troubled sleep. In fleeting dreams he searched for his lost girlfriend, María López – and in those dreams he saw two eyes of crimson fire. They, too, were searching.

For her or for him? To destroy or to help him?

21

He awoke with a start when shaken by Atalotl. To the east, towards the lake, the sky was brightening. The girl would soon be horribly slaughtered should they fail. He jumped up, but Atalotl raised his hand – a sign not to be too precipitous.

"Stay calm," the man warned. "Look normal. And keep the bracelets covered with the sleeves of your tunic. Someone might recognise them. The priests fear those Golden Jaguar bracelets more than anything. They're useless fighters themselves."

They walked calmly through the dusty, early morning streets of Tenochtitlan. There were children playing tag and street traders already setting up their stalls. Adam looked anxiously at the sky. A pink glow rimmed the skyline in the direction of the lake. María had little time left. Atalotl stopped and turned to the boy:

"Here's the map. If you succeed, cover Arima with the robe of a priest. No one must see the jade skirt of the *Chalchiuhtlicue* maiden. Have courage – and may the disgraced deity of our brave city be with you, Adam. Now look up above that building opposite and you'll see the top of the Temple of the Sun God. That's where they'll tear out Arima's heart. As soon as you pass round the building you could encounter the Golden Jaguar. He'll probably just creep up behind you and when he pounces he's quicker than the blink of an eye. The temple square might seem totally empty then suddenly the jaguar's massive jaws are crushing your head into a thousand fragments of bone and brain. If you're lucky enough to see the beast first, show him the bracelets. Command him to save Arima! It'll depend on the strength of your will, Adam. Now I must leave and pray to our ancestors I see you again – and the princess."

"I will save María! I love her!" Adam said quietly. "You've no idea how much!"

Atalotl smiled.

"And Arima?"

"*And* Arima!"

When the boy reached the square, the horror of the task ahead struck him with a force worse than a jaw-punch from Spike – but he, Adam Winters, class nerd and weakling that he'd always been, felt no fear. The vast temple was at the far end of the square. A group of five ghoulish, black-cloaked figures – Aztec warrior-priests – stood on the platform at the top of the steep, stepped pyramid, two of whom were dragging a struggling girl towards a large, flat stone blackened with congealed blood and resting on blocks. The girl, who had long dark hair, was dwarfed by the priests, and the pinking sky illuminated the pale green of her jade skirt giving it a strangely eerie sheen.

That stone? The altar? Where—?

"NO!" shrieked Adam, sprinting across the square.

He ran faster than he'd ever run, his gaze fixed upon the gruesome, unfolding scene. He saw María being forced down onto her back across the stone altar, a priest holding each of her arms and legs. With her head hanging over one end, her silken hair swirled as she fought to break free. The fifth priest stood over María. He held something with both hands, his arms stretched high above the girl's bared chest.

And the man waited for the sun to rise above the lake.

Adam had already scaled half a dozen of the steep steps but realised he could never reach the platform in the minute or so before the sun would light up the top of the pyramid. The glow in the east had changed from salmon-pink to bright gold as a sinister sliver of sun peered above the horizon.

"STO—!"

Before he could finish the word, a painful blow jerked Adam's head sideways. For a second he thought that it must have been knocked off his shoulders as he tumbled down the steps and crashed onto the stone paving below. He eased himself up – then saw him:

The Golden Jaguar of the Sun!

He was huge. Completely spotless, his golden fur gleamed in the ghostly morning light. He crouched metres from where the boy lay sprawled on the ground. His muscles tensed as he settled himself onto his haunches preparing to spring. For a brief moment Adam seemed mesmerised by the penetrating eyes of the beast – coal-black apart from vertical slits of crimson fire which cut each staring eye in half. A finger of shimmering gold touched the temple platform as the sun slid majestically above the waking city. Suddenly that strength, which had smouldered deep inside the boy ever since he'd slipped the second bracelet over his right wrist, overcame the hypnotic stare of the giant feline. He held up two firmly-clenched fists into the gaze of the Golden Jaguar so as to ensure the crude, paired cast-gold images of the beast's namesake were visible to the unearthly creature. He thought of María and his love for her as he stared into the eyes of the great cat. A surge of power flowed from him to the jaguar and he saw a change in the præternatural animal. The Golden Jaguar became Adam's servant. He willed the boy to give him orders. Adam commanded the beast to scale the Temple of the Sun God, destroy the evil priests and save the girl:

"Rescue María! I love her."

The Golden Jaguar turned and, like a missile launched from an unearthly catapult, bounded up the temple steps; a golden missile that shone in the soft light of the early-morning sun; a terrifying missile of steel-hard sinews and muscle. Before the priest wielding the vicious obsidian knife had a chance to strike María, the beast leapt over the stretched body of the girl and hit the hooded figure with such force that he was sent spinning like a devilish dervish before tumbling in a neck-snapping fall down the steep steps at the far side of the platform of death. Petrified, the other priests let go of María and fled towards the doorway of a small stone structure. The cat sprang, bringing down one of the screaming men before silencing him forever by sinking his huge teeth into the man's head, their ivory points easily piercing the man's skull as if it were made from polystyrene. Another two men toppled from the edge of the platform in panic, hurtling to their deaths below. The last remaining priest, rigid with fear, slowly backed away as the jaguar stalked him before hurling his great body at the cowering figure. With one blow from a massive clawed paw, the beast flipped the man's head round so it faced the wrong way. All went quiet.

The Golden Jaguar crouched in front of the altar, his toe-curling snarl a warning that he would protect the girl at all costs, but Adam was alarmed by her stillness. He scrambled up the last few steps, soon reaching the top. María had a pulse, praise the gods. Putting his face close to María's, he felt her warm breath on his cheek although her eyes remained closed.

Must've fainted from terror, the poor girl!

He stroked her hair then whispered into her ear:

"María, it's me! Adam! I'm so sorry! I *do* love you. Everything's gonna be all right."

María's eyelids flickered. Adam lowered his head onto her naked chest, his cheek touching one of her soft young breasts, and he remembered how he'd wronged the girl. He'd failed to trust her in New York before going alone to that awful party. Stupidly, he had even imagined Spike fondling those same sweetly-innocent breasts. Then he recalled the song she'd been singing after the cold-steel blade sliced into his chest. It was about love – *her* love – *their* love.

"Forgive me. I should've trusted you. I dunno what came over me. When I saw you with all those media guys – then hearing about Spike – guess I was afraid — I thought—"

Not caring to reveal his real fear of María yearning for some Spike-like guy to make love to her, he listened instead to the frightened beating of the girl's heart. It sounded so faint, so fast. Like a startled horse galloping way in the distance, fleeing to escape the warrior-priests. Never would he allow those cruel Aztecs to rip that warm, loving heart from his girlfriend.

At last she spoke, faintly:

"Forgive?" she questioned.

"María, please forgive me," he repeated without looking up. "I've been so crass!"

He felt her fingers stroke his cheek.

"Adam?"

The girl's voice sounded stronger. He raised his head. Her eyes were open. How happy he felt to look into them again – and—

Oh God, how beautiful she is!

"Adam, where are we?" she asked. "I was so afraid. I thought—"

She turned her face away, saw the body of the bloodied, black-hooded priest on the ground, and gasped.

"Adam!" she cried, sitting up and flinging her arms around the boy.

"It's okay," he reassured. "The guy's dead but we'll have to get away quick. Before others come. You'd better put on that bastard's cloak. Stay here a moment."

Adam left María to retrieve the dead priest's garment. She screamed. He swivelled and saw her staring at the Golden Jaguar, rigid with terror.

"It's all right," he called out. "He's protecting you. Saved your life!"

Golden Jaguar of the Sun

María was still trembling when Adam lifted the cloak over her. Her pretty face, framed by the hollow blackness of the large hood, appeared deceptively small and painfully vulnerable.

"Protecting me? Yuk! This stinks!" she complained, grimacing.

"Might get better in Macy's, huh?" joked Adam.

"Adam, what *are* we doing here? You know, I was afraid you didn't—" She slipped down from the altar and stood before Adam, taking hold of his hands. "You were acting so weird. I really thought you loved someone else. I was worried—"

Adam silenced her with a kiss on the lips.

"Never!"

"Why are you wearing that funny costume? Looks so – so kinda boys' movie stuff. Freaky!"

"I like it when my girl objects. More normal. But we'd better hurry. They'll soon be coming after you."

María, descending the steps barefoot, struggled to keep up with her boyfriend. Down in the square, she held onto his arm as they ran towards the awakening streets of Tenochtitlan. The Golden Jaguar slunk soundlessly after them, watchful over the girl he'd been commanded to protect.

Adam halted and took out the map. They could reach the lakeside by heading for the sun but he knew he must also keep to the north. In the city centre, to the south, Aztec priests, warriors and crowds of commoners would be waiting by the lake where the *Tota* tree was to absorb the blood of a beautiful girl, the *Chalchiuhtlicue*-maiden. After the blood, the jade skirt and jewellery that María was wearing were to be hurled into the water, for jade belonged to the female water deity. What remained of the girl would be thrown to the coyotes for it could be of no further use to any of the gods. This was to be a ceremony of life to bring on the rains and restore food to the land – and a ceremony of death for a young girl.

They sped along empty streets, across a deserted market square, towards the sun, the lake and freedom. They reached the shoreline. Not a hundred metres away was a huge gathering in a space that opened onto the central harbour. Everyone jostled for better views of the awaited gruesome proceedings. Adam took María's hand again and, staying close to the buildings, he ran with her from the harbour and the noisy Aztecs, followed by the gleaming Golden Jaguar.

The boy was relieved to find his native friend, Atalotl, crouching alongside the canoe under the bridge. The man stood and bowed to María. He glanced at the Golden Jaguar without fear for he saw only a tamed beast. Adam spoke to the creature who with eyes aglow turned and bounded back towards the crowded square.

"Your highness, we have to hurry," Atalotl told María. "They'll know something's wrong by now. They've had to wait too long for your blood. I saw a group of warriors head back into the city towards the Temple of the Sun God."

Adam helped María into the canoe. Then he and Atalotl took the oars and paddled strongly. The canoe slid easily over the still water. He heard shouting in the distance. He turned. There was consternation amongst the crowd beside the harbour and he spied several canoes, similar to the one they were in, gaining on them. Something cut into the water beside their canoe with a swish-plop. An arrow floated to the surface.

"For heaven's sake get down, María!" he urged. His girlfriend looked so defenceless hunched under the voluminous black cloak. Suddenly, Atalotl cried out:

"AAARGH!"

The shaft of an arrow stuck out at right-angles from his left shoulder. He stopped paddling. Their canoe swung round, pointing back towards the island city. For a moment

28

Adam thought all was lost until he spotted the head of the Golden Jaguar behind the nearest canoe. In no time the beast reached the craft. He reared his huge bulk out of the water, dwarfing the astonished Aztecs. With a single cuff from a massive paw, he reduced it to a collection of splintered fragments of wood that bobbed amongst the bodies of warriors. All four other canoes fled before the creature but none made it back to the land. One by one, frantic, flailing warriors were torn apart by the jaguar's teeth, turning the water red.

"So the *Tota* Tree drinks the blood of vermin instead!" remarked Atalotl, gripping his shoulder.

The Golden Jaguar leapt ashore at the harbour of Tenochtitlan causing a Mexican wave of panic to spread through the terrified onlookers. Meanwhile María, also the *Chalchiuhtlicue* maiden Arima, was carefully removing an arrow from Atalotl's shoulder using her father's obsidian knife. Tapping into the strength welling inside him, Adam turned the canoe around on his own and continued to paddle until María had completed the painstaking operation. When they were half-way across the lake he heard a rumble of thunder. The sun had disappeared behind a bank of darkening clouds and soon he was paddling in a drenching downpour. Atatotl laughed.

"Their sacrifice to the Water Deity was prevented and still she gives up her rain! Now they'll have no excuse to return to our city. We might just forget to pay our tribute to the city of Tenochtitlan, huh?"

Back in Atalotl's city, María ran sobbing from the canoe into her parents' arms. Adam removed the bracelets and handed these to Mixihuetl.

"Take the bracelets," he said. "You'll need them in this place. They're where my strength came from. María gave me one. Her grandpa told her to. The other we found thanks to the Old Woman of the Hills."

The chieftain held up his left hand. Miguel López was also left-handed.

"Thank you, Adam, but keep them. That strength came from you. As for Arima's grandfather – well, he died before she was born."

María looked away when her father glanced at her, as if unsure of who or where she truly was.

"Adam, don't leave now," the man pleaded. "Tomorrow we'll have a great celebration."

Mixihuetl turned and whispered in his daughter's ear. She nodded and smiled at her boyfriend from a different time and place.

"The whole city will join with us. For my daughter's wedding," the chief explained. Adam looked as if he'd been hit by a runaway chuck-wagon. Were they now going to give María to some ancient Mexican Spike-equivalent? The girl read his anxiety, shook her head and grinned. "Tomorrow I give the hand of my daughter to Adam Winters, the bravest warrior in our land."

"But I'm only fifteen. Too young to be married," Adam protested without conviction. Wild thoughts of making love to María befuddled his mind. Not Spike, but Adam Winters lay in bed with her!

"Adam, why did you risk your life for the girl?"

There was only one answer:

"I love her," he replied quietly.

"That's enough. But there's something very special about Arima. We never really understood this until you appeared from that other world. It has to be you. Right? This is what Pedrocoatl was trying to tell us before you got back," continued Mixihuetl. "The ceremony of the tying of the knot will take place tomorrow."

The following day María, in a pink and gold dress embroidered with exotic tropical birds, looked ravishing. Their wedding was a dream-weave of magical threads. The shaman-priest who married them, a cheerful elderly man called Pedrocoatl, was a carbon copy of Papa Pedro, an old Mexican friend of Adam's who had an antiques shop in Houston. In fact, the boy was certain it *was* the old man; as certain as he was that Arima was María and Mixihuetl was Migual López. And when the guy insisted they rebuild the city temple and dedicate it to a new God – María's God, the God of Love that the bearded ones from the East spoke of in Tlaxcala and which some reckoned signified the return of Quetzalcóatl – Adam knew he and María straddled two worlds. He wasn't the least surprised when the old man winked at him and, with his hand, made a sign of the cross, for this was more than merely being transported back in time. Maybe he now stood in a dimension shared by interwoven universes – and if the girl belonged to both, then so did her God. Like his father, Adam had no real religion, but since being with María he'd begun to doubt his disbelief.

That night, the young couple lay together on a bed of colourful plumed feathers and beautifully-soft alpaca wool, draped with patterned cotton sheets inlaid with gold. They were exhausted after the day's events and María, her face inches from Adam's, looked at the boy with those warm, brown eyes which had been in his mind ever since the day he first noticed her at middle school.

So they were married? If only! How he wished to take her in his arms and let free the desire consuming every fibre of his body – but he couldn't; that trusting look, the love, the fear – the uncertainty. He wanted his soul to fall into those eyes, to achieve union without harming her – become as one in some other way.

She touched two fingers to his lips. Her way of telling him she shared his thoughts.

"Not yet," she whispered. "Not here. I, too, know there's another place. And another me. We must wait."

María reached up with her hand and stroked Adam's cheek. Still smiling, she closed her eyes. Adam kissed her eyelids, rolled over and squinted at the low, stone ceiling above. Her eyes were also there, looking down at him.

María? Arima? Who are you, my love?

***

"Awake at last, honey!"

Adam opened his eyes. It was Ann Winters.

"Where—?"

The boy sat up, took in the stark hospital room, then flopped back staring at the white ceiling.

"María too," Ann continued. "She fainted when she got that dreadful picture of you and that blonde on her cell phone. Then we heard about the stabbing. The police said you were dead and the poor girl passed out again. Nothing could bring her round. They've worked miracles here. María recovered consciousness when you came off the ventilator this morning. Thank God you're both okay. And Adam, that girl really loves you. You have no idea."

"I—" Gripped by shame, he turned his face away. "I think I do know, Mom." He looked back at his mother. "It's okay. Now she knows how I feel too, I guess."

"Adam Winters, the first thing you do when you see her is apologise! Why, I—"

"Mom, we've more than made up already. I think. Kind of, anyways. Don't worry. I'll always trust her from now on. I was being so monkey-ass dumb!"

Something caught his attention on his bedside cabinet. *Two* golden bracelets. So it wasn't just a dream. Somewhere, in another dimension, he and María were man and wife.

Getting married was the only episode he clearly recalled, although he sensed panic and fear. Not of being knifed but of losing his girlfriend forever through death.

And he also remembered a beast...

Chapter 3: Art and Jeannie

*"**You** fool! What on earth possessed you when you made those bracelets of the beast in the fire I gave you? Now they've let her go!"*

Tezcatlipoca chided his servant on Earth for his folly.

"I had to protect myself from the power of the beast. Anyway, we'll see to it the boy gets his comeuppance."

"We?"

"The two of us. We work together now."

"Aren't you forgetting something?"

"The beast? We can do without the beast!"

"No. The reason why she must not only die but be destroyed."

The servant looked away from the ancient Great Sun God.

"Quetzalcóatl?" he queried.

"Far worse! Go now. Remember – get close to her!"

"We've chosen already. A husband and wife."

"Her parents?"

"Parents, my lord? What fifteen year-old girl listens to her parents?"

***

María López was the eldest of seven Mexican siblings who only stopped talking, shrieking or tumbling about when then they were asleep. The first time Adam went round to her place in Houston, just a few blocks away, he thought he'd entered a madhouse, yet he loved it. He sensed the energy of the López family in the very air of the place, in the children's shouting, now in English, now in Spanish, in the sound of María's mama, Carmen, singing in the kitchen behind a mountain of washing – and in María.

How boring white American girls were by comparison. She always had something to say and every word had

passion, although words alone weren't enough for the girl.
The accompanying hand gestures, facial expressions and
body language added so much more.

María's father, Miguel, was the owner of a highly
successful Mexican restaurant and worked all hours, so
Adam rarely saw him. The man doted on his eldest daughter,
however, and the boy had been warned by María that he'd
have to earn her father's respect. It was the Mexican way.

"Still thinks of me as his little girl," she explained.
"Don't get me wrong. He likes you, only – well—"

"Well what?"

"Keep your distance from me when he's around."

Adam faked glum – so María kissed and cuddled him
back to his usual jokey-yet-unconfident, self.

"Only when Papa's around!" she stressed. "Otherwise—"

She went quiet and blushed. He liked it when the girl
blushed – though he might have blushed himself if he'd
been privy to her thoughts as they embraced. But he
respected her religion, her determination to remain a virgin
until properly married – and he knew she'd *never* go against
her papa.

Which was why it came as a surprise that day in the
hospital in New York. He got the gist of what she said in
Spanish to her father over her cell phone as she sat at his
bedside:

"No, Papa! I'm staying here in New York till Adam's
better! Yes, Papa, I do understand! I'm so sorry – okay – all
those arrangements for nothing! But Papa, I can't leave him
here on his own. I just can't! That's final!"

María placed her free hand over Adam's.

"What do you mean by 'serious', Papa?"

María winked at Adam.

"Well, then I am serious! No, Papa, that's what a
quinceañera's all about, anyway. Coming of age – so, I'm
sorry Papa, but I can't – he'll just have to be *chamberlán* to

another girl. That's all. Plenty of us Mexican *chicas* around in Houston."

She went unusually quiet after coming off the phone.

"Fernando?" Adam queried.

Fernando was the Hispanic boy the López family had always assumed the girl would one day hang out with – mad about her, same neighborhood, same church. Later, a few weeks into their first semester at Senior High, Adam felt the full force of María's Mexican connection. After seeing her home one evening, he was set upon by a gang of Hispanic dudes in league with Fernando. He'd have been beaten to a pulp but for the intervention of Sam Royal, an African-American guy who, driving past, stopped and intervened and who took Adam, swollen-faced, back to the López home. María swore revenge on Fernando for what he'd done. The following day she slapped him with full Mexican fury in front of his buddies, told him he'd brought shame on their community and forced him to apologise in public to Adam.

Sam, married to a blue-eyed blonde, fully understood Adam's cross-ethnic love problems. A computer scientist, he ran a karate club evenings and weekends, and he and Adam became great pals. He coached Adam for free, and was dumbfounded by the speed and ability of his new pupil. Within weeks, without a single belt to his name, Adam won the Texas junior karate championships. By focusing on the Golden Jaguar bracelets before a contest, he was unbeatable. His opponent would've already lost as Adam imagined yet another Spike-like hunk making out with María. Sam, unaware of the power of the mysterious bracelets, merely wished to make a point by promoting his star pupil: that karate wasn't about belts or bits of paper but flowed from the heart.

María, too, became friendly with Sam and family, often baby-sitting for the five year-old Royal twin boys who would beg their parents to go out just so the girl could come round and play with them.

It was María's friendship with Adam's old chum Papa Pedro that clinched the white boy's acceptance by the Mexican Hispanic community.

Pedro was a respected elderly Mexican guy who owned an antiques shop and became almost more of a father to Adam than his own overworked dad, Johnny Winters, a computer scientist in the oil industry who, like María's papa, laboured all hours. When not working, he'd be slumped in front of the TV and Adam couldn't remember when they'd last had a meaningful conversation.

Most weekends, Adam, who also loved antiques, would spend hours in the old Mexican's shop just talking with Papa Pedro. The man's knowledge and wisdom seemed depthless, but what the boy enjoyed most was listening about the guy's past – and about Mexico. As Pedro talked, Adam heard strains of Mexican music play in his mind, saw men in sombreros and donkeys in dusty, winding streets lined by dirty, white-washed houses. Also, he could feel the tension and the volcanic violence of the place. Like many local Hispanics, Pedro was an illegal immigrant. Adam loved the story of Pedro and his wife being smuggled across the border into Texas hidden in a truckload of water melons.

Over the previous two years, Papa Pedro had given Adam extra Spanish lessons for free. 'In case one day you meet some fine Mexican girl,' he used to say. And when, after seeing María for the first time, he told Adam 'that girl's kinda special – know that?' it seemed there'd been something prophetic about his relationship with the old fellow. Not just a father figure but a priest substitute for a boy who never went to church – and now the man who had married them in another dimension?

When Pedro's wife, once a great beauty, died, Adam shared in his grief. That was shortly before Adam got beaten up by Spike and replaced the bully as María's boyfriend. Adam took the girl to meet him after they'd returned from New York, primarily to buy her a fifteenth birthday present. Her bust up with her papa over the cancelled *quineañera* had blown over, and Adam had promised a surprise gift by way of compensation. Something he and Pedro had planned.

The girl was crazy about quality antique dolls and the old Mexican had found just the job. A Victorian doll with blond ringlets and a blue crinoline dress that should have cost far more than Adam could afford. But they did a deal. If María could introduce Papa Pedro to her family, Adam would have the doll for the price of two cans of coke. Afterwards, the antiques dealer became a good friend of Miguel López and Adam no longer felt like an alien gringo.

What really happened whilst he and María had both lain unconscious in hospital, Adam could not recall. He'd been left with a lingering awareness of closeness to the girl such as he'd never before experienced, mixed with the shame of having distrusted her. As for acquiring the second bracelet, how this happened remained a puzzle. He never discussed the bracelets with María for he believed their strange power might be at variance with her devout Catholicism. Nevertheless, he knew they were somehow connected with the girl.

Once, he asked her what she remembered about that blank period in New York:

"I kinda remember a hollow opening up beneath me when I saw that picture of you and that blonde girl, and – oh my gosh, Adam, when the police came and said you were dead it was like – it was like I fell into that hole – then woke up in hospital and your momma was sitting there saying you were gonna be fine." María's eyes moistened. "Don't ever leave me like that again, Adam. Please don't!"

"D'you remember nothing else?"

María frowned.

37

"Fear!" she answered. "Just fear. And a pink and gold dress."

Adam chuckled.

"Fear and a pink and gold dress, huh?"

"Yeah, but not together. The dress was a kinda happy feeling."

They didn't talk about it again but María had changed. Even Art and Jeannie noticed it.

Adam and María had met the extraordinary couple in San Antonio a few weeks before when María was performing in the talent show contest that won the girl her recording contract. Art and Jeannie were at the same hotel for an Austin Healey Rally. Art, the owner of a highly successful haulage business, loved his red Austin Healey almost as much as he loved his vivaciously-funny wife, Jeannie. She was a plump blonde who never stopped laughing and Art, a wild-looking man with red hair and a crazy beard, seemed more like a prospector from the gold-rush of the eighteen-forties than a business-man of the twenty-first century. But Art and Jeannie were simply lovely and they both adored Adam and María whom Jeannie first met in the hotel pool:

"Oh my, you are pretty," Jeannie said on seeing María. "You must be Mexican or something?"

"How did you guess?" María asked, sounding fed up. She preferred to think of herself as American.

"Cos I ain't ever seen a white girl as lovely as you. Now, does *he* appreciate you, I'd like to know?" the woman added, looking pointedly at Adam.

"Oh, he likes the *fajitas* in my dad's restaurant!"

"And her dad shares ownership of two more restaurants in Mexico City with María's uncles," Adam added proudly.

"Ah, but that sure ain't why you love her, huh?"

Jeannie smiled at Adam. She had one of those smiles that ensures folk feel both warm and good inside. Art said that his wife's smile still made him go all weak at the knees,

Golden Jaguar of the Sun

even at the age of forty-seven. And they would tease each other endlessly as childless couples of that age do when still very much in love and totally happy with each other.

"Can't get Art to go anywhere near water," Jeannie pretended to complain that day when she met Adam and María in the pool. "Says it makes him wet."

After Spike had unexpectedly turned up in San Antonio with his Austin Healey-owning wealthy cousin, Nat, in the vain hope of winning back María, Art thought he might have to intervene when it appeared the heftier, athletic Spike was about punch his studious rival in love all the way back to Houston. Then he witnessed María lose her fiery Latin temper as she stood up for her new boyfriend:

"Don't you dare call my boyfriend Snowflake again!" she warned, glowering at the football-playing hulk looming above her.

"Baby, y'all look great," persisted Spike ignoring her remark. "Jus' leave little Snowflake behind an' you an' me we'll have real fun drivin' around in Nat here's Austin Healey, an' your lovely hair a-blowin' in the wind. An' then we'll go dancin' together all night in a club down town, huh?"

At which María slapped Spike hard across the face for the second time.

"Adam's pinky is worth more than the whole of you, Klaus O'Driscoll, you flathead!"

Spike tensed, his anger visible, but Art, a broad, strongly-built man, only had to take one step towards him and Spike slunk off, cursing.

"Hey, Jeannie! That girl's jus' like you. Knows how to stand up for herself!" Art declared.

"And since when did I stand up to you, Mr Art Weissenbach?" responded Jeannie, giving her husband a playful punch in the ribs.

Golden Jaguar of the Sun

Art and Jeannie had María giggling for most of that weekend in San Antonio. And Adam couldn't believe it when they turned up unannounced at the hospital in New York.

"You drove all the way from Des Moines, Iowa?"

"Sure thing, Adam! Can't remember whether we used the excuse of seein' our friends, Adam an' María, for a three day fun drive in my old gal (he called his car his 'old gal', Jeannie being his 'young gal'), or the other way around, but here we are!"

"How did you know?"

"I do read the newspapers, son. When the young gal lets me."

"Adam, you sure you're okay now?" Jeannie asked.

"I'm good, Jeannie. Home in a couple of days, they say."

"And you, María? What happened to you? We heard you kinda fainted on hearin' about Adam, and that you had those clever doctors scratchin' their heads wonderin' why you hadn't come to."

María shrugged her shoulders.

"As I told Adam. It was like I fell into a hole."

"Love!" Jeannie said after a pause. "That's what it is. You know, in the old days it was called an 'understanding' between two people."

Understanding? If only I understood María better. Special, Papa Pedro said. Yeah, but what the heck did he mean?

"Well, there's a whole Adam Winters fan club out there now!" Art informed the boy.

The man proceeded to tell Adam about the publicity surrounding his action at the party in Brooklyn. Big coverage on all the news channels and in the national press, and to cap it all the NYPD had recommended him for a bravery award. Because of his courage and quick thinking, the drug pushers had been arrested within hours and the whole gang in New York was being methodically broken

40

apart by the police. Young Chrissy, the one who'd lured both Adam and Lee to the party, and in league with the pushers, had put her own life at risk by co-operating with the police.

"I think she really cared about you, Adam. Seems you have a way with women, huh?"

Art winked at María, but the girl looked the other way. The mention of Chrissy's name made her Mexican blood boil.

"Only ever be one girl for me now, Art," Adam replied, taking hold of María's hand. "Only one!"

"I'll be after you, Adam my boy, if you ever let María down again. Hear that? She's special, see!"

Art held up his large fists like a prize fighter and winked.

Special? Art too?

"I won't," promised Adam.

If he'd known then how hard this was going to become – if he'd had even an inkling of the true reason why they'd been brought together and who the girl called María really was, would things have been different?

"They say it's nothing short of a miracle you're still alive, son. That knife cut through some pretty serious stuff. Lost more than half your blood. In fact—"

"STOP IT!" María's face looked drawn when she interrupted Art.

"Sorry, I just had to – no, never mind."

Be sure? thought Adam, finishing Art's sentence in his mind. *Be sure of what?*

Even in San Antonio he'd had a curious and irrational feeling that Art and Jeannie were not at the same hotel purely by chance – and that María served a purpose for them plus vice versa.

Art and Jeannie stayed on in New York until seeing off María, Adam and Ann Winters at La Guardia Airport. Before saying farewell, Art took Adam aside and reiterated what he'd already said more than once. This time he was serious: "She's truly special, Adam. You've gotta know that, son, but not the reason. Not yet! And because of her, you're special too. Can't say more. One day you'll understand. Be good to María. Stay with her always. Ain't never gonna find a woman like that again. Hear me?"

Adam never did forget Art's words.

The publicity was an embarrassment for both Adam and María, for conceit was something foreign to them – and they had no idea then how dangerous the media attention would be. In fact, they'd forgotten all about the whole business prior to the launch party for María's album at a new restaurant opened on the other side of Houston by Jorge López, María's owl-wise cousin from Mexico City.

María had always been so very fond of Jorge, a truly gentle soul, and she was over the moon when she heard he was moving to Texas. She could think of no better place for the local launch of her album and was delighted she'd finally get to wear her white *quinceañera* dress for the party, knowing how happy this would make her papa.

The restaurant was bursting with reporters and journalists, Mexican relatives and friends of both families, for it was as much a party to honour Adam's bravery as María's musical achievement. But as soon as Jorge started to play the girl's album something extraordinary happened. The excited jabber of Spanish and English stopped. Everyone went silent, stood still and listened, for they were spellbound by the haunting beauty of María's voice.

Then there were the speeches. Bruno, the guy who'd recorded the album, was down from New York and gave a moving address about two young people who had "changed his life forever". He thanked María for showing the world that a great singer can also be a humble and loving human being and he thanked Adam for saving his kid brother, Lee, from a fate worse than death. Chloe, Adam's ten-year old kid-sister, amused everyone by saying how pleased she was that Adam had such a pretty girlfriend, and that he "really does need a girl, you know, cos he never listens to me!"

María adored Chloe, but there was much more to the remarkable little girl than she was aware of. Chloe's artistic skills were almost as phenomenal as María's musical ability, but it was Chloe's strange 'sixth sense' that really set her apart – as María would one day discover.

Adam had never before felt so completely happy as at that party at Jorge's restaurant, but the best was to come at the very end when Johnny Winters stood up and made an announcement:

"They say you can move mountains if you really try—" he began.

"Sit down, Dad," whispered Adam, embarrassed. He had no idea what was coming next. Ann Winters knew, and, grinning, told Adam to "shush".

"See, when Adam was lying there in hospital and we thought he was gonna die I got to wondering what I could do for him if he pulled through. What he would wish for most in the world. Now it took a lot of phone calls, a lot of persuading, but in a week's time, son, you'll be starting at the same private Catholic Senior High as María."

Stunned, Adam sat motionless, his eyes brimming with tears of happiness. He'd assumed he would be going on to the public school and María to the expensive private Catholic school (with Spike) that had a reputation for music, and that this would be the end of it! María pushed her chair back, ran to the boy, flung her arms around him and kissed him on the lips, long and loving. That was the photograph that appeared on the front page of the *Houston Chronicle*.

Johnny Winters, unable to afford the fees for a private school, had sworn secrecy with Adam's mysterious benefactor.

Chapter 4: The Second Album

*"**So** you persuaded the old guy to pay for him to go to the same school as the girl. Was that wise? Haven't they had enough attention? Shouldn't they be kept apart till the time comes?"*

"Impossible. Besides, he needs to be challenged. How else can we be sure?"

"Challenged? His love?"

"No. His strength."

"Ah, that. And he doesn't even believe. Have we made the right choice? Does he really know what he's up against? Or who his enemy really is?"

"His enemy? Sees his enemy every morning in the mirror!"

***

Adam Winters awoke with a start. It was dark and sweat from his brow had dampened the pillow. His hand trembled as he reached for the clock with luminous hands beside his bed. Two-thirty in the morning – the morning of his first day at Senior High. He flopped back onto the pillow. Thank God it was only a dream. But, oh Jesus— María dead in his arms? Only a dream, only a dream, he kept on repeating to himself, but he still shook from the horror of it and in his brain hovered other frightening images: of an eerie, terrifying place where he feared he would lose María forever; of two fiery eyes seeking him out. Finally he managed to force his mind to see the girl he knew and loved so much: María López – her awesome eyes, her lively smile. Somehow he managed to drift off to sleep again thinking about María, his nightmare all but erased from his mind.

After the incident with Fernando, Adam had been befriended by another Mexican boy, Álvaro. It was he who spread word around about Adam's ability in karate; Álvaro who ensured Adam got respect from the Mexican contingency at the school and Álvaro who constantly warned him:

"Be careful, Adam!"

There was still anger amongst some at school that a Mexican girl with María's looks and fame had taken up with a white nerd. But what happened the day before Halloween forced all of this to the back of the boy's mind.

When he returned from school after walking María home, his family was seated around the kitchen table. Everyone went quiet, as if discussing something which they didn't quite know how to put to Adam.

"What's up, Mom?" he asked, placing his school bag on the table. "Why is everyone so glum?"

"Adam, I think you should sit down first."

"Mom? What is it? Dad lost his job or something?"

Adam knew there were often lay-offs in Johnny Winters' company and no one ever quite knew where the axe would next fall. His father shook his head.

"It's Papa Pedro," blurted Chloe. "He's dead."

"Chloe!" cautioned Ann Winters.

She'd wanted to break the news a little more gently but it was too late. For a few moments Adam sat staring into the distance, as if trying to make sense of what his little sister had just said.

"Did she – did Chloe say – erm – what?"

Adam felt unable to articulate any sort of meaningful sentence although he knew exactly what Chloe had said and what she meant. His mind didn't want to believe it. Ann Winters got up, came over to Adam and rested her hands his shoulders.

"This afternoon, honey. About two o'clock. Jorge phoned. Guess she'll know too, by now. He and Jorge were very close. Particularly after—"

Ann paused and looked down at Adam.

"Adam," she continued as her son gazed vacantly ahead, "there was something Papa Pedro didn't want to tell you. Said you'd enough worries and problems on your plate."

"But Mom, I saw him just the other day. He'd lost weight and looked so much fitter. It can't be. You've got it all wrong."

Adam turned to face his mother. There were tears in her eyes. She was telling the truth. But he didn't want to face that truth for, after María, Papa Pedro was his greatest friend. Surely you can't lose a friend just like that?

"Honey, Papa Pedro was not a well man," said Ann. "He had cancer. Was losing weight because of it. He'd known for a while. They said it was untreatable. You see, he loved you and María so very much but he didn't want to burden you guys with his problems. And the last thing he wanted was pity. He made us promise not to tell you until he'd passed away. And you know what, Adam? He was just so pleased that you and María continued to see him despite being swamped with work at St Joseph's. Made him real happy, that did."

"Today? How? What happened?" asked Adam. He felt strangely calm.

"Had a haemorrhage. So sudden. Called Jorge who rushed him to hospital but it was too late. He hoped the end would be quick and it was. Somehow I don't think he wanted to go on much longer. He still missed his wife terribly and after seeing you and María get together, well, I don't think he felt there was a need for him to hang on. It's like he—" Ann paused.

"Welcomed death?" Adam offered. She nodded and smiled. "Told me once," the boy said. "After his wife died. Said one day he'd welcome death. Guess that time came."

When Adam phoned María, she'd already heard and was crying at the other end of the line. She seemed curiously concerned about Papa Pedro being totally alone at the end of his life.

"But he had Jorge to comfort him," said Adam. "Mom says Jorge was really good to him at the end."

"It's not that, Adam," sobbed María. "It's – well, it must be such a lonely thing, dying. To leave this world all by yourself."

Adam, disturbed by the girl's obsession with death, particularly after the dream he'd had, went round to the López place after dinner. For a couple of hours they sat in María's room and talked and talked to a backdrop of shrieking and laughter from the girl's brothers and sisters. Hearing them so full of life seemed to make things worse. María became even more preoccupied with dying and the fear of leaving behind all memories of life.

"You know, it's funny how Papa Pedro always told me to live in the present," began Adam, trying to cheer her up, "but – well, I don't think he could ever let go of his wife. Told me recently he still loved her like crazy even though she's been gone for nearly six months. D'you think now they're, well – you know – kind of—?"

"Together again?" María interrupted, wiping away the tears with the back of her hand. She smiled – then frowned. "Dunno. But promise you'll never leave me like that, Adam. Like Pedro's wife left him. See, back there in New York—" María looked down at the floor. "What really happened to us in New York?" she asked. "I still have nightmares about it. Seems there's another place in those nightmares. Like some sort of high up temple. Men in black cloaks. A feeling of emptiness all around me. Papa Pedro dying kinda brought it back to me, all those nightmares.

"I only know what they told me. About being knifed and losing blood and—"

María placed two fingers over Adam's lips to silence him.

"Don't, Adam, please don't," she whispered. "Just hold me."

The funeral came as a relief, as if after it they could move on, forget death and live again. Although Papa Pedro had no immediate family in Houston, he'd been such a popular figure that a sizeable crowd turned up. The priest gave a heartfelt address and managed to get across what an extraordinary and loveable man Papa Pedro had been and how his life should be an inspiration to all. In some ways, Adam felt Papa Pedro wasn't completely dead. Something of the spirit of his old friend lived on in him and possibly in others present. Afterwards, when Adam and María were standing beside Papa Pedro's grave, hands clasped together, Jorge approached holding a guitar case.

"Pedro wanted you to have this, Adam," he explained. "Told me just before he died. Said there's a note inside. Here! Take it."

Jorge handed Adam the case that bore a silver plaque engraved with the initials 'S.F.' Before returning to school that afternoon, María and Adam took it back to his room. Inside the case was an awesome red electric guitar. For a few moments they sat staring at it, speechless and puzzled. María, tearful again, retrieved a scrap of paper underneath the guitar. It bore an untidily scribbled message in Spanish. The girl read in silence then looked up.

"Papa Pedro asks us to take the guitar back to Mexico City," she said. "To bury beside Santiago, the son of his friend, Conchita Fernandez. The boy was a singer like me. Got killed in a car crash two years back. Conchita wanted Papa Pedro to sell it but he says he couldn't. Believed the boy's spirit was still somewhere inside the guitar – so he wants it returned to its owner. 'It's the right thing to do. I feel it here,' he says." María patted her chest then handed her boyfriend the note. "Says 'trust only those you love.' Why?"

"For me, María," replied Adam, his guilt resurfacing. "A threat, more like," thinking of Art and his fists.

He studied the girl for a few uncomfortable moments. There was something in her eyes. Was she trying to recall what lay buried deep in her mind? Seeing her like this, he, too, felt it. Terrifying – but had it yet happened? A hidden memory or a premonition? Something to do with death?

"Adam, I still get those nightmares. They're awful."

Suddenly, she buried her face on Adam's shoulder and wept and the boy held her close. He'd never told her about his dream of holding her dead in his arms, but the idea that it had been a premonition had become a conviction. Why else should they have shared a similar dream?

Adam wiped the girl's tears with his handkerchief then chuckled whilst struggling to brush away dark thoughts:

"I can just see the old guy patting his chest as he wrote 'trust only those you love.' That's you, María. You know that, don't you?"

She kissed him and a smile brightened her face.

"So you will come to Mexico with Papa and me? Maybe a little less jealousy on your part will keep you safe next time."

Adam's expression changed.

Teasing me? No, no! Not that again! Just back to her old self, I guess! But do I really know that self? A little less jealousy, huh? To keep me off my guard?

***

María phoned Adam the day after the funeral. Typically Mexican, she made no mention of Pedro. It was as if the whole business about the death of the old antiques dealer had been sealed into her past and had nothing to do with the present. She so bubbled with excitement Adam could barely get a word in edgeways:

"Oh, you'll never guess! We've another reason for going to Mexico now! The two of us! Ain't it just awesome! Over the Christmas recess! Spoke to them today and—"

"María, what?"

"Jorge's arranging the flights. We'll have nearly three weeks there. Extra time off school. Can't believe it. You will do it won't you? I said you would."

"Do what? I dunno what—"

"The album, Adam! The new album! I told them 'yes' straightaway. Only just off the phone to Jorge. Please, Adam. Had to let them know immediately. Oh, I'm so excited!"

"New Album? Mexico? María, what are you talking about?"

"Best label in Mexico. Subsidiary of the label in New York. They've asked me to do a new album of Mexican songs. Wanted to start next week but I told them it'd have to wait till the Christmas recess. Oh – and I said only on one condition." María chuckled at the other end of the phone.

"What's that, María?" Adam was getting her drift and felt more than a little uncomfortable.

"Guess!" she replied.

"Oh, you didn't say that – did you?" María began to laugh. "María, how can I sing? And in Spanish – for Mexicans?"

"*¡Perfectamente, mi amor!*"

"María, you should've..."

"No," the girl insisted firmly, "I shouldn't have. You would've said 'yes', anyway. I know it! I told them I'd make the album only on condition we sing together. At least for some of the tracks. So – gonna be busy, *chico*!"

"Hmmm!" grunted Adam.

The girl was right about one thing. If she made up her mind, he, Adam, would agree. As for the singing bit, he had a good voice. Lack of confidence had discouraged him from singing anywhere close to other humans, but María changed that. They often sang together in his room with María playing the guitar. Even he had to admit they sounded better than most America's Got Talent boot campers.

Soon their school was abuzz with talk about María's new album, '*Lo Siento Dentro di Mí*'. The girl would be writing all the songs herself.

"'I feel it inside me!' For Papa Pedro," María explained. "Wanted to do something for his memory. This seemed the best way."

Amanda, María's best friend, in her usual jesting manner pretended she was upset that María would be making the album with Adam:

"Shucks!" she exclaimed, "I'd hoped you'd leave the dude behind so I could look after him for you!"

"No way, Amanda! Why d'you think I'm taking him with me?" She winked at Adam whose face turned cardinal red. "Besides," she added. "I'll need a strong guy to look after me! Anything can happen in Mexico City!"

"Anything?" queried Amanda. "Wow, Mexico City here I come, guys!"

Amanda, a plump girl with a passion for photography, an outrageous hair-do and a tendency to wear things intended for figures several sizes smaller than hers, couldn't have been more different from María, yet Adam liked her. His own best pal, Álvaro, was the polar opposite. Never joked about anything and in addition to lacking the fiery yet happy-go-lucky Mexican temperament, he was forever moaning about being a 'disadvantaged Hispanic'.

"We run this goddamn place (Houston), but who get the top jobs? Who get all the privileges?" the boy once asked. "Goddamn white guys! Sorry! You're different, of course, Adam. More like one of us."

"Bit of a chip on his shoulder, if you ask me," María grumbled after an earful from Álvaro.

"He's a real pal," protested Adam.

"Not saying he isn't, but—"

"But what?"

"Be careful."

"That's just what Álvaro says!"

Adam felt more than a little cross with María but soon forgot it when she held him close and kissed him.

"Be careful! That's all I ask," she repeated before disappearing for an extra music class.

Álvaro seemed over the moon that Adam would be accompanying María to Mexico City.

"Cool, man! You should meet up with my cousin, Alejandro," he suggested. "Important guy! Knows all the right people! He'll be a great help to you both. Could take you to the recording studio each day. Get you an armed guard."

"Armed guard?" Adam was puzzled. He knew his friend never joked about anything. "We ain't going to Colombia, Álvaro. Just Mexico City! Besides, María's got plenty of family there."

"I've told Alejandro anyways. He can't wait to meet you two. He adored María's first album!"

Another handsome hunk? Shit!

The piercing pain of jealousy pricked again! No way would they meet up with the guy.

***

The boy who had transformed from classroom geek to national hero flew with María and her papa to Mexico City. María's Tío Federico and Tía Bea welcomed Adam into their family as if he were one of their own. Miguel López returned to Texas later the following day after a frantic time sorting out business affairs with his brother. Things were going well for the López family – almost too well, for they planned to open two more restaurants in San Antonio and Dallas. Miguel teasingly asked Adam whether he'd considered running a Mexican restaurant himself, for he seemed to enjoy Mexican cuisine that much. María appeared embarrassed by this but Adam laughed it off, saying archaeology was more his thing and that he didn't think fossilized *fajitas* would go down too well.

With María's father back in Texas, that left María's uncle and aunt, Jorge's sister Ana-María, who worked in a designer boutique, and the crazy twins Camilo and Javier, approximately the same age as Adam although they seemed painfully young. Definitely not into girlfriends, but they were good fun. They called Adam '*el profesor*' since he was far more knowledgeable than them about ancient Mexican history.

There was a constant bustle, as in the Houston López residence. Fortunately Adam and María had worked hard on the tracks for the new album back home in Texas otherwise they'd have had little chance of getting the songs up to scratch in Mexico City.

One of the first things they did in Mexico was to contact Conchita Fernández about returning Santiago's guitar which they'd brought from Houston. They had already met the woman at Papa Pedro's funeral. Tío Federico drove them to Santiago's cemetery after picking up Conchita on the way.

She was quiet, in many ways quite un-Mexican, and she kept turning round to Adam to say "*¡Gracias, gracias!*" María chatted away in Spanish and the woman finally opened up a little, telling them stories about Papa Pedro that Adam hadn't yet heard. As a young man he'd rescued a child from a blazing building and once he'd fought off armed muggers in Mexico City, but the saddest thing was his sorrow that he and his wife had never been able to have children of their own. Conchita explained this was why he used to call himself 'Papa Pedro'.

Then she told them about the Old Woman of the Hills.

After Santiago's death, her husband had taken the boy's guitar to the Old Woman of the Hills who had "unearthly powers and knew about things long forgotten". She could communicate with deceased ancestors and José Fernández had hoped she'd be able to magically return his son's beloved guitar to the boy on the other side of the grave. Conchita had shown him the way since her husband had a hopeless sense of direction. The Old Woman said it was beyond her powers to pass material things across the "wall of death", but she could free the guitar from its sadness and allow it to be played by others. Curiously, before that day no one alive had been able to produce any sensible music with the instrument whereas afterwards the sound it created was awesome. Somehow this troubled José who, now believing it to be possessed, asked his old friend in Houston to sell the instrument in his shop.

María seemed strangely upset by the story. Adam realised that native Mexican superstition would be at variance with her religion, but he sensed that wasn't what disturbed the girl. The boy reckoned she knew more about the Old Woman than she let on but he didn't press her further. They'd both had enough of death.

Tío Federico parked his car in front of the cemetery, remaining there whilst the others went inside, Adam carrying the guitar. The cemetery was unlike any place the boy had ever seen in Houston. It was enclosed within stark, white-washed stone walls, above which crosses on the taller monuments and the occasional head of an angel were the only indication from the outside that this was a place of burial and not a prison. Within those walls it was very different. There was a feeling of peace that contrasted absolutely with the noise and energy of Mexico City. Adam gazed at the monuments and tombstones, all of which bore inscriptions of the names of departed loved ones, the dates when they'd entered and when they'd left this world, and messages in Spanish which, although unable to fully make out, he knew were there to comfort the relatives left behind. Sadness magnified by silence pervaded the cemetery. In the setting sun the monuments cast sharp, dark shadows across the path, and these seemed like reminders of death. The boy knew death was the great silencer of all things, but he wondered whether, if he were to listen really hard, he might actually hear the sadness of death; harder still, and perhaps also the voices of those who'd died, whispering across the terrible emptiness that separates the dead from the living: the 'wall of death'.

In his mind flashed another place in another dimension where he'd waited for what seemed an eternity whilst an old woman tried to communicate with a departed soul across that same wall. Adam knew this hadn't been just a dream and that it was to do with María being in danger, but the vision vanished immediately. Had this been in the past, a previous life all but erased from his memory, or could it have been an awful premonition of the future? So many disturbing thoughts entered the boy's head but when he looked at María he saw only life. She so radiated vitality she became an incandescence that vanquished all fears of darkness and dying. For the first time Adam felt certain there was something about the girl that could even overcome death.

The boy could scarcely believe that only eight months back María had been no more than a pretty girl in his class whom he longed to speak to whereas now he felt closer to her than to anyone else in the world. How ironical that he'd only started to have such feelings for the girl when her then boyfriend, Spike, began his intensive bullying. If his mother hadn't told him about Spike's tragic private life he might have considered thanking the bully. Not only had the teasing helped Adam realise his love for María, but it had also made him more determined to win her love. In a funny kind of way it had given him strength. However, knowing what he now knew about Spike he had no wish to gloat. He simply wanted to be with María – always.

Conchita Fernández took Adam and María to show them where her beloved son, Santiago, had been laid to rest. María genuflected and crossed herself in front of the tomb. Adam, although not a Catholic, did likewise. It made him feel closer to the girl.

Adam followed Conchita and María into the office beside which stood a chapel. The widow introduced them to a priest whom she'd arranged to meet and whom she obviously knew well. Solemn and restrained, they were a world away from the noisy López household. The priest wished to see the guitar and Adam removed this from the case after showing the man the initials 'S. F.' on its lid. Conchita reached out and lovingly stroked her deceased son's initials. There were tears in the old lady's eyes. The man gently took the guitar in both hands, smiled at the widow and spoke softly in Spanish. Adam didn't quite catch what was said but he knew it must have been something comforting. Later, the boy learned how Papa Pedro had left Conchita Fernández money to have the red guitar interred beside Santiago's tomb. Above it was to be a plaque bearing a simple inscription: *La Guitarra de Santiago Fernández*.

Having returned the red guitar to its case, and closed the lid, the priest placed the case on a small table behind him. María and the old lady disappeared with him into the chapel to pray, leaving Adam staring at the worn case. It felt like saying "goodbye" to old Papa Pedro all over again.

"Adam, do you believe in God?" María asked as they walked back to the car, her large brown eyes both loving and questioning.

"Chloe's always asking me that!" he replied evasively.

"And what do you tell her?" queried María.

"Well, I used to say 'I don't know'."

Golden Jaguar of the Sun

"And what do you say now? To me?" the girl persisted.

"María, I—" He paused. "I believe, but I don't know what it is I believe in."

She smiled and whispered in his ear. He put his hand over the ear as if this might keep her three magical words there forever.

"I love you, too," he whispered back.

"That's enough, then!" she laughed.

In Mexico City, Adam and María did meet up with Alejandro, Álvaro's cousin. Adam had no choice in the matter. Álvaro must have got the girl's cell phone number from Amanda, for it was his cousin who called María. Thankfully he was older than Adam expected, probably over thirty, and quite unlike Álvaro. Typically Mexican, he was more easy-going and his English was perfect – better than Adam's Spanish. Most important of all, no one could have described Alejandro as remotely handsome. A receeding chin and prominent teeth reassured Adam there was little danger of María transferring her affection. Also, Álvaro was proved right. He was a godsend in the urban jungle of Mexico City. María, however, seemed unsure about him – much to her boyfriend's relief for his charm made up for his lack of looks.

"I dunno know what it is, Adam. Almost over-friendly."

Nothing seemed too much bother for Alejandro. With Jorge now in Houston, they had no 'private chauffeur' on tap. The man apparently had all the time in the world to adopt this role and drove them to and from the recording studio every day, plus on days off showed Adam the sights in and around Mexico City. His generosity was without limits. He took them out to lunch each day, bought Adam a book about the Maya and even offered to buy him an acoustic guitar though this was declined. But the boy felt uneasy when, the day before the completion of the album, Alejandro produced for María a beautiful pearl necklace with a ruby set in gold. It looked perfect around her pretty neck, matching her red dress, but Adam's jealousy hit the gong. María was too taken aback to comment. Alejandro said the necklace would be just right for the album cover shot. The girl had already told him she'd be wearing the red dress her mother made for the San Antonio talent show – the same one she'd worn for the cover of her first album.

"I'm sure he means well," Adam suggested, trying to ignore stabs of jealousy. "Says I'm such a good friend of his 'miserable' cousin. His word. S'pose it's like repayment for listening to Álvaro's moans about how badly the Mexicans are treated back home. Funny how the other Latinos at school don't care much for him."

"You're too kind. That's the real trouble!" María responded tersely.

She said nothing to her uncle or aunt about the necklace, hiding it in her red handbag after briefly slipping it on for the cover photograph at the recording studio.

Adam got stuck into the book about the Maya and for this alone he was grateful to Alejandro. The beautifully illustrated tome so fired his imagination he stayed up till the early hours each night absorbing every detail. He learned about the Mayan belief that the creation of the Earth resulted from a discussion between two gods, the god of the sky and the god of the sea. What an interesting discussion that must've been, he reckoned. He read about these gods' dissatisfaction with an Earth filled only with animals and birds and about how the Maya believed these two gods first experimented by producing mud people then people made from wood before finally coming up with an acceptable design for the human race: one that could commune with and pay respect to the gods.

"And what did 'pay respect' mean, precisely?" María asked suspiciously.

"Yeah! You're right. Wasn't only the Aztec gods who demanded blood from those poor bastards who got sacrificed. They thought of human blood as a sort of Life-Force for the gods. Used it to appease them. But the Maya weren't as bad as the Aztecs."

"Yuk!" she exclaimed. "They were all bad!"

"But—" Adam began, stretching back on his bed and staring at the ceiling. "—but the funny thing is only people who'd met a violent end were allowed to go straight to paradise. Perhaps those who were sacrificed really believed it was the best way to get to heaven."

María, sitting on the edge of the bed, looked down at her boyfriend then shook her head.

"I think they'd have been terrified. I know it!" The fear in the girl's eyes told Adam perhaps she really did know. But how?

"Funny thing is, Maya folk believed people who kinda died naturally ended up in a terrifying place – an underworld called Xibalba. Means 'Place of Fear'. The poor dudes who landed up there had to face a whole heap of crap to prove themselves before being allowed to float up to heaven. Most never got there. Goodness and – erm—"

"Love?" María offered, her liquid eyes melting the boy's insides.

"Yeah. Love. These things didn't figure at all. But—"

The boy could resist no longer. He sat up, took María in his arms and kissed her – and kissed her and kissed her till she complained she couldn't breathe.

"They got it wrong about the ancient Maya predicting the world was gonna end in 2012. Just the end of some astronomical cycle. But the Brotherhood of the Sword of God – a whacko religious sect – they now say first of January two thousand and seventeen's gonna be the big day. So, Señorita López, we're gonna have to 'do it' before then – even if that means getting married first."

The girl said nothing. He kissed her again – and again and again – until something inside warned him to stop. He sat back and he looked at her.

"Why are you looking at me like that?" she asked quietly.

"We've gotta – you know – 'do it' before that happens! That end of the world stuff. Married or not."

"Shhh!" she hushed, gently placing her hand over his lips. "You know how I feel, Adam. There'll only ever be you – but we must wait. Please understand. Anyway, I don't believe in crazy predictions."

She got up and disappeared off to her room. Oh, how he ached to be with her all night but he respected her feelings. As he drifted off to sleep he wondered how those Sword of God weirdos reckoned it would happen. Nuclear war? A cosmic cataclysm – collision with a giant asteroid? More likely, a solar storm wiping out electricity across the civilised world. Whatever, he and María had to be properly 'together' before January two thousand and seventeen.

Curse all religion! I have to make love to her!

But his curse got no further than his brain.

Adam slept fitfully that night and in one of his vivid dreams he saw María and Alejandro in each other's arms on the top of an ancient Aztec temple. María was naked apart from a short skirt of green jade and Alejandro was attired like a warrior-priest straight out of his book. When Adam interrupted the copulating couple, María seemed annoyed. "You don't belong here," she told him. "Just white gringo trash. Go away!" Next, two piercing black eyes with fiery red slits hovered above the couple as the girl began to climax. The eyes seemed to be searching for him. A voice accused him of weakness and of failing the girl.

When he awoke he was wearing both golden jaguar bracelets, one on each wrist. He must have got up in the night, opened his bedside cabinet drawer and slipped them on, although he had no recollection of this. Because of the dream, he kept them on.

The big day: completion of the second album. They'd gotten used to the routine after New York and the guys at the studio in Mexico City were every bit as friendly as Bruno and the New Yorkers had been for María's first album. María wore the ruby and pearl necklace for the media photos, quickly removing it afterwards and hiding it in her handbag. Again a party was held, but nothing as daunting as the one in New York. Far more informal and this time Adam successfully suppressed his simmering jealousy whenever the girl smiled and giggled with the media boys. Alejandro joined in but seemed put out that María wasn't still wearing the necklace. She blushed whilst explaining how she thought she'd have been overdressed sporting such awesome jewellery but reassured him she'd worn it for press shots.

Why did she blush? What hold had this man over his girlfriend?

After the party, Alejandro offered to drive them home. As they walked to the car park, he explained how taxi drivers in Mexico City were not to be trusted when it came to celebrities. There'd been no space in the studio parking facility but it was only a short walk to the public one. Adam felt like a 'man' for the first time in his life, his fabulous and famous Mexican girlfriend holding onto him for support as she took small, girly steps in her red high-heeled shoes. These were a perfect match for that stunning red dress which perhaps revealed more of the girl's shapely legs than Adam wished for in Alejandro's presence. Tía Bea had shortened this a little on Ana-María's suggestion.

It happened so quickly Adam had no time to think. On turning a corner, he heard a screech of tires. A black van jerked to a halt alongside them, the van door opened and simultaneously María was grabbed by the arm and pulled away from him. The girl screamed and Adam, frantic, tried to hold onto her but someone stronger gripped his arm from behind and he was forced to let go. The boy's reflexes were fast. He swung round, brought one leg up between his opponent's legs, twisted an arm, and shot his other hand towards the man's neck. Dodging the blow, the man overbalanced and fell sprawling to the ground. Adam swivelled to catch hold of María but all he saw were her bared legs sticking out from the open van, her dress up around her waist exposing her underwear. Her red shoes kicked helplessly as she got dragged further into the vehicle whilst her screams cut into him like flying daggers.

Alejandro shouted Spanish obscenities as he struggled with another bastard who, like Adam's assailant, wore a balaclava. A blow to the jaw sent Alejandro staggering across the side-walk. The man who'd grabbed Adam was now up on his knees. He pulled a knife and Adam stepped back, knowing only too well what a knife could do. The dude got up and edged towards him. María's feet had vanished into the van, her squeals muffled, then drowned, by the revving of the van's engine. Alejandro yelled out:

"*¡Para!*"

"*Un revólver,*" exclaimed the man with the knife in alarm. A sharp shot rang out as the two black-hooded figures leapt into the back of the black van when it swung free from the sidewalk. Alejandro, still on the ground on one knee, pointed his gun at the van and fired again. The van swerved, gathering speed, screamed round the corner, and was gone. The sound of the disappearing vehicle dwindled, soon replaced by silence.

Alejandro stood up and came over to Adam. The boy could neither move nor speak. Barely able to take in his next breath, he stared at the empty road where he'd just seen his girlfriend bundled into a black van. Then the man did an extraordinary thing. A motorcyclist appeared from the direction taken by the van. Adam's new friend stepped into the road and pointed his gun at the rider. The bike skidded to a halt just in front of him.

"Did you pass a black van?" asked Alejandro in Spanish.

The terrified motorcyclist merely nodded.

"Off!" ordered Alejandro, waving his gun. The man stumbled in his haste to dismount. In no time Alejandro was astride the bike and away, leaving Adam and the bewildered motorcyclist standing together on the side-walk. The biker removed his helmet and approached Adam. The boy still trembled with impotent rage. The man spoke in Spanish but at first Adam could only speak in English:

"They've bloody taken her!" he kept repeating. "Those bastards have taken María."

"You know the swine who took my bike?" the biker asked in Spanish.

"*Sí,*" Adam replied, his Spanish returning. "*Es un amigo.*"

The motorcyclist angrily paced up and down, muttering and kicking at the edge of the side-walk, but the man's plight was trivial compared with María's. She was in real danger. Adam had no idea who these people were. He must have been standing there for a good twenty minutes, numb with fear for his girlfriend, listening to the ranting of the motorcyclist, when his ears picked up the whine of a motorbike. The sound scaled a crescendo before the bike roared round the corner. Alejandro deftly swung the machine in an arc and came to a standstill beside Adam, the engine still putt-putting.

"*¡Muchas gracias, señor!*" he said, stepping off the bike and graciously returning it to the other man. The motorcyclist put on his helmet, grunted something, got back onto his bike and sped off.

"Had to try, Adam," explained Alejandro, "but they were already gone. Could be anywhere by now."

He rubbed his face, red and swollen on the side where the gangster had slugged him, before placing a comforting arm across Adam's shoulders.

"Don't worry, Adam!" he said. "This is Mexico. I know how these gangsters work. They'll want some money – a ransom – from María's papa. Then you'll get her back. Happens all the time, my friend. A favourite Mexican pastime!"

Adam barely heard what Alejandro was saying. Though tears welled, it was as if these belonged to another person. Inside he felt different. There he was strong and his only thought was to get María back undamaged. There was also raw anger, but Papa Pedro's voice from the past echoed somewhere inside his skull, instructing him to control the anger for "anger can only do more harm" as the old man often said. Sam Royal had given the same advice for karate. The boy glanced at the Golden Jaguar bracelets around his wrists and realised it was these giving him a strange inner strength. Perhaps they might lead him to María.

Alejandro made a cell phone call.

"The police," he informed Adam. "Gave them a full description of María and of the vehicle. Now we'd better get back to her uncle's place. They'll call soon, I know it. I must be there when they do. Just so long as we don't put a foot wrong she'll be fine."

They ran to Alejandro's car in the public car park and Alejandro drove like fury, taking side streets, impatiently skirting around slower vehicles. Meanwhile, Adam phoned Tía Bea. He couldn't believe how calm he sounded as he recounted the awful news. From somewhere deep down a mysterious power had welled up and given him a confidence and determination that felt unbeatable. María *would* be rescued – *he* would find her.

Back at the López family home it seemed as if Adam had walked into a madhouse. The boy was just so thankful

Alejandro was with him as, together, they tried to calm everyone down. The man was proving to be a true friend. María's cousin, Ana-María, had returned early from work and she and Tía Bea were hysterical. Tío Federico was shouting into the phone to Miguel López. An elderly woman friend, unknown to Adam, had joined the scene and was also shedding floods of tears, but none of this was getting them anywhere. Alejandro spoke soothingly to the women, took the phone from Federico and talked sagely to Miguel López. Gradually some sort of order prevailed.

Alejandro gave Miguel his cell phone number then put down the other phone, explaining that they should keep it free at all times until they'd heard from María's kidnappers. He called the police again from the cell phone and soon afterwards the López's phone rang, causing Adam's heart to miss a beat. Alejandro answered. He nodded, looked at Adam then handed him the phone. It was María.

"Adam!" she cried. "I'm so frightened. Please make them do everything these men say. Please. I'm – OW!"

There was a scratching sound followed by a gruff male voice that gabbled in Spanish. Adam could no longer hold back the tears after hearing María's anguished sobs. He gave the phone to Alejandro and joined the weeping women. By the time three police officers arrived, twenty minutes later, the full picture had emerged:

María's captors were demanding three million US dollars in ransom. Since the police were now involved (how did the kidnappers know?), they informed Alejandro that María would be moved to a more 'secure' location. They said they knew the López family had the money and they'd have to pay up if they wanted to see the girl alive again. All of this Alejandro relayed to Adam and the family as he spoke with the kidnappers.

Meanwhile, the police arrived: three armed officers.

"Yes, yes, pay up now. Straightaway!" Adam pleaded. Tío Federico stood shaking his head. "Please! Now! Just give them the sodding money. Get María back," the boy insisted. He looked from Alejandro, to the police officers, to Tío Federico and back to Alejandro. "We'll have to wait till they call again, Adam. Until then—" Alejandro turned to address Tío Federico. "—I suggest the family gets the money ready ASAP! They want it in US dollars. At least—" He turned to face Adam again. "At least we know María is – well, she's alive."

Alive but damaged? Adam recalled the white flash of his girlfriend's underwear as she got dragged kicking into that van. He fought to control his fury. He had to stay calm – to think.

"Your cell phone, Alejandro," he requested. "Tío Federico – Conchita Fernández's number, please!"

"Adam, have you gone crazy? Why would you wish to trouble that poor old woman?"

"She knows someone who can help us find María. That's why." By raising his eyebrows, Alejandro made it clear he reckoned his young friend had completely lost it.

Against a background of shouting, wailing and weeping, Adam phoned Conchita. Thank God she was in. In slow and carefully-worded Spanish he spoke to the old lady:

"Adam Winters – yes, Adam – Papa Pedro's friend. Yes – Santiago's red guitar. Look, something terrible has happened. To María – yes, *María*. We'd just finished recording her second album when she got kidnapped – *kidnapped!* Dragged off in the street and taken away in a van – a black one – it is awful, but – but I'm just hoping you can help find her – yes, *you!*"

Adam stroked the face of the jaguar on the gold bracelet around his right wrist as he spoke. Something immensely powerful stirred inside him.

Golden Jaguar of the Sun

"Conchita, you know how your husband took Santiago's guitar to that Old Woman of the Hills outside Mexico City to have it blessed? Made special?" Adam stood with the phone to his ear whilst Alejandro stared at him, stupefied. He obviously reckoned the boy had turned certifiably insane. "Yes, I'm sure she'll still be there. I just need to know how to get to her – yes – yes – in about forty minutes."

He returned the cell phone to Alejandro.

"Can you take me – like right now?" Adam asked.

Alejandro's chinless jaw fell open.

"Erm – I really should stay here, Adam. By the phone. With María's family."

Adam glanced at one of the police officers who merely shrugged his shoulders. Exasperated, the boy turned to go upstairs.

"I'll take a taxi then! Go by myself!" he muttered tetchily before leaving the room.

"Okay, *okay,* Adam! But please tell me what this is all about," Alejandro called out, following Adam upstairs into María's bedroom. The boy appeared to be searching for something.

"Ah – here she is!" he exclaimed, picking up the Victorian doll he'd bought for María at Papa Pedro's. He knew how much the girl loved that doll.

"I'll call my mom first and then we go," he told Alejandro. "Take your cell phone and leave the number with Tío Federico."

From the expression on Alejandro's face, Adam could tell that his friend was unhappy. The man wasn't used to being given orders.

"Look, I know what I'm doing. I'll explain later. Honest I will!"

Alejandro shook his head in despair as Adam phoned his mother. The boy had never known her so upset.

67

"Adam, I just don't know what to say. It's all so awful. Poor Carmen is beside herself with worry. And you, honey – must be terrible for you. Look, we've gotten a flight for Mexico City tomorrow. Can't let Carmen come alone. Jorge's gonna try and make it as well in a day or two. Oh, I do pray we have María back safe by then."

"Mom, I'll find her. I know I will."

"Adam, please, *please* be careful. These men will be dangerous. Far worse than in New York."

"I'll get her back! Promise María's momma from me. I've – I've got it worked out."

"Adam?"

The boy had no time to explain his plan. He and Alejandro left the López household in a state of fox-in-a-chicken-house panic. On the way to pick up Conchita Fernández, he spelt out what must have seemed a lunatic notion to the man:

"She'll take us to see this Old Woman who lives in a cave in the hills. Conchita says she remembers the way. José, her husband, had a terrible sense of direction. She had to show him how to get there when he took Santiago's red guitar to be blessed. Released from the dead man's spirit so it could be played again. I have a hunch the Old Woman is still alive – that somehow she'll never die. In fact, I know it!"

"Pfff! Superstitious Mexican bullshit!" exclaimed Alejandro making no attempt to conceal his scorn. "I'm sorry, Adam, but you really are mad. *¡Loco!*"

He tapped the side of his head.

"So – not heard of the Membrane Theory, then? Eleven dimensions?" probed Adam.

"Eleven bollocks, gringo! You care about María? Then listen to me!"

"I did! You and Álvaro. And look what happened! They bloody took her! You had a gun, for God's sake!" Adam started to count up to ten inside his head. Something María had him do whenever he felt his blood boil – which was pretty often. "Alejandro," he continued after ten, "this Old Woman has special powers whatever dimension she's in. I'm certain if she holds this doll of María's – the one I got for her from Papa Pedro – our old friend in Houston who died – she'll be able to tell me exactly where María is. Then we can go there together. You and I. With the police. We'll rescue her."

"You're completely crazy! A blessed guitar? You know nothing about us mad Mexicans! And that Old Woman – if she ever existed, she'll be a dried out pile of bones lying in some forgotten cemetery. Everyone dies sooner or later, *amigo!*"

"She'll never die," insisted Adam, a conviction he felt even more strongly on stroking one of the Golden Jaguar bracelets again. Something informed his brain that she and her cave were outside the dimensions of Life, Time or Death. Alejandro nodded thoughtfully.

"I'd like to help, Adam, even if this ghost of a woman does tell you where they've taken the girl. You know I would. But these guys'll be armed. And we can't go without the money!"

"I'll go alone if I have to," persisted Adam.

"No! I can't let you do that."

"Tell me, do you always carry a gun?"

Alejandro glanced at the boy.

"In Mexico City, *Sí.*"

"Fat lot of good it did," Adam added caustically. "Would do better getting a few lessons from Sam Royal."

"Sam who?"

"Never mind!"

"Look, I'm trying to help you. Don't make things so personal, gringo!"

"Call me gringo once more and – and María will slap you so hard your own mother wouldn't recognise you!"

69

Alejandro chuckled.

"That, I think I would enjoy, huh?" The twinkle in the man's eyes was difficult to decipher.

An hour later, Adam was back in his friend's car. Conchita Fernández sat up front directing Alejandro who drove on and into the hills beyond the city limits. They were heading for the vague destination of "a cave somewhere up there" which the old lady indicated with a wave of the hand in the direction of the arid mountains ahead – and perhaps another dimension...

Chapter 5: The Old Woman of the Hills

"I can't believe what I'm hearing," roared Tezcatlipoca. He eyed his servant on Earth with suspicion. "The beast no longer obeys you? How come?"

The servant felt confused. Things had changed. Tezcatlipoca seemed less threatening. Was the strange power in the girl truly greater than that of The Great Sun God and Quetalóatl combined? He remembered wishing he'd been chosen by Quetzalóatl before the good god got banished.

Adam had been having occasional, weird flashbacks for some time but now they came more frequently and were increasingly vivid.

Flashbacks of concealed memories? Often, as he absent-mindedly traced the outline of the jaguar's head on one of his bracelets, he'd see coal-black eyes staring from the face of a large cat-like creature with glistening golden fur. They would suddenly vanish, replaced by other horribly-real images – as real as they were strange: a huge lake, fringed with mountains, upon which, in the distance, he saw a strange island city: a vast and terrifying square, empty, at the far end of which stood a giant red stepped pyramid. Over this hung an aura of desolation and despair like a cloud distilled from droplets of fear. Seeing such images the boy sensed María was facing death and that time was running out. Although fleeting, he knew they weren't imagined; they were fact, and from his past, yet commonsense told him this was impossible.

It happened again as Conchita told Alejandro to pull the car into a lay-by on that deserted gravel road in the foothills of the mountains. From the car, Adam saw a well-worn path winding up the steep slope. Certain he'd already been there he could feel his legs still pounding the same path, his mind heavy with dreadful urgency. He half-remembered how María's life had been in the balance somewhere else in another dimension. Conchita observed his confusion:

"Some say the Old Woman's mad, Adam, but she isn't. Her wisdom's awesome. Trust her," she urged.

After Adam and Alejandro left the car, Conchita called out to the boy from the window as he hurriedly set off up the path clutching María's doll in one hand and a map of Mexico in the other:

"Listen carefully!"

The path soon became steep. Adam led the way and Alejandro had difficulty keeping up with his young friend who part ran, part scrambled up the slope. Normally, the boy had no head for heights but now, as they climbed higher, the drop down to the road didn't bother him. By the time they were within sight of the cave, Alejandro's car had become a blue dot way below.

Adam climbed onto a stony ledge in front of the cave, soon joined by Alejandro. For a few moments they stood staring at the dark cave entrance and the heap of meagre offerings of food and clothes left outside. Another déjà vu, but this reassured him that his idea wasn't completely jumping jack-rabbit mad. Alejandro looked doubtful.

"*¡Qué locura!*" he muttered.

"Wait here!" the boy said.

Adam had total confidence in what he was doing. Stooping to avoid bumping his head on an overhang, he entered the cave. There was a small torch attached to his key-ring and he switched this on. What the boy saw took his breath away. Even in the faint light he could make out extraordinary paintings adorning the walls of the cave's antrum. Although the entrance seemed insignificant, the antrum was huge. The walls were so high they disappeared into the gloom above and he was unable to make out a ceiling. Slowly, his eyes grew accustomed to the dark and the images on the walls became clearer.

They were beautiful beyond belief. People with Mexican faces and elaborate ceremonial costumes, some wearing large plumed headdresses, communed with weird mythical animals, many recognisable as eagles, lizards, snakes and pumas. Allowing for the dull light, Adam saw how colourful the pictures were. He wished he had time to gaze for longer but finding the Old Woman was of more urgent concern.

"*¡HOLA!*" he called out.

The only reply in the eerie silence was a muffled echo.

"*¡AYUDAME POR FAVOR!*"

Still nothing from the darkness ahead. Adam was beginning to think his idea *was* crazy, as Alejandro suggested, when he heard a faint sound. It became more defined: something scraping over rough ground. He saw the outline of an approaching shape. Gradually this took the form of a very old woman bent forwards over a crooked stick which she held in front of her, tapping at the ground, feeling her way. The Old Woman of the Hills – the woman of whom Papa Pedro had spoken, the one who had returned life to Santiago's grieving guitar. And when he saw her face, her eyes fixed upon him, he knew he had seen her before and that he'd been right to come.

The Old Woman stopped a few feet from Adam, looked up and smiled. There was warmth in that toothless smile that sparked off yet another déjà vu and he now remembered: María was about to be slaughtered and butchered on an ancient temple altar.

The woman spoke in a weird language. He had no idea what this was but felt he should both know it and understand the oddly familiar words. He shrugged his shoulders. She smiled again.

"*¿Nahuatl no, espagnol sí?*" she asked quietly.

"*Espagnol, por favor,*" he agreed, nodding.

"*¡Ven aquí!*" the Old Woman urged, beckoning to Adam to follow her. He could see why she went so slowly for they seemed to be walking into solid blackness. Even with his torch switched on he could barely make out the ground in front. Soon he became aware of a shaft of light emerging from the side of the cave ahead. As they approached this, he saw that the cave veered to the right. Once round the bend he found himself in a spacious cavern lit by a long slit-like crack high in the ceiling, through which filtered a pale blue sky. The walls of the cavern were covered with fantastical paintings like the ones near the entrance, their colours more intense in the brighter light. The place was sparsely furnished with a mattress, table and chairs, an eccentrically-leaning cupboard, a cooking area and stacks of dusty old books plus documents along the length of one wall. The Old Woman noticed Adam staring in awe at the paintings.

"*¿Te gusta, las pinturas? ¿Están preciosas, verdad?*"

"*¡Sí, preciosas y ancianas!*" replied Adam, wide-eyed.

She glanced at María's doll dangling pitifully from Adam's hand.

"*¿La Princesa de nuevo?*" she asked, pointing at the doll. "*¿La Princesa Arima? ¿María?*"

Princess Arima? María? In this dark place he was convinced his girlfriend had been in danger before, but how did the Old Woman know? And who was Princess Arima? The woman seemed to regard her and María as one and the same.

He was taken to the stone table where they sat side-by-side as he related in Spanish the events of that bleak afternoon and begged her to locate the 'secure' hiding place where the kidnappers had hidden the girl. At first she merely muttered away to herself and what she said made little sense. Then, quite suddenly, she pointed to the doll.

"*¡Dame la muñeca!*"

Adam pushed the doll towards her. The Old Woman took it and closed her eyes. She began to rock backwards and forwards, murmuring incomprehensibly in Nahuatl. He heard the name 'Arima' repeated several times and he had an extraordinary sensation of being in a totally different dimension, as if he'd awoken in a world beyond that of dreams. The woman opened her eyes and stared at him for a few moments. Held in that stare, he felt himself floating in timelessness, adrift in a parallel reality. She broke the silence:

"The Golden Jaguar bracelets. You have these now?" she asked in Spanish.

They were covered by the sleeves of his jacket. No way could she have known about them. Adam rolled up his sleeves and showed her the bracelets. She smiled.

"*¡Bueno!*" she exclaimed. "And your friend? He is true?"

So she knew about Alejandro? Adam assured her the man had been a sincere friend to María and himself, and, since the girl's capture, a rock to her family. Her scant white eyebrows knotted into a frown.

"A necklace?" she asked. "There's a ruby necklace?"

Adam, both amazed and worried, nodded.

"*Un regalo,*" he replied.

Perhaps she could see into María's mind and this unnerved him. Why should the girl be thinking about Alejandro's present which had caused her such embarrassment? Jealousy attempted to resurface as the Old Woman pointed to Adam's folded map.

At last! *This* was why he'd come. He spread the map out on the table, turning it round for the woman. She touched a spot with a skeletal finger.

"*¡Aquí!*" she said. "*La Princesa Arima está aquí.*"

"*¿Arima?*" queried Adam. "*¿Es María, no?*"

"*¡Sí, sí!*" the old woman answered. "*María. Arima. ¡Aquí!*"

She repeatedly poked at the spot. Adam took out a pen and marked it with a small cross.

"*¡Sí, la cruz!*" the woman exclaimed. "*Santa María. Santa Cruz.*"

Her warm smile returned. She sat for a long, long time and the boy was reminded both of a Buddha statue he'd once seen in the New York Met plus that famous picture of the *Mona Lisa*. He left her sitting frozen in some other time to examine the paintings on the walls. Although they portrayed scenes and images of a very different world, the power behind the pictures was undiminished. They spoke of Life emerging from an empty primordial darkness and, through the power of the gods of Nature, clinging on to the space it had found in this world.

Someone spoke in near perfect English. Adam swivelled to look at the Old Woman, now standing. He had no idea she could speak English. It was so bizarre. He returned to the table.

"They hide the princess in an old temple in the jungle. Chiculhuán. Great danger. Nearby is an airstrip. They take her by plane today. You go quick. Fly tomorrow. Princess Arima is in grave danger."

That temple she dreamt of? Where she's to be killed? Sacrificed?

Adam turned the map around. The cross was located in the Chiapas region of southern Mexico, near Guatamala. It was miles from any sizeable town. How on earth would they get to such a remote place? No proper airport anywhere nearby. His heart sank to an all-time low.

"Fly! Airstrip there," the Old Woman insisted. "Tomorrow!" She pointed to the Golden Jaguar bracelets. "There you call for Golden Jaguar. Always he searches for you in The Forest Without Time. Always he wants to protect the Princess Arima. Her love, it changed him forever. Now he guards that love, not the temple. He can find you if you use the bracelets. You must call. Call for the Princess."

"María?"

"*¡Sí, María! La misma. Pura. Santa María.*"

The Old Woman had reverted to Spanish and seemed puzzled when Adam spoke again in English. He couldn't make her out but he had to trust her however mad she might be. The information she'd given was his only glimmer of hope.

He looked at his watch. It had stopped. Tapping it a few times failed to bring it back to life. He folded the map, retrieved María's doll, bowed politely to the Old Woman and thanked her in Spanish. She remained seated at the low wooden table, muttering in Nahuatl as if she'd now also forgotten Spanish. When Adam turned round, before heading for the cave entrance, that strange smile again puckered her wrinkled face and it seemed to connect with the strength hidden inside him.

The boy had been so long in the cave he feared Alejandro might have driven off out of sheer frustration.

"I thought you wouldn't find the old fossil!" declared the Mexican who stood in exactly the same position as when Adam had left him an hour or more earlier.

"What d'you mean?" asked Adam, ducking the overhang at the entrance to the cave. "I've been gone ages!"

"Like less than a minute!" laughed Alejandro. He held up his watch and tapped it. Adam saw that the sun was in precisely the same low location in the sky as when he'd gone into the cave. The Old Woman's words, 'Forest Without Time', resounded in his head. Without any doubt, he'd just emerged from a different dimension.

No time to ponder. He showed Alejandro the map, indicating the spot marked with a cross.

"That's where they've taken María. I know it. It's called Chiculhuán. An old temple. Must be Mayan. In the Chiapas jungle near Guatamala. There's an airstrip closeby. Just hope the police believe me. We have to fly there tomorrow."

He'd expected little support from his sceptical friend and was surprised by Alejandro's sudden change in heart:

"Adam, I've been thinking. You might be right," he said. "That's the kinda place where they *would* take her. Away from any town or city. Away from the police. Parts of the Chiapas are under Zapatista control. Government doesn't much care about what goes on there. Bigger problems to worry about. You know, I was thinking in the car about these guys. They're no ordinary criminals. Big time – and you know what that means here in Mexico?"

Adam's eyes narrowed at his friend.

"Drugs!" exclaimed Alejandro. "Narcos, I'm sure of it. They'll be hit men for some struggling drug baron from South America looking for quick cash to stake out an area in Mexico. Take on one of the big cartels. *Gángsters de drogas.* That's what makes them so dangerous, Adam. The ordinary police'll be out of their depth and could make things worse for María. If a whole load of armed officers suddenly showed on their doorstep they'd have nothing to lose by killing the girl – and everything to gain. If María were dead, those police dudes wouldn't be risking their own lives in a shoot-out. Like you said, Adam, you and I can do this. I saw how you felled that guy who had a knife. We'll take the money with us, pray they hand over the girl and that'll be it. But we must be prepared. See, I still have friends in the Special Drugs Unit. They could get me a plane."

To hear Alejandro talk about María getting killed felt like having someone rip out his soul, but the man was right. Turning up at some secret hideout with a small army of police could be the worst thing to do. He thought about what Alejandro said whilst they slipped and scrambled down the steep path.

"Okay," agreed the boy, climbing into the car. "We leave together tomorrow! No police!"

Before driving off, Alejandro made a phone call. He spoke too fast for Adam to understand a single word of the Spanish – or was it even Spanish? Meanwhile Adam thanked Conchita for bringing him to the Old Woman's cave. He showed her the map and the spot marked with a cross.

"*Sí*," she said, nodding. "*Las Chiapas. Son peligrosos.*"

Adam didn't tell her everything that had happened in the cave. There were bits he felt he should keep to himself. Like María, she was deeply religious and he wasn't sure how much of what he'd experienced would sit comfortably with her beliefs. Alejandro came off the phone and faced Adam.

"All fixed! Tomorrow afternoon! In the morning we collect the money and after lunch we drive out to a military airstrip."

He called Tío Federico. Adam listened:

"Yes, Federico, we need the money by tomorrow morning," Alejandro said in more intelligible Spanish. "Every cent! But tell the kidnappers it'll take two days. That way we'll be ahead of them. As yet we don't know where they want the drop off point to be. Probably somewhere in Mexico City. They'll get a mighty big surprise when we turn up on their doorstep with the money, *vale*? Then we bargain with them. 'Give us the girl, and we give you the money. Harm the girl and we blow us all up!'"

Adam was taken aback by what he overheard but Alejandro later explained that having worked in a Special Drugs Unit he knew how to call these guys' bluff and Adam had to believe him.

Back at the López place things were no calmer. Having Camilo and Javier home from school, more excitable than ever, wasn't helping. Adam discovered his mother and Carmen would be taking an earlier flight and he was thankful he'd soon be seeing her again, though perhaps for the last time. She had to understand he'd risk anything, including his life, for María. Should he fail to rescue the girl he'd never again be able to live with himself.

The boy struggled to get a few winks of sleep. It was important to be alert the following day but for most of the night he lay wide awake praying María was all right, going over their past times together.

Finally he lapsed into a fitful sleep, awakening after everyone else. Alejandro had already appeared and remained in total control. The police had checked out the man's credentials and frankly seemed only too pleased he'd take over the operation till the girl got released, particularly since he'd once been a special agent in the government's ceaseless struggle against the murderous drug cartels. As far as the chief of police was concerned, nothing could have been more harmful for his personal reputation than for the daughter of an important business family spanning Texas and Mexico to be killed by *los gángsters de drogas*. The deal was that should anything bad happen to María then they, the police, 'knew nothing' about Alejandro and Adam's plan. For the family it was a dilemma – whether to go with the crazy notion of surprising the gangsters in their presumed hideout, its location identified by a mysterious old woman who lived in a cave in the hills, or await instructions about a drop-off point in Mexico City and hope that afterwards María would be returned safely.

Whilst Tío Federico was away collecting the money, having spent a greater part of the night contacting high-up officials in his bank, the phone rang. Alejandro grabbed it from Tía Bea before she could speak. He had to be sure she didn't say a single wrong word. After putting the phone to his ear he handed it to Adam. It was María. She was crying and the boy had difficulty making out what she said:

"Please do what they say. They're evil, these men. Oh Adam, I love you so. Please help me. Please—"

Golden Jaguar of the Sun

"María, Tío Federico's getting the ransom money. Call for the Golden Jaguar straightaway if things get desperate," urged Adam. "Call loud 'n' clear!"

Whether or not she heard him Adam never knew for a man's voice replied:

"Ze Golden Jaguar? *¿Qué es esto?*"

Alejandro snatched the phone from the boy.

"*¡Nada, no es nada!*" he assured the brute at the end of the phone. "*¡El chico está loco!*"

Alejandro scowled as if Adam was completely unhinged. He gabbled in Spanish into the phone, saying the money would be ready in two days, explaining that he was a family friend and the police would have nothing to do with the hand-over of cash. It was finally agreed that María's captors would phone at the same time the following morning to arrange a drop-off point.

"Only after then will they talk about handing her over," Alejandro explained. "You were right to suspect they may still not release her after that, Adam, but are you mad? What was that Golden Jaguar business? A rich guy's car or something? You made the dude at the other end of the phone all jittery!"

"Oh, it's nothing! A fairy story we once read together," lied Adam. "Just to let her know how much I care about her."

"From now on only I speak on the phone!" insisted Alejandro. "You could've gotten the girl killed!"

Later that morning, Tío Federico had still not returned. Adam began to worry. To challenge the gangsters without the ransom money would be suicide. Worse, even. It might prove fatal for poor María.

Adam's mother and Carmen López arrived from the airport by taxi just as he was turning this over in his mind, thus helping to divert his thoughts. Tía Bea and Carmen wept in each other's arms whilst Ann Winters hugged her son then sat and listened to the story to date.

Although seeing his mom didn't numb the pain of losing María, some of the strength and optimism of the boy's mother rubbed off onto him. Also, Alejandro promised he'd do everything humanly possible to bring María back safe and unharmed. Adam felt reassured when the police praised his past work in the Special Drugs Unit. Together they'd make an ace team. His girlfriend's negative feelings about the man were completely unfounded – as was his goddamn jealousy. Besides, no girl could go for a guy looking like that, however saintly he might be. Yeah, Alejandro was surely a saint sent from heaven – or by the creator of the Golden Jaguar, perhaps?

Tío Federico finally arrived back with the cash: three million dollars in a black leather attaché case. He said he'd had to move mountains to get hold of such a sum, but there it was! He embraced his sister-in-law, assuring her no effort or expense would be spared to ensure María's safe return.

They had a quick lunch, though Adam ate little. He just wanted to get going. His mother prepared a small backpack with the barest of essentials. Alejandro held on to the case of money and together they left after hurried and tearful farewells. Only when they were in the air, in a small prop plane, did Adam feel the lightening of spirit that accompanies that sense of relief when at last something seems to be happening. He prayed that putting all his faith in the Old Woman of the Hills had been the right thing to do. If not, María was doomed.

But praying wasn't in his natural comfort zone. Like his dad, he never went to church.

Chapter 6: Jungle Temple

*"**Can** the beast be trusted?" the old man was asked. "They have a saying down there that a leopard never changes its spots."*
"He's no leopard," came the reply.

Adam remained silent for most of the flight. Apart from Alejandro, there were two other men in the plane: the pilot and a dude in military uniform armed to the teeth. Adam guessed he was Special Drugs Unit on secret mission with them. Alejandro, also armed, had explained how this man would stay with the pilot to guard the plane. The boy could tell from the conversation that the three men were well acquainted.

He drifted off to sleep, waking up when the plane juddered in a pocket of turbulence. It flew low over the trees. Mountains showed in the distance. Adam looked at the map on his lap. They were approaching the jungle-covered mountains of the Chiapas spanning southern Mexico and extending into Guatamala. The location of that cross on the map had to be out there somewhere.

The crinkled bio-carpet of forest seemed to go on forever, the plane almost skimming the tree tops coating the hills. After cruising like this for an hour or more, the plane banked and began to circle. Adam gripped his seat belt. For a few moments all he saw from the window was a flash-past world of green – no horizon. Gradually the plane righted and sky reappeared. Ahead was a long, broad clearing in the forest. The airstrip? The plane shuddered on coming in to land and moments later they were bumping and bouncing along the runway, rapidly slowing. At the far end of the runway the plane turned and taxied back towards a small brick building with an attached wooden shed. The engine spluttered then went silent. The propellers stopped turning. Adam, eager to get going, hurriedly unfastened his seat belt and grabbed his bag.

"Wait!" cautioned Alejandro.

The military dude fumbled for something under his seat and pulled out an AK-47. He stood up, exchanged a few words with the pilot, opened the plane door and leapt to the ground. Adam peered from the window and watched as the man, his gun at the ready, approached the building and kicked open the door. He slipped in sideways, re-emerging moments later, one hand raised.

"As I thought," confirmed Alejandro. "No one there."

The uniformed guy also checked the wooden shed before returning to the plane and climbing back on board.

"*No hay nadie,*" he reassured.

"*Now* we can go," Alejandro said, giving Adam the thumbs up. "Follow me."

He stopped to speak with the pilot who pointed to a spot about halfway along the edge of the runway. Adam's friend jumped from the plane with a case full of dollar bills in one hand and a revolver in the other. Adam stuffed the map into his back pocket and followed with his backpack – the same one he took to New York with María the previous summer. The thought of this both saddened and spurred him on. They ran towards the building. Alejandro double-checked that the building was truly empty then headed off in the direction indicated by the pilot. He turned and waited for Adam to catch up.

"The pilot saw the temple from the air," he called out.

"Chiculhuán?"

"*Sí.* And he was certain the path to the temple starts from just along here at the edge of the runway. If the path's good it may take only an hour or two. If bad, it could be dark before we get there. Better hurry. Just hope we can rescue the girl and leave before sunset."

Golden Jaguar of the Sun

Adam's elation at the thought of this hovered, fragile as a newly-blown bubble.

Please make it come true, the boy said to himself over and over, though whom he was addressing he had no idea. The Old Woman of the Hills? The Golden Jaguar? God? And where the heck did God feature in all of this, he questioned? If it hadn't been for María's strong Christian beliefs, the boy would have given up on God long ago.

Sure enough there was an opening in the forest a hundred yards further along the edge of the runway, and from there a good trail, wide enough for a small vehicle, disappeared into the jungle.

Alejandro spoke in a soft whisper:

"From now on no talking. No noise whatsoever. We have to surprise them. They'll have scouts along the way and they must've heard the plane. Just hope they think it's one of theirs and won't suspect anything – but we can't be too careful."

The pair slipped silently into the jungle along the well-cut path, all eyes and ears. Bird calls and screeching howler monkeys helped to obscure the soft tread of their sneakers on the wet ground. From time to time Alejandro stopped, holding up his hand as a caution to Adam before continuing on once reassured it was safe. They proceeded in this stop-start mode for over an hour until, without warning, Alejandro grabbed the boy's arm and pulled him backwards into the undergrowth. He put a finger to his lips and for a few seconds Adam held his breath.

The sound of approaching voices from the path ahead filtered through the trees. Adam's heart raced. Would these be his last moments on earth? Was he about to be shot? It wasn't the fear of death that bothered him. He'd already been on the doorstep of death in New York. All he cared about was María's safety and her release. It was the fear of doing something wrong, of jeopardizing her rescue – and her life – that had whipped his mind into frenzy. Nevertheless, getting himself killed would rather spoil her chances of survival.

Four men in camouflage flak, bullet belts slung over their shoulders, holding assault rifles, appeared from round the corner. They seemed to be enjoying some kind of joke. Adam prayed this had nothing to do with María. Alejandro touched the boy's arm, warning him to stay put, then leapt out onto the path in front of the men, pointing his gun and lifting up the silver case. For an awful moment Adam thought his friend was about to be mown down by gun-fire when the other men raised their rifles, releasing safety catches. Alejandro, showing bravado to the extreme, grinned and waved the case in the air.

"The money!" he shouted in Spanish. "I have it! Three million dollars! You have the girl?"

"*Sí, sí. La chica mestiza. ¡Muy guapa!*"

One of the men laughed. Adam seethed to hear his girlfriend demeaned as a '*chica mestiza*'.

"Adam! Please!" called Alejandro. Adam stepped proudly out from the jungle foliage onto the path, a few feet from his friend. He was the only one without a gun. "And I have *el chico*," Alejandro continued, swivelling round and pointing his gun at Adam.

Adam's jaw dropped.

"Oh, Adam, my little friend, this has been *so* easy! And so much fun! You played right into my hands! Well done and *¡muchas gracias!* Now my mission is completed. Game's over. Tie him up, *mis amigos*," he ordered in Spanish.

Adam stood motionless, open-mouthed, trying to think of something to say but too confused to formulate any sensible words. It felt as if his world had collapsed around him. Staring at Alejandro whom he'd trusted so completely, questions danced in his mind. Where had he gone wrong? María, naturally, had been right all along. Why hadn't he listened to her when she warned him about that shitty little Álvaro? Why hadn't he picked up on Alejandro's effusive generosity? Conceit? Was that it? Using the Mexican as a benchmark to show the girl he could be even better than her in the saintliness game?

María, I've failed you. It's all my goddamn fault!

One of the thugs sauntered up to Adam, deprived him of his backpack, pulled a cord from his belt, yanked the boy's arms behind his back and tied the cord firmly around his wrists. The gangster left the map stuffed into Adam's back-pocket. The boy was frisked and, reassured that he had no fire-arm, the man rejoined his comrades after chucking the backpack into the forest.

"Oh, by the way, Adam, let me introduce my friends! They've been dying to meet you!" Alejandro laughed. "Dying? Well, not literally, thank God. Not *them*, anyway!"

"You bastard!" Adam shouted. "I trusted you. So did María's family. So did the police and the guys on the plane!"

"Forget them, Adam! My old uniform came in handy, mind you. Ramón's men too, *chico.*"

"Ramón?"

How Adam despised the man for destroying his only chance of getting María safely home. In the depths of despair, he nervously fingered the bracelets around his wrists, touching the jaguar heads. Immediately an image of the Old Woman of the Hills appeared in his mind, as clear as if she were with him there in the forest.

Is your friend true, she'd asked? She knew. She had tried to warn him. He'd have to believe in her from now on – and in the Golden Jaguar.

The Forest Without Time? Where the heck is that place – that other dimension? Is there any hope left for María here in this jungle hell?

He hung his head in shame for having been so stupid and barely listened to what his ex-friend was telling him:

"My cousin, Ramón Molina! The big boss! You see, Adam, you pissed him off big time in New York. Those guys you gotten put away, they were *his* boys. And when that girl Chrissy squealed – oh man! Remember her? Too keen on you, she was. Went and broke up the whole goddamn ring and Ramón, well, he got kinda upset. Not a man to upset, my cousin. Seem to have a way with the girls, don't you, Adam? But not any more, my little *chico*. This is the end of the road for Adam Winters. But you can feel real proud that Ramón's coming all the way from Colombia to do the job himself. Says he wants that pleasure so we have to keep you fit and well until then. Should arrive by private plane early tomorrow."

"Kill me if you must but let María go, you filthy coward!" said Adam, rediscovering the power of speech. "Take her back to her family. She had nothing to do with that business in New York."

"Ah! How stupid of me. I forgot to tell you where the girl fits in," continued Alejandro. "Álvaro was a great help there. 'How can we truly hurt this Adam Winters before dispatching him,' our cousin Ramón asked? 'Through the girl,' said Álvaro. 'Adam's besotted with her'. So Ramón, he can show María who's the real man right in front of you, Adam. Give her what all girls crave for! He's good at that, you know. Lots of experience! Then she'll be his girl! Álvaro said you might find that a bit painful to watch! Afterwards she can enjoy seeing Ramón get rid of her little *chico* because she won't need him anymore, huh? You see, she'll be well and truly Ramón's by then. Oh, she'll learn to love the big guy like the rest of them. Ramón will take the girl back to his penthouse in Cali. She'll join the others and soon she'll be begging for more precious time in Ramón's bed. They all do!"

If Adam's wrists weren't bound he'd have aimed a punch at Alejandro, gun or no gun. All he could do was stand impotently listening to what was going to happen to his girlfriend, a virgin for sure.

Jesus, why wasn't I more careful?

"Oh, and Ramón gets his necklace back! More valuable than the girl, that necklace! At least it won't grow old. Know what happens to Ramón's girls when their boobs begin to sag, Adam? Lucky for them there's plenty of guys in the streets of Cali less fussy than Ramón! But that's a while ahead. 'Very pretty', my cousin said when he saw her picture on that album of hers. That's why he sent the pearl necklace with the ruby. 'It'll match her red dress,' he told me. Said to make sure the girl wore it for the publicity shot. Plus she can sing for him. He likes her voice. Really he does. So the lucky girl might get more personal attention from the big boss's private equipment than those others in his penthouse. Until he's fed up with her. Álvaro says she's bit of a temper, mind you. Might need taming, don't you think? Guess you'd wanna see how we real men do that before – you know? Ha ha ha! Vicente's our tamer, by the way!"

Adam found it hard to believe the man was actually talking about María.

"You filthy bastard!" he spat. "She's only fifteen! No one bloody touches her!"

"She looks older. And Álvaro says she's sixteen! You telling me my cousin's a liar?"

"She's only fifteen," Adam repeated quietly.

The poor girl never got her *quinceñara* because of him, and now this! He fought to control his anger, recalling Papa Pedro's wise words on the subject. In his mind he also turned over what Sam Royal said about karate:

"Your opponent will use your anger against you, Adam. Stay calm. Wait. Sooner or later he'll make a false move. Be prepared and strike quickly when he does."

He twisted his hands within the cord binding his wrists until he could feel the Golden Jaguar bracelets, his only weapon. By the grace of God, the man who'd tied his wrists together had failed to notice the bracelets covered by his long sleeves. He had to use them – or rather, the Golden Jaguar – but, as with karate, only at precisely the right moment.

"Oh, and thanks for the money," added Alejandro, lifting up the case and shaking it. The other men laughed, their eyes sparkling with thoughts of fistfuls of US hundred dollar bills.

"Come in useful, it will, *chico*, but sadly there's not enough to repay the debt you owe my cousin."

It was a further thirty minute walk along the path to the jungle temple. Adam tried to lag behind in the hope that he might slip unnoticed into the forest, but those guys with guns were watching his every move. Besides, all he now wanted was to see and be with María – before she got raped.

No! Ramón must never touch her! God or no God, he'd bloody make sure of that. By the following morning they'd have formulated some sort of a plan of escape. Alejandro had only succeeded in stoking the fire of his determination with foul words; merely fanned that mysterious power stirring within him.

One of the men ran on ahead. Adam heard shouting. They rounded a bend. Through the foliage he glimpsed a massive stone structure. Twenty yards further on and they were in a large clearing in the centre of which stood a vast, crumbling pyramid: the Mayan temple of Chiculhuán. A steep stairway led to a platform at the top and from ground level he could see a small stone building up there. It was similar to the larger Aztec pyramids he'd visited near Mexico City, only steeper.

At the edge of the clearing were a few tents and a camp-fire.

"The workers' quarters and restaurant," joked Alejandro, seeing Adam staring at these. "But you, my young friend, can now relive history. Follow me up these steps. This is where the Maya took their prisoners to be sacrificed. Let's just say Adam Winters is being sacrificed for love, huh? Is there a god of love, *chico*? Of course there is! María will soon yield to her very own god of love, my handsome cousin, Ramón Molina! 'Yes – oh yes, yes – YES!' she'll cry out when he takes her. He's particularly good with first timers, you see. Yeah, you can thank Ramón for showing you what beautiful girls like María really desire – before you die!"

Adam knew Alejandro was taunting him, trying to wind him up. He was learning fast. *'Shut the bastard out of my mind,'* he told himself as he climbed the steps to the temple platform.

To see María again was a mix of awful and wonderful: awful to see her so mistreated and upset, with her long, black hair straggled and un-brushed, her ruffled red dress spattered with muddy stains, but wonderful just to see her. She sat with her back to the wall of the small stone building he'd seen from below, legs crossed, arms behind her back with her red, high-heeled shoes placed neatly beside her. What struck the boy most of all was how stunning she still looked even in this sorry state.

"Adam!" she called feebly, her morale clearly crushed "What's happening? Why are you here? Why are your hands tied too? What are they gonna do to us? And Alejandro – why's he here?"

The girl turned her tear-smudged face towards Alejandro and looked beseechingly up at him. Alejandro merely grinned lecherously as Adam sank down beside her. How the boy wished he could hold his girlfriend in his arms and tell her everything was going to be okay.

"He's one of them, María. And so is Álvaro back home."

María's eyes flashed anger. *A good sign,* thought Adam. *They haven't completely destroyed her spirit.*

"Well, enjoy your five-star accommodation whilst you can, *mis amigos*," Alejandro joked. "I must love you and leave you, as they say. Ha ha! Love you! That'll be Ramón's job tomorrow. As María will discover. Bet she can't wait, huh? Meanwhile Vicente here will look after all her other needs. Don't you go upsetting Vincente, now, Adam. He can turn *ve–ry* nasty."

A large, swarthy man with a big, bulging belly appeared at the doorway of the stone building, looked scornfully at Adam, grunted then went back inside.

"*¡Hasta mañana!*" Alejandro cheerfully called out before making his way back to the steps and disappearing over the edge of the platform. At last Adam was alone with María.

"Does the big guy speak English?" he whispered. "Looks pretty dumb."

María managed a smile.

Oh man, she is lovely. Special! Yeah, that's what the Old Woman said too! Special and pure! Jesus, Ramón's never gonna have her! Never, never – NEVER!

"I don't think so," she answered. "I tried speaking in English very slowly and clearly and he didn't seem to understand a thing. His Spanish is kinda funny, too. I think he's pure Mayan. Like the others. Probably Zapatistas who've turned to crime. Vicente spends most of the time in the little building behind us, thank God. Sure dunno what he gets up to in there."

"Doesn't look like the sort who'd play chess on an i-Pad!" Adam pointed out. María laughed and her laughter injected strength into him.

"María, we must have an escape plan by tomorrow morning. Alejandro's cousin who heads the gang is coming from Colombia by plane. Alejandro told me."

"Ramón? Yes, I heard about him. Will we be freed then? Did you bring the money?"

How could he destroy María's only hope by telling her the truth?

"Sure Ramón'll free us," he lied. "Alejandro has the money. But we must have a plan anyway."

"Adam, these men are dangerous. They're all armed. Just don't get yourself shot! I've hardly gotten over what happened to you in New York. No more bravery awards – please!"

Adam leant towards the girl and whispered in her ear:

"The Golden Jaguar, María. Like I said on the phone. It's all true. That story you told me on the plane last summer."

"You're crazy!"

"Shhh! Remember Santiago's guitar?"

"*¡Sí!*"

"About José Fernández having it blessed by an old woman who lives in a cave in the hills?"

"*¡Sí!*"

"Well, I saw her myself. Alejandro, of all people, took me. When I thought he was our friend."

"She'll have been dead for years. It must've been some other old lady."

"It was her. I know it. She tried to warn me about Alejandro but I stupidly ignored her. She even knew about the necklace. Knew you were wearing it."

Adam tried to visualise María's pretty neck without Ramón's accursed pearl and ruby necklace around it.

"I wish I could chuck the thing away. They demanded I put it on. For *him*, they said. Wouldn't tell me who the heck 'he' was at first till Vicente let the cat out of the bag."

"What did he say?"

Maria remained silent but tears began to well. Adam said nothing about the necklace coming from Ramón – or what the bastard planned to do to her. Perhaps she already knew. Was it true he could turn any girl crazy with desire?

"Look, it's the same Old Woman. I'm telling you. There's something very strange about her, but she's good. You can tell from her eyes."

"Not very clever about Álvaro and Alejandro, were you?" María pouted, looking the other way. Adam liked it. Her old spirit was still there and that would be important for their escape the following day.

"No, I wasn't, but believe me this is different. There really is a Golden Jaguar. Sometimes I see his eyes in my mind. It's to do with the bracelets. I'm sure of it. When I rub them I feel this – well, a sort of—"

What? What do I feel? Is it all in my imagination? María, look at me – I need to see your eyes!

"How come you've gotten two, Adam?" she interrupted, turning to face him. "I was too scared to ask you before. They kinda frightened me."

Jesus man, your eyes! How I bloody missed them! But why did you really give me that bracelet? Only because it scared you? No – Adam, don't! For God's sake don't lose trust in her again!

"Dunno. Perhaps that was the Old Woman as well. Look, the Golden Jaguar wants to protect you, María. I believe I can make him appear with the bracelets if I empty my mind. Communicate with him. There's some sort of magic about them. Something to do with – I dunno – with other dimensions, I guess. And with you."

María looked at him long and hard. She knew he wasn't lying for this was a boy who never lied, whatever his other faults.

"I want to believe you, honest I do, but it's so difficult. Stuck out here in the jungle with all those jerks with guns and that psycho Vicente!" Tears now streamed. "It's so awful when I need to go to the bathroom. He follows me down to the jungle and just watches. Says I might run away. He's an animal."

"Has he – have any of those other gangsters – touched you like? In that kinda way?" Adam asked, fearing the worst.

Inside his head he saw Ramón Molina, a handsome Hollywood star lookalike, slowly undress the girl. Would she fight him off? Or was Alejandro right? Is this what she really wanted?

María shook her head but continued to sob; little comfort for Adam who knew she was only being kept a virgin for the big guy the following day.

"Adam, I just wanna be outa here. I wanna be with Mama and Papa and the kids. I don't think I can take this any longer."

"María, be strong. You can be. You must be. You will see your folks again, I promise. Do you believe me? Look at me."

She looked at Adam through her tears then nodded.

"*¡Si, mi amor!*" she answered quietly.

For a while they remained silent. Adam used the silence to concentrate his thoughts on the Golden Jaguar. Those coal-black eyes with their fiery red streaks had to belong to the Golden Jaguar. Even though the eyes only appeared in his mind he could feel their awesome power and he felt certain he could unleash that power whilst wearing the bracelets. He closed his eyes and thought about the face of the jaguar on the bracelet whilst tracing its outline with his fingers. Those eyes reappeared in his mind, fixing him with a terrifying stare. The whole face of the beast was now visible and so much clearer than before. Using his mind, he let himself sink into the jaguar's eyes. He allowed something within, his soul perhaps, to penetrate the fire there, and beyond that fire he sensed a strength that was invincible. A voice spoke inside his head – a deep, echoing voice, the voice of a praeternatural beast. Strange words appeared and Adam understood these as he'd understood the Old Woman of the Hills in that other dimension:

"Princess Arima – is she in danger?" the voice asked.

Adam's thoughts followed that voice beyond the fire of the eyes to a place where he felt like a god.

"Arima? María! Yes," he replied. "Come quick. She *must* be saved."

The fire flickered, became brighter; it grew, as if about to explode out of the boy's skull until, quite suddenly the image vanished. At the same time, far in the forest, came a distant sound, a disturbance – impossible to describe.

Adam opened his eyes. María was staring at him. Alarmed and frightened, she trembled.

"What *was* that about, Adam? You were talking funny – and then that weird noise?" she asked.

"It's okay, María. You will be rescued," Adam replied.

María moved up closer to Adam, closed her eyes, and nestled her head on his shoulder. In a few minutes she'd drifted off to sleep. The poor girl! He hadn't even asked her whether she'd slept since her capture.

Golden Jaguar of the Sun

Chapter 7: The Beast from Another Dimension

He was the first Great Sun God, the Giver of Life on Earth. He should be Master of the Beast created by his servant on Earth. If the girl could change both the beast and his servant, what else might happen?

Whilst his girlfriend slept, Adam logged a mental map of the temple layout. He needed to absorb every detail, for when the time came such knowledge might mean the difference between life and a living death for the girl. In the centre of the temple platform, about ten yards from where they sat, was a stone altar. It was worn away on one side, broken-off fragments of stone littering the paving. Beside María, adjacent to the doorway of the little building where Vicente did whatever he got up to on his own, was the fallen stone carving of an ancient Mayan animal effigy, possibly a serpent. Adam noticed the jagged base of the statue sticking up from the platform – precisely what he would need to cut through his bond at the correct time. On the other side of the doorway was the statue of a squatting figure with a curved nose and large staring eyes. The boy observed that the dense jungle was close to the temple pyramid along the edge near the sacrificial altar. This was where they'd make their getaway. The pyramid was steep but with care they'd surely make it step by step down to ground level whence they could vanish into the forest. He'd need a knife of sorts to cut through the jungle growth and one of the stone fragments near the altar might suffice.

Then?

On the map, to the north of the point where the Old Woman had placed her bony finger, was a dot with a minor road leading to it. He believed this to be a small Mayan village. If not, they'd be lost in that jungle hell.

It was late, the sun was low and he was aware of the direction in which it was sinking. That would be to the west and they had approached the airstrip from the east. Thus he had a clear idea of the direction to take. And water? Other provisions? He had a feeling they'd find these in Vicente's lair. Sure enough, as soon as the sun had set, Vicente emerged carrying a bucket in one hand and a bottle of water in the other.

"*¡Coma! ¡Beba!*" he growled, giving María a kick on the butt with his boot. The girl awoke with a start and Adam narrowed his eyes. María sat up, dazed, blinking.

"Looks like feeding time at Houston Zoo with roles reversed," muttered Adam.

María stood and obediently turned around. Vicente put down the water bottle and the pail before untying the cord binding the girl's wrists at the back.

"This is the only time we have our hands free. We get to go to the bathroom afterwards," she explained, facing Adam as she smoothed down the ruffles in her dress before massaging her wrists where the cord had been. She flexed her legs a few times, shaking out the pins and needles. A thought came to Adam:

"María, tell Mr Ape Man that Alejandro said I'm not allowed to have my bond untied because of my karate. Give him all that junior Texas karate champion trash," he said hurriedly. "Say you'll have to feed and water me. We can sort out the toilet business later. Whatever happens, he must not see the bracelets."

María grabbed Vicente's arm as he approached Adam. She spoke rapidly in Spanish. Vicente looked at Adam, baffled.

"Say Alejandro will be *very* angry with him if he unties me. Say you don't want him to get into trouble. Use your charm, María."

María did as he said, although the following morning it would turn out to be her undoing. She smiled sweetly at Vicente and clearly no female had ever done that before. He grinned back, showing a mouthful of irregular brown teeth pointing in different directions, with toothless spaces in between filled by red, fleshy gums where bits of stale food lingered. Adam saw María try to control a retch as she looked up at the smirking fiend, but somehow she managed to maintain a pretty smile. She softly stroked the man's hairy arm and said how she'd hate to see him get into trouble with Alejandro, explaining how she'd heard the man would kill for less serious offences. It worked. Vicente shrugged his shoulders, pointed to the bucket, to the bottle then Adam.

"Go ahead. Feed the animal!" he ordered in guttural Spanish.

He folded his arms and laughed, watching the girl's every move. When she turned to see whether he was still there he rewarded her with another revolting grin. Uneasily, she returned the smile.

María carefully spooned beans in chilli sauce from a tin into her boyfriend's mouth. She giggled when Adam said he preferred eating at her father's restaurant. Vicente laughed along with her, not wanting to miss out on the joke and perhaps hoping it might ingratiate him with a pretty girl. After the beans, Adam chewed on a crust of stale bread and pulled a face, once more making María, then Vicente, laugh. María put the water bottle to Adam's lips and the boy drank till he'd had his fill. María, still standing, scooped up the remainder of the beans for herself, ate some bread plus a bruised apple which she'd found in the bucket. She ate slowly to savour the pleasure of standing upright with free hands. Except for meals and toilet, they had to stay down on the stone floor all the time and found it painfully uncomfortable.

After a taste of jungle cordon bleu cuisine (Adam's words), María stepped into her red high-heeled shoes. She and Adam were led down the temple stairway to an area stinking of urine, behind the tents and the camp-fire around which *los gángsters* sat and ate. The smell of cooking meat teased their nostrils – a two-way onslaught on the olfactory senses!

"Can I choose from their menu next time, please?" joked Adam. The girl giggled again and Vicente also had a go at giggling though it sounded more like a frog being strangled.

"So this is the bathroom," María said, flashing a timid glance at Vicente.

"You first. I promise I'll close my eyes." Adam gallantly whispered. "And please ease up on the smiling. Ape-face is getting a little too keen on you." He glimpsed anxiously at Vicente now staring fixedly at María. "Just imagine he's a monkey hanging from a branch attempting to figure out what you're doing!" he added.

María found a tree to squat behind. Vicente moved his position to ensure he could keep her in view.

"Okay! Finished!" she called out after a short period, hurriedly smoothing down her dress when she realised her captor had her within his sights. "But how are you gonna–?"

"You'll have to help me," interrupted Adam.

Embarrassed, she approached her boyfriend, stopped then giggled again. How he loved her innocence – and how he hated those men for what they planned to do to her the following day. When a fleeting image of the gang boss publicly deflowering the girl invaded his mind, those ephemeral, internal eyes of fire branded anger onto his brain.

"Gonna have to work this out," María said, frowning. Vicente lost interest and wandered off to speak with his mates around the camp-fire, but he repeatedly peered back at the teenage captives. Adam banished thoughts of making a dash for it. For certain, they'd get shot.

"Look—" he began whilst María gazed at his lower half wondering how to proceed. "Unzip my pants, yank 'em down, turn me around and look the other way. I'll manage somehow. When I say so, reach out, pull 'em up again, fix the zipper and – well, there you go!"

María was unable to suppress a further burst of giggles despite repeated shushes from the boy. She managed to accomplish the first part of the exercise without too much difficulty but her frivolity had caused a renewal of interest from Vicente.

"Okay! I'm good!" Adam called out when he'd relieved himself. María reached to the side, looking away. "To the right – no, not so far," he directed. Her hands flailed about blindly searching for his pants. When they finally came into contact with his legs she giggled again. "Hey, don't tickle me! Down a bit!"

The girl burst out laughing. Vicente glanced at the playful pair and shouted something, his voice abrasive. María fell silent.

"He says to hurry up," she explained after finding Adam's pants and pulling them up. She turned and grinned at her boyfriend. "Never done *that* before!"

"Glad to hear it!" said Adam.

Goddamnit, I swear I'll kill the lot of 'em if they try to rape her in the morning!

Vicente returned through the tangle of undergrowth.

"You're wasting my time," accused the fiend, grabbing María's arm and pulling her roughly back towards the temple steps. Adam reckoned he'd have to watch him carefully. At the top, María held her hands behind her back for Vicente to rebind her wrists with a cord.

"*¡Ay!*" she yelped. "*Demasiado tirante.*"

The Neanderthal loosened the cord.

101

"*¡Sentarse!*" he barked.

Adam and María sat down together, the boy in front of the broken-off snake statue and, most importantly, between the door of Vicente's hideout and María. From what Alejandro had said, it seemed unlikely the man would try anything with her during the night but he couldn't be sure. His suggestion that she smile at the brute may not have been such a great idea. Adam's job now was to protect the girl, having gotten her into this mess through his goddamn 'bravery'.

Bravery? Bloody stupidity! Why, oh why, didn't I trust her in New York?

Vicente disappeared into the building and re-emerged with a couple of blankets which he flung over María and Adam.

"Lights out then, Mr Ape Man?" queried Adam.

Vicente blinked then grinned at María.

Darkness was rapidly reclaiming the jungle. María waited until Vicente had vanished for the night.

"Watch this!" she said. She grabbed the edge of the blanket between her teeth and flung her head to one side, dragging some of the blanket with her mouth. After doing this several times she'd created a curious pillow substitute. Then she caught the edge of the blanket again, tugging it this way and that until, on lying back, she looked almost snug in a coarse woollen cocoon.

"Had to do something to amuse myself last night," she explained. "Couldn't sleep a wink!"

"Hey, cool!" exclaimed Adam. "Let me try!"

He snuggled close to María and attempted the same thing but instantly spat out the blanket.

"Yuk! Tastes like horse-shit!"

"I wouldn't know," chuckled the girl. "They all say it tastes bad at first. Gets better as the night wears on."

María pressed her face up against Adam's cheek and kissed him. It was the most beautiful thing that could have happened just then, but what about the following day? Would she be hungrily kissing her god of love, Ramón, and on the lips – or even worse? Jealousy bit for the thousandth time. Plus he was acutely aware of Vicente being but a few metres away in that small building.

"Don't let Mr Monkey Brain see you do that," he whispered. "Might give him ideas!"

"Adam, stay next to me all night," María pleaded. "Just make sure I can feel you touching me. I get so scared."

Jealousy? Wasn't that how this all began in New York?

"Yeah," he replied. "And you make sure you get some sleep. We'll both need our wits about us tomorrow morning. When the time comes, do exactly as I say. Trust me!"

The girl nodded and fixed Adam with an expression he knew so well. If he'd been more than a mere teenager with zero experience of women he'd have been able to read her eyes; eyes that slowly closed as she drifted off to sleep. They spoke of one thing only: an unfathomable love for the boy beside her.

Adam snuggled up against her unspoilt body and began to doze.

Weird dreams played havoc with his exhausted brain. First, he was on that huge lake which had reappeared so often during fleeting visions. Paddling a canoe as if every second counted, he was with someone he'd never seen before but knew this man to be a true friend, not a coyote in disguise like Alejandro. When they spoke it was in an alien language yet they conversed freely as the canoe skimmed across the dark water in a desperate bid to save María. She was in peril and time was running out. The dream vanished, replaced by another in which he found himself in an enormous empty square enclosing a vast temple. Terrifying things were happening at the top of the pyramidal temple.

He saw María up there, bare-chested, and he ran to stop those black figures of death from...

"NO! NO! LEAVE HER ALONE!" he screamed.

Adam awoke with a start. Sweat trickled off his forehead and he was panting as if still running. María stirred, briefly opened her eyes, mumbled something then drifted off again.

Thank God – just a bad dream, but, oh man, why so real?

He turned his head sideways and kissed the girl's closed eyelids. She smiled in half-sleep.

For a while the boy lay back staring at the stars. They seemed unusually bright and strangely permanent. The very same stars must have looked exactly the same to the ancient Maya, he thought as he recalled stories of Mayan mythology from Alejandro's book; stories that involved the cosmos, mythical spirits based on forest animals, gods and warriors and leaders from long-forgotten civilisations. Even if the Maya had gotten it wrong about two thousand and twelve, would he yet live to fulfill his dream to one day become a Mesoamerican archaeologist?

All illusion, he told himself. *Some of those stars may no longer exist.*

He was seeing them as they were hundreds of thousands of years ago. How odd to look at things that perhaps no longer exist. Would he also soon no longer exist? Would María become Ramón's – what? Whore?

Never!

He began to count stars and fell asleep, his slumber no longer packed with nightmares. Now the girl in his dreams was free. The beast was there too. The great Golden Jaguar of the Sun, huge and terrifying, but it was with them as if a part of him, replacing the class nerd that got thumped and humiliated by Spike. Adam felt unbeatable. In another dream there was a grand ceremony. María wore a beautiful pink and gold dress and her parents were also present. Papa

Pedro too. Adam knew this to be about himself and María – about their being together – about their love.

When he next awoke he felt sublimely at peace until the full horror of their plight smashed into his consciousness. He turned his head. María was sitting up, beaming down at him.

"Adam, I just had such an amazing dream," she announced. "We were together, and—" She gave a timid chuckle. "And I was wearing this pink dress with gold bits on and weird birds and – well, I sort of – I mean we – erm—" She sounded embarrassed. "I think we were kinda getting married, you and me. It was so—" She sighed. "If only it could come true!"

The girl burst into tears.

"It will," insisted Adam, hesitant to tell her he'd had exactly the same dream. Who was he kidding – her or himself? All he could think about was what they were going to do to her that very morning. By comparison, his death seemed unimportant. Ramón might arrive any minute and still he had no escape plan. "One day," he added. "Before January, two thousand and seventeen it's gonna happen. Remember?"

Happen? Between María and Ramón? Please, God, don't let them do that to her. That's all I ask. Kill me if you must, but protect María. She believes in you.

"Yeah, but I don't want the world to end then. I want a life with you, Adam. A *whole* life – not a little bit of one."

A little bit? Jesus, María, what have I gotten you into? Stay strong when the time comes. When you find out about Ramón. Perhaps we've only gotten a few more hours together on earth.

But having the same dream? An omen – or a fast-fading wish?

At that precise moment he heard the snarl of a large beast from the forest – very close.

"Do they have mountain lions here?" María asked. Alarm had widened her eyes.

"A jaguar!" replied Adam.

"*The* jaguar?"

Adam was about to say something when Vicente emerged from the stone building carrying the food bucket and a bottle of water.

"Here we go! Room service again!" Adam exclaimed.

They went through a replay of the previous evening only María didn't smile at Vicente and this appeared to annoy him. After releasing her bonds, he tried grinning again but she merely scowled. Whilst she was feeding more beans to Adam, Vicente came up close to the girl and pointed to himself:

"*¿Guapo, sí?*"

Adam thought *guapo* meant handsome.

"Perhaps just a hint of a smile to keep Mr Animal Brain happy," he spluttered through a mouthful of beans.

María looked as if she'd prefer to vomit over Vicente but she managed a slight flicker of the lips that sent the man into a state of ecstasy. They finished their breakfast, María put on her high-heeled shoes and they went through the toilet fiasco as before but without the hilarity. Adam remained tense and alert, aware that the few remaining sand grains in the hour-glass of his life were draining fast.

They returned to the temple platform. María's wrists were re-bound. Adam heard an aircraft and knew what this signified. He glanced up but saw nothing, his view restricted by the forest canopy. The plane sound grew louder. He sat with his back against the sharp edge of the broken off statue, feeling the hard stone with his fingers. María squatted beside him, keeping her shoes on as he'd told her to. The high heels could be turned into weapons as a last resort. Vicente stood, hands on hips, ogling María – in part a good thing, for Adam was able to move his hands up and down unobserved, firmly rubbing the cord over sharp stone. Vicente spoke to María in his repulsive Spanish. Adam understood. The girl's eyes revealed both distress and disgust.

"The plane – that's Ramón," Vicente continued, pointing at the sky. "I know Ramón says you must become his girl over there (he pointed to the altar) before he kills *el chico* and that no one else is to touch you first – but I see you smiling at me, so please, before the big boss comes and does the job, a nice kiss for Vicente too, huh?"

María sat open-mouthed, aghast. Vicente crouched low and offered up a pair of thick, purple, pursed lips. Incandescent with rage, the girl spat at him. Vicente jumped back, wiping the spit from his face. Adam took note of his agility for one so fat.

The boy furiously rubbed the cord over the stone. The threads began to give but it was made of tougher material than he'd reckoned with. He focused all thoughts on the Golden Jaguar and tried, in his mind, to see those burning eyes. He called aloud in Nahuatl to the beast. Vicente was too focused on the object of his lust to listen.

"ONLY ONE BOY WILL EVER TOUCH ME LIKE THAT," María yelled in Spanish, "AND HE'S SITTING RIGHT HERE BESIDE ME!"

"Ha! Spirited!" responded Vicente. "A true *mestiza*, right? Come, *mi chica guapa*, a little kiss before Ramón takes you! Girls say he's good at it, you know! I can tell you're a first timer but he'll soon have you crying out for more!"

He stooped down and attempted to force María to kiss him, gripping her shoulders between filthy, spade-like hands before stumbling backwards with a hoarse cry, slapping a hand over his mouth. His eyes turned from stupid to evil. María, terrified, pressed herself up against the wall as if hoping this might magically open up and allow her to escape. When Vicente lowered his hand, Adam saw a trickle of blood on the man's lower lip where his girlfriend had bitten him.

"*¡Bestia! ¡Tigresa!*" barked the slavering swine.

Adam frantically chafed the cord up and down over the edge of the broken statue whilst the cringing girl froze with wide, fearful eyes, filling with tears, fixed on Vicente.

"NOW!" the boy yelled in Nahuatl. "AT ONCE! MARÍA! PRINCESS ARIMA! SHE NEEDS YOU!"

Vicente strode up to María, grabbed a handful of her hair and pulled her up from the ground.

"OW! YOU BRUTE!" squealed the girl as Vicente dragged her staggering in high-heels across to the stone altar.

"STOP, YOU BASTARD! LET GO OF HER!" Adam shouted in Spanish. "GOLDEN JAGUAR! COME QUICK FOR GOD'S SAKE! MARÍA – ARIMA! SHE'S IN PERIL!" he cried out in that other language.

Vicente pushed María face down across the altar and held her pinned with a thick, hairy arm as her red shoes kicked out in futile attempts to keep the ogre away.

"LEAVE HER ALONE!" yelled Adam.

Vicente undid his belt and whisked it free, careless for the knife-sheath and gun-holster which dropped to the ground.

"No one does that to Vicente! I'll tame the little tigress for Ramón. Then he'll reward me, huh? But I mustn't mark those pretty legs. Might make the big boss angry!" the evil man teased as he pulled the girl's dress up over her back. "Virgin white, ay?" he remarked gazing at her underwear. "Virgin for not much longer, *mi pequeña tigresa.*"

He gripped the belt by the buckle and struck María's butt so hard it sounded like a rifle shot disturbing the still morning air of the Chiapas jungle. The girl screamed. To her boyfriend it seemed as if the white purity of her soul was being defiled by the monster. His fury boiled over as he funnelled every particle of strength from his body into his arms, rubbing the weakening cord over the statue. That's when he first heard a chilling growl from the edge of the jungle less than a stone's throw away.

"Your tiger friends, *mi chica*?" laughed Vicente, striking María again. The girl had stopped kicking but her cries and sobs fanned Adam's anger.

"See how we tame the little tigress!" boasted the drug gangster as he turned to wink at Adam. "Vicente knows what she needs."

A final forceful thrust against the stone and the cord was severed, the boy's hands freed. When Vicente struck the girl a third time, Adam sprinted towards the altar, grabbed the knife-sheath and the gun-holster and in an instant had the gun out. He flicked the safety catch then pointed the weapon at the fiend whose arm was raised to deliver another loud lick with his belt.

"DROP IT!" Adam shouted in Spanish.

"Ah, *chico* – Ramón's little tigress needs taming, that's all," insisted a surprised Vicente, holding his arms up with the heavy belt dangling from his right hand. His Satanic smirk displayed a curved row of horror movie teeth whilst still blood oozed from his lower lip. "See how she's stopped struggling!"

"Drop it, I said," warned Adam, edging towards the man who'd just beaten his girlfriend. Vicente opened his palm, spread his fingers and the belt slipped to the ground. María turned her tear-streaked face towards Adam, staring in disbelief at the gun in his hand.

"Quick, María! Here! I'll cut you free."

Adam shook the sheath off the knife held in his left hand. María straightened up and ran to Adam, turning to allow him to cut the cord binding her wrists. One upwards flick of the knife sliced through the girl's bond. María rubbed her wrists and smoothed down her red dress. Then, with a ferocity that heartened Adam, she went up close to Vicente and slapped his bloodied face with full force, jerking his head sideways. She was about to slap him again, when Adam called out:

"BACK, MARÍA! HURRY!"

María turned and ran to Adam. She held on to the boy for she too had heard the sound. Vicente barely had time to spin round and glimpse the huge, gleaming gold body as it shot up and over the edge of the temple platform. The beast smashed into the man, throwing him against the altar. Dwarfed by the Golden Jaguar, Vicente was cuffed aside as if no more than a baby rabbit. María gasped and gripped Adam's arm when the jaguar pinned the man to the ground. Vicente turned his head to look up at the creature. Adam saw the man's eyes. He'd never before seen such terror and he was pleased. He hated Vicente for what he did to María more than he'd ever hated before – and for a moment he forgot Papa Pedro's wise words about hatred.

"Kill him!" he whispered.

"What did you just say?" María asked.

Adam had spoken in the language of the Old Woman of the Hills and of the Golden Jaguar. He was about to say something else when María shrieked and hid her face against the boy's chest. Vicente's head disappeared between the jaws of the Golden Jaguar. There was a crunching sound. The man's limbs ceased jerking. Adam closed his eyes and put an arm around his sobbing girlfriend.

"Forgive me, Papa Pedro!" he whispered in English. "Please forgive me. I've just killed a man."

"You?" questioned María.

"I willed it, María. *I* killed him."

When he looked up, the Golden Jaguar had abandoned the lifeless body of Vicente and crouched, head low, fixing

Adam with fiery eyes. The boy felt María's body tremble as she held on to him even more tightly.

"Please don't be afraid, María. He'll never harm you. Not so long as I have these bracelets. Now he only wants to protect the girl I love. That's you! You see, he thinks you're a —" Adam grinned and stroked María's tangled hair as she stared at him. "Thinks you're a princess. With the name the Old Woman uses. Princess Arima."

"He won't turn on me if he finds out I'm not her, will he?" the girl asked. Adam hugged her close.

"Nope! For him you are and always will be—"

The boy was cut short by the sound of excited men's voices coming from the camp of *los gángsters*. He no longer heard the plane. It must have landed. Ramón would be on his way. They had little time left.

The Golden Jaguar crawled on his belly towards the edge of the temple at the top of the stairway. The men's voices closed in – mounting the steps.

"María – behind the altar!" Adam whispered.

Holding hands, they ran to hide behind the altar. A man's head appeared, followed by another then a third. One of the men shouted as he ran up onto the platform, firing at the Golden Jaguar. The shots had no effect. He might as well have fired blanks for the huge creature swivelled and sprang. The man had no time to scream. He'd have died instantly as the Golden Jaguar gripped his throat and flung him to the side, snapping his neck, before rearing up, turning and felling his next victim. The third man stumbled in his panic to escape from the beast, shooting randomly in all directions. He, too, was quickly silenced. The jaguar returned to the edge of the platform, twitching his tail, peering down like a king surveying his land. Then he turned and slunk slowly back to face Adam, now standing in the open in front of the altar. His eyes looked searchingly into the boy's. The fire in them still burned, albeit reduced to a smouldering glow. Adam gazed into that glow.

"It's not over. There'll soon be others and Princess Arima must escape from here. You have to stay with us," he whispered in Nahuatl.

"Adam, I didn't understand one word of that! What did you just say?"

María, eyeing the Golden Jaguar with unease, came and stood beside Adam.

"If only he understood Spanish too, like the Old Woman!" Adam replied. "I was warning him there'll soon be more of those bastards. Alejandro and the others must've gone to meet their boss Ramón. We'd better hurry. I'll see if there's food and stuff in the building. Wrap it in one of those blankets. Need water as well. Then we've gotta try and find that village. Look – I'll show you!"

He removed the map from his back pocket and pointed to a dot accessed by a track or small road to the north of the cross marking the site of the temple.

"If the Old Woman was correct with her cross it should be – erm – in that direction," he decided, waving vaguely at the jungle with the morning sun to his right.

He stuck the knife into his jeans belt and, still holding Vicente's gun, entered the stone building. Here he discovered its true purpose: boxes upon boxes of polythene packets containing a white powder. Drugs! All the sordid, chemical wealth Ramón and his gang had amassed that would be used to trap and enslave innocent kids like Lee, but Adam had no time to ponder over the evil of Ramón's organisation. He rejoined María with armfuls of food – tins of beans (his guts groaned), corned beef, cheese, fruit, wrapped sliced bread and bottled water; also, a torch, a tin opener and a box of matches. He bundled everything into a blanket before securing this with Vicente's belt. The belt doubled as a strap to hold the bundle. María, understandably nervous of the belt, disappeared into the building. When she let out a shriek Adam rushed to the entrance, but, thank the Lord, it was a shriek of delight.

"My handbag!" she exclaimed, holding up a small red bag. "Plus—" She opened it and peeked inside. "—My cell phone!"

Adam held up his hand.

"Listen!" he warned. "That sound!"

The Golden Jaguar began to pace up and down at the top of the stairway. Adam had seen lions do that at Houston zoo; guarding their territory should they feel under threat, his Dad had once told him.

"Sounds like a giant wasp to me," María said. "Heard it earlier. Woke me up but got fainter so I guessed the wasp was going away."

"No goddamn wasp!" exclaimed Adam. "A motor-scooter! Several of 'em! They're here already." He took María by the arm and they ran from the building. "Back behind the altar!"

They retreated to their hiding place, Adam carrying the gun and María the bundle of provisions. The wasp sound grew and grew until the jungle resounded with the ear-splitting noise of scooters curving into the clearing below. Each stuttered to a halt. The engine sound was replaced by agitated shouting. Someone yelled the names of men – men whose bloodied bodies lay sprawled across the temple platform. Other voices called out in alarm. Soon, these were ascending the temple steps. Adam put his arm around María and held her close. No way was Ramón going to ravage his girlfriend.

There was gun-fire. The men had spotted the Golden Jaguar. Their guns, useless against the beast, merely made him snarl – a blood-curdling sound that would have reduced the most fearless of ancient warriors to lumps of quivering jelly. Two men, who'd reached the top of the stairway, fired constantly. Within seconds they both lay dead. Two more appeared and ran shrieking towards the stone building, randomly blazing their weapons. With one easy bound the Golden Jaguar leapt onto the back of one, bringing him down headless. The other, in a futile attempt to save his friend, turned and aimed shots at the burning eyes of the animal from another dimension. The jaguar growled then sprang and another gangster was silenced forever.

Adam peered from behind the edge of the altar whilst María, trembling, hid her face against his shoulder. Two more figures came into sight, both with guns. One was Alejandro. The other – a small balding, middle-aged man, even uglier – the boy took to be Ramón. Ramón, with his gun held in both hands, approached the Golden Jaguar. Alejandro stepped back, turned and ran from the scene.

"Coward!" Adam whispered.

Ramón must have heard him for he instantly spun round and fired. The side of the altar, inches from Adam's head, exploded into a shower of dust and stone fragments. María let out a cry.

"¡LA CHICA!" shouted Ramón. Ignoring the Golden Jaguar, he ran towards the altar. The jaguar leapt and grabbed Ramón's right arm between his powerful jaws. He shook his head and for a few seconds Ramón was like a rag doll dangling from the beast's mouth, his limp body swinging crazily. The man's gun, no more than a child's toy against the Golden Jaguar of the Sun, clattered to the stone platform. Adam emerged from his hiding place and shouted to the Golden Jaguar in the language of the Old Woman of the Hills. The jaguar dropped his prey, turned and faced the boy, sinking subserviently onto his haunches. The fire in his coal-black eyes still blazed. Ramón lay in front of the beast, writhing and groaning and clawing at his torn arm. María ventured out from behind the altar, her face betraying a curious concern for the injured gang leader. Adam

114

approached the Colombian, pointing Vicente's gun at his head. Stooping, he picked up Ramón's weapon and handed this to María. Alejandro had vanished but Adam warned María to watch out for him.

"Now tell me why I shouldn't kill you!" the boy demanded of Ramón in Spanish. The man only grunted, gripping his arm. He was in agony. "I'll tell you, then," Adam continued. "Maybe that cowardly cousin of yours will come back for you if you're still alive. Then we'll have him as well. We'll make sure—"

Interrupted by a burst of engine noise, he grinned on hearing a motor-scooter speed off into the jungle.

"Too much of a coward, huh?" suggested Adam. "Either way, I'm gonna get you to the police alive so they can break up your filthy racket. And free those poor girls you keep locked away in Cali. Get up!"

Ramón's legs flailed like a baby's. He was unable to stand. María gasped and raised her hand to her mouth when she saw the state of the man's right arm. With the bone shattered, it dangled on strands of skin, tissue and torn tendon. His useless hand touched an expanding red pool into which blood spurted from a partially-severed stump of flesh that protruded out of the ripped sleeve.

"Adam, we have to do something," the girl said faintly.

"Stay here! Point the gun at him and shoot if he tries anything. Like this!" He gently cupped his hand around hers, positioning her small fore-finger around the trigger of Ramón's gun. "Just press it if he does anything more than breathe. I'll go fetch one of those dead guys' belts to use as a tourniquet."

Moments later he was back with a leather belt. He cut through Ramón's sleeve using Vicente's knife then paused whilst staring at the arm. If he could stop the bleeding Ramón might survive. He tightened the belt around the stump, pulling against Ramón's cacophony of screams until the blood flow ceased. He disappeared into the stone building and emerged with a rag which he used as a bandage.

"String?" he asked, glancing at María.

She shook her head.

"Oh – I've an idea!" she suddenly exclaimed, unfastening the priceless pearl and ruby necklace that decorated her slender neck. "Use this!"

And so Ramón got his necklace back to tie a rag around an arm which he would certainly lose if lucky enough to live. Adam dragged the groaning man to his feet.

"We've gotta give him something, Adam. I've pain-killers in my handbag. For period pains."

Adam couldn't believe what he heard.

"María, you really must be a saint like the Old Woman said," he goaded. "After what Vicente did, and what this bastard was going to do to you – you still care about him?"

He was gonna rape her, for Christ's sake! Can't she even hate him? Perhaps she hopes he'll – no, Adam – cool it! Not that again! Please God, not that!

Ignoring Adam's loaded question, the girl turned and fetched her handbag from behind the altar.

Why can't I accept the simple truth? That I've just so much to learn from this girl – that she really is special as so many folks are trying to tell me, the boy tried to persuade himself as he watched her gently place a couple of pain-killing pills between Ramón's lips, followed by sips of water from a bottle. Now playing nurse to the man who had threatened to deflower her with force, this made no sense to Adam. When the bastard was sufficiently recovered to stand, all three, followed by the Golden Jaguar, descended the steeply-stepped pyramid and headed off into the jungle in a direction where Adam prayed they'd find a small village.

116

Chapter 8: Jungle Village

The one-time priest leaned forward for a better view.
"Yes, he has strength now with help from the opposition – and courage – but something's wrong, I'm telling you. What if he blows it? This will be our last chance."
"Have faith, brother," replied the old man. "And take care with your choice of words. In the face of what lies within the girl there is no opposition."

It soon became clear to Adam how impossible it would be to cut a path through the jungle with only a knife. They'd made little progress after an hour and he began to despair. Should they turn back and try their luck at the airstrip? Suicide! He knew there'd be more armed men there, including Alejandro. By now the fiend would have gone for reinforcements, and the boy realised that Alejandro, however cowardly the man might be when confronted by the Golden Jaguar, would try anything to prevent him from contacting the police. Retracing their steps was not an option. Alejandro had known all along about the temple of Chiculhuán and the terrain; he'd be well aware of the village marked on the map, the most obvious place to escape to from this jungle nightmare. However, the villagers would be ordinary folk unlikely to take kindly to drug cartels; maybe even Zapatistas totally against drugs. It had to be the village if they could reach it.

Hopelessness engulfed Adam. He turned to face the others. Ramón had somehow managed to struggle on behind them. Whimpering like a child, the revolting little squirt had to be tougher than he looked. María followed Ramón, holding the man's gun in one hand and trailing a bundle of provisions behind her with the other. Struggling through the jungle in high-heels was difficult for the girl, even at the pace of a tortoise. Behind her slunk the Golden Jaguar, ever watchful and flicking his tail. When they came to a halt, María reached out to support Ramón.

"Adam, we're gonna have to do something," she pleaded. "He's in awful pain."

Even though the same man had planned to publicly rape her before killing Adam, the girl couldn't bear to see him suffer. Moments earlier her boyfriend had smiled contentedly to himself on hearing his grunts of pain.

Why does she worry about the bastard? Could it have something to do with what the Old Woman of the Hills said? 'Santa Maria' – 'pura' – 'special'? Like Art and Papa Pedro said? Sure, she's special – but if so, who really is she?

"María, it's gonna take days to cut through this shit. Even then, I can't be sure we're going in the right direction. I just dunno what—"

Adam stopped mid-sentence, his attention diverted by the Golden Jaguar. The beast was standing protectively beside María and staring at him, trying to tell him something. When the boy cleared his head of all other thoughts, including his old enemy jealousy, words appeared in his mind: the words of the Golden Jaguar.

"What an idiot I am! The Golden Jaguar knows the way. He knows exactly where we're going and look at him! He'll make us a path by forcing his way through the forest. Oh man, how dumb can you get?"

Adam stepped aside as the beast pushed on through the forest leaving a perfect trail for him and the other two. The boy laughed and gave María a hug, but she broke free and insisted he help the injured Ramón by half-lifting him onto his shoulder and dragging him along. Adam complied, reluctant – no, seething – with his status reduced to that of luggage bearer.

Saint or no saint, she bloody wants him! Will she become his whore after all? Christ, man, what's happening?

Luckily Ramón was smaller than Adam. A burden, but one with which he could unwillingly cope. The boy looked ahead at the curvy back view of María whose stubborn determination to help the gangster boss draped over his shoulder was driving him crazy. At least with his girlfriend in front he could keep a watch over her whilst jealousy carved dark inroads into his dancing mind. How odd that he and the Golden Jaguar should have reversed their roles – himself protecting the girl from her own desires, for by now he'd convinced himself she wanted the drug baron to 'take her' as had been the bastard's original plan.

Frequently the beast would stop and look back to reassure himself Princess Arima was safe. Once, caught in the stare of those fiery eyes, Adam was certain the Golden Jaguar was trying to tell him something. Could the beast read his mind – his jealousy? But those jealous taunts blocked the beast's thought-words.

Thus they traipsed through the forest, each uneasy in his or her own way, until Adam, exhausted, called out to the Golden Jaguar in Nahuatl:

"Stop! Gotta rest – eat – have some water!"

"What did you just say?" asked María, turning to grin at her boyfriend. "You gonna major in that funny language or something?"

Adam wanted to laugh but couldn't when he saw the concern with which she looked at Ramón.

"Jaguar and I think we should stop and have lunch."

"Suits me just fine," agreed the girl.

Suits her? So she can 'do it' with him, huh?

María unfolded the blanket, spreading it out neatly on the path.

For her and him to make love on? Will she ask me to look the other way before the heavy breathing starts?

"Fancy these?" the girl asked Adam. She held up a tin of beans in chilli sauce. The boy pulled a face. María knelt, her butt too sore to sit on, and chose a packet of sliced cheese and a packet of wrapped bread. He nodded. "That's more like it," he agreed feeling as flat as a slice of cheese himself. The boy helped Ramón down onto the blanket at an acceptable distance from his girlfriend and sat squarely in between them.

"You go ahead and I'll feed scum-bag," he said.

But before she started eating, María took another couple of pain-killers from her handbag.

"Please give him these, Adam."

"What if I don't?"

Adam's eyes flashed anger. María said nothing so the boy felt obliged to feed Ramón the painkillers as well as bread, cheese and water. Shattered, the injured man lowered himself onto his back. He looked dreadful. Beads of perspiration peppered his brow and he breathed in shallow gasps. His partly-detached arm had become smelly and gangrenous and there was no doubt death would overcome him unless they were to reach the village pretty goddamn soon.

After stuffing bread and cheese into his mouth, and gulping down water, Adam availed himself of the natural bathroom facilities of the forest. He recalled the look in María's eyes on seeing him the previous evening, plus her naïvity and apparent purity whilst helping him unzip his pants, and he inwardly smiled. He must've got it wrong about María and Ramón. Surely the Old Woman, by calling her "Santa María", had been trying to tell him his girlfriend was without unclean thoughts. He'd go along with the girl; show her that he, too, could be a 'Christian'. He felt almost happy as he zippered his pants, whistling one of María's latest songs.

Making his way back, he froze. María was still kneeling, but her position was changed. Ramón's head rested on her lap – and – oh God, she was stroking his hair and singing softly to the guy who'd planned to rob her virginity. Adam broke through the tangle of forest bushes and yelled at the girl for the whole world to hear:

"WHAT – WHAT THE HELL HAVE YOU TWO BEEN UP TO? HAVE YOU 'DONE IT' WITH HIM? ARE YOU HIS NOW? A GODDAMN DRUG DEALER'S HOOKER?"

María looked calmly up, still stroking the man's head.

"Adam, he's dying. He's human. Don't you understand?"

"So he damn well should die if – if you and he – if—"

"Please don't be like this. I can't bear to see anyone suffer. That's all. You'll only ever be the one for me. That has to be. I'll never cheat on you. You know that, right?"

"I – I know nothing! Get away from him! He was gonna rape you! You heard what Vicente said!"

"This isn't about you or me, Adam. It's about a dying man. A man in agony."

"Get up! I'll carry on dragging the bastard for you if that's what you want, but if you've decided to become his whore—"

Adam couldn't believe he was saying these things. He wanted to stop because he knew he was hurting the girl and that she was right, but his brain wouldn't allow him to see reason. María stood up, silent. He was expecting her to wallop him across the face in feisty Mexican fashion, but she didn't. He wished she had. Surely she could have said something – at the very least responded in some way to his cruel words. Why didn't she? Was there truth in what he'd said? Was there guilt in her dignified, unreadable expression? And when she'd laughed the evening before as they shared the gangsters' toilet facility, had this been because she considered him too small 'down there' to satisfy her?

Adam helped the drug baron to his feet and María gathered the provisions in silence. She picked up Ramón's gun and for an awful moment he imagined her shooting him and making off into the forest with Ramón. Instead, she turned and followed the Golden Jaguar. The boy struggled on with Ramón and two Adams. Both loved María, but one only wanted the girl for himself, fearing every male within a hundred yards of her, whilst the other yearned to know her better and would always be there for her.

Ramón was barely alive when, an hour or so later, they heard voices of excited children, the contented sound of turkeys, of dogs and the occasional burst of shouting. The Mayan village, thank God, and so close after all. Adam knew all along that the Old Woman would have been pin-point accurate with her location of the temple of Chiculhuán.

María was overjoyed. She abandoned the bundle of provisions and ran on ahead. The Golden Jaguar sank to the ground, discreetly concealing himself in the undergrowth, whilst Adam stopped and held on to his loathsome burden. He heard the alarmed screams of young children and grinned. What would those kids make of María, her long, black hair wild and un-brushed, emerging from the forest wearing a dirty red party dress and high-heeled shoes, carrying a posh matching handbag and brandishing a gun? He was aware of other voices, including María's gabbling in Spanish, and in no time two men with Mayan faces came running from the direction of the village to see to Ramón.

The village was small. There were about twenty or so palm-thatched long huts and one white-painted house with a thatched roof. María was gabbling in Spanish to a group of three Mayan women dressed in white *huipiles*. They stood in a plaza strewn with plastic bottles, bits of junk and several lazing dogs. A *jabali*, a skinny grey-haired kind of pig, strained on a string attached to a small tree.

Golden Jaguar of the Sun

Adam, dragging the provisions, went over to María whilst the two men carried the half-dead Ramón to the white house where, they were told, a man called Manuel would fix him. The boy so wanted to apologise for the awful things he'd said but now wasn't the time. One of the women, short and slim and in her late twenties, smiled as he joined his girlfriend.

"*¿Se habla español, no?*"

"*Sí, un poquito,*" Adam replied.

María laughed, gave the gun to one of the women and put an arm lovingly around her boyfriend as if the vile things he'd said earlier were of no importance.

"*¡Como un hombre mexicano!*" she proudly announced.

Has she forgotten and forgiven? If she can forgive Ramón will she do the same for me?

The villagers spoke modern-day Mayan, quite unlike Nahuatl. Even though he wore the Golden Jaguar bracelets he couldn't understand a word. Fortunately the young woman, called Lela, spoke fluent Spanish, as did several other villagers. She took Adam and María, both pooped, to her hut.

It was a crude, basic dwelling with a single main living area. A small bedroom – or rather, 'sleeping area' – was curtained off from this by a colourful woven blanket. Here, three hammocks hung from hooks on the wooden rafters. Fires of charcoal and wood smouldered both outside and inside and there was a small outside toilet and a galvanised bathtub. María's eyes lit up at the sight of the bathtub but Adam was more interested in the pile of fresh tortillas beside the fire in one corner of the hut.

Two bilingual children aged four and six, Carla and Pepe, took to María like eager puppies. She was so used to her own younger siblings she knew instinctively how to win their confidence. At first they were wary of Adam but when

123

they sensed how much María loved the boy they decided to like him too.

"So important they learn Spanish!" Lela explained. "One day they'll leave this hole and make names for themselves."

María asked about her husband, seeing no sign of a man about the place. The woman looked away, sad beyond tears.

"Killed," she announced after a pause. "*¡Los gángsters de drogas!* They come into our village in a truck. They want food, money and women! My husband, Pío, he says 'no! no! no! So they shoot him. Still they take our food, our money and they take Anna, my friend. Such a pretty girl, Anna. They take Anna to Colombia. To Cali. Six weeks ago. Her poor husband, he couldn't live with this. Hanged himself."

Lela kept looking from María to Adam as the three sat drinking *taxallate* – a drink made from corn and cocoa. So far, the pair hadn't given their story. Besides, there were bits Adam felt needed clarification, such as what the girl truly wanted of him and of Ramón. Nevertheless, it slowly emerged.

María told of her delight at having been asked to make the new album in Mexico and how she'd insisted Adam sing some of the tracks with her. Adam attempted to explain his misplaced trust in Álvaro and his smarmy cousin, Alejandro, María's kidnapping in Mexico City, his failed rescue bid and subsequent incarceration in the jungle temple.

When it came to the bit about the Golden Jaguar, the boy glanced at María. He could tell from her expression that the same thought was going through her mind: this was one secret they should not divulge. Instead, he said how, after seeing the ogre Vicente beat his girlfriend, and having severed his bond, he had to kill the man. He described how he'd made a grab for Vicente's gun and left it for Lela to deduce Vicente had been shot. Adam wasn't one for telling lies (was this why he had such trouble suppressing jealousy?). He honestly believed it was his command that caused the Golden Jaguar to kill Vicente, an unarmed man. The guilt of killing became piggy-backed onto the guilt already burdening Adam: the guilt of failing to understand the girl he loved so much.

When they came to the bit concerning Ramón, Adam fell silent. María spoke up, saying Ramón and his men were "soon overpowered by Adam" (*if only!*) and that Ramón's arm "got caught in something". Not a hint from the girl that she thought of the drug baron as anything other than an evil creature who deserved his comeuppance.

So why all that tenderness in the forest, for heaven's sake?

Ramón's mutterings to the village men about some sort of a giant cat with eyes of fire had been put down to delirium.

"So the man they're helping this very minute, that's the big boss of *los gángsters?*" queried Lela, cut up to know her husband's murderer was possibly having his miserable life saved by Manuel in the white house.

"*¡Sí!*" answered Adam. "And it's so important he does live. He's the key to this filthy drugs racket. Gotta hand him over to the police so they can get the information they need to break up the ring. And your friend, Anna – maybe they could rescue her from the sonofabitch's penthouse in Cali."

Lela looked dumbfounded.

"I'd gladly kill him myself, but you're right, Adam," she agreed. "The police can make use of his knowledge. Top guy! He'll know everything."

"We're very worried Alejandro got away," Adam added.

At this point Adam and María learned what they'd been dreading most of all: that there was no available phone. They'd already discovered there was no signal for María's cell phone and now they heard how the gangsters had cut the phone lines to the village and destroyed their solar panel, a gift from the Zapatistas. The only truck they had was away with a man called Plácido who drove to tourist towns with woven baskets, hand-crafted material and other goods to sell in the markets. He wasn't expected back for a week or so. There were some rusty old bicycles that Adam and María might have borrowed but a cycle ride to the nearest town would've been long and dangerous; more so with Alejandro on the loose.

"You must stay here with me till Plácido returns," Lela insisted. Adam agreed. Carla and Pepe were ecstatic.

"María! María!" they chanted, climbing up onto the girl's lap and hugging her.

"*¡O, Mis hijos!*" scalded Lela, thinking they were annoying the girl.

"It's okay!" reassured María. "I'm used to this. Got a house full of children back home. I'm the eldest of seven."

"I don't understand. Normally they're so suspicious of strangers. They really have taken to you!"

Adam understood perfectly well. It took two small children to show him how wrong he'd been. Not only was his girlfriend beautiful, she was friendly, kind and gentle.

Plus special?

Like everyone else he too felt something but did he *understand* her in the way he understood his parents, little Chloe, Pedro, Art and Jeannie – even the Old Woman of the Hills? The person closer to him than anyone else could ever be was enshrouded with mystery.

Because of the children, María rapidly reverted back to her old self. Even when she and Adam were alone together, she made no mention of her beating, of Ramón, or of her boyfriend's behaviour in the forest. The unconfident Adam promised the other Adam he'd apologise when the time was right. As far as understanding the girl, Papa Pedro had once told him the human spirit is indomitable. Papa Pedro had always been so right about everything. María was simply indomitable and he could forget all that 'special' nonsense.

Golden Jaguar of the Sun

The boy was particularly concerned that Ramón should be kept alive after hearing Lela's story. The Mexican police and Interpol would be able to locate the drug baron's penthouse and free Anna and those other young women, but when they heard what Manuel had to do to save Ramón's life something unexpected happened: something that kicked Adam's other self back into a flurry of jealousy.

María fainted. After she'd come to on the floor, Pepe and Carla, both crying and seriously worried she had suddenly died, jumped up and down with excitement:

"*¡Viva, Mama, viva!*" they yelled, repeatedly kissing the dazed girl. Adam watched glumly as they sat María up, now several shades paler than a Mexican girl should be.

"Cut off his arm with a saw?" she asked weakly, as if unable to believe what Lela had just told them.

"Good!" exclaimed Adam. "Maybe a little justice has been done if the jerk survives!"

"They think he'll live because the gangrene has been taken away," explained Lela. "Manuel knows so much about these things. Always wanted to be a doctor when he was a boy – but no money, no proper education. We're a poor people, Adam, and *los gángsters* they make us poorer. If Manuel had become a doctor he'd have been the best in the world. Mostly, he uses plants and herbs we grow here but he has antibiotics too. Plácido gets them in town. He's been using them on that demon. Yes – I'm afraid he'll pull the bastard through—" She appeared angry at the thought of this before adding, with resignation, "but only for police! So he can rot in jail for the rest of his life."

"Here's hoping," added Adam, glancing at María. Her face seemed to agree with Lela.

Lela lent María some of Anna's clothes: pretty, tasseled white cotton *huipiles*, jeans and tops. She was sure Anna wouldn't have minded. María was over the moon when she could have a bath and wash her hair – to Adam's regret on

127

the other side of the drape – plus change into clean clothes and Anna's sneakers.

When the girl finally emerged, her sleek black hair dripping, Carla became excited.

"Let me brush it for you!" she begged. "Please let me brush it!"

"Sure thing!" agreed María.

The child stood behind María, eagerly stroking the older girl's hair with a brush. Adam laughed to see such an intensely serious expression on little Carla's face. After a short while, Pepe realised he was missing out on something.

"Let me have a go too!" pleaded the Mayan boy. "It's not fair! I want a go!"

Soon María had both children tugging and pulling at her hair with their mother's brush and comb. Adam could tell from her facial contortions that this pained her but she didn't complain. She was tough – yet also vulnerable by caring about others.

More than special? Truly a princess from another dimension?

The children and the Golden Jaguar saw it: something that could not be put into words – something that would one day take the world by surprise. But Adam remained blind. Perhaps he loved her too much – or perhaps not enough.

***

Adam and María became much-loved guests in the small village. Pepe and Carla would proudly parade them between the village huts, each child hanging onto one of María's arms as they showed her off to the other children, chanting '*Santa María! Santa María!*' Yes, '*santa*'. At first Adam tagged along behind feeling supernumerary, but when the village boys heard that he preferred soccer to American football his popularity rose to almost equal that of María. He became a sought-after team member in their soccer games although arguments often arose as to whose team he should be in.

This led to the occasional skirmish and Adam would be forced to intervene.

María helped Lela with her housework, washing and cooking. Like her mother, she was a fantastic cook. *Bodes well for the future*, the boy thought as he watched her prepare a particularly delicious meal of pork, beans, vegetables and chillies grown in the village.

Adam felt bad that his and María's parents would be stuck in the nightmare of having no contact from them, uncertain whether their prayers would ever been answered. If only he could let Chloe know they were all right. Perhaps she did. He alone was aware of her extraordinary telepathic power, but it was unpredictable. The boy wondered whether the police might instigate a helicopter search of the jungle. Unlikely, given that the Chiapas was such a huge area, much of it under Zapatista control. Besides, Alejandro had brokered a deal with the police chief which meant they'd wish to distance themselves from the operation until the last possible moment.

Adored by the village children, the two teenagers grew to love the other villagers. They loved their gentle friendliness as they admired their honesty and fortitude in the face of poverty and constant intimidation by drug gangsters. Even the Zapatista rebels seemed to have lost interest in them but Adam swore he'd never forget these people so excluded from the outside world. He would forever treasure memories of their extraordinary resilience. The heyday of their civilisation had been so long ago they seemed hardly aware that once the Maya had been a great and proud people, but for Adam their present humility in no way belittled them.

Chapter 9: The Spider

*"**We** won't need the old Sun God any longer when Quetzalcóatl returns," growled one of the gods. All the others stayed quiet. All, that is, except Tezcatlipoca. "Forget Quetzalcóatl! As for the girl, she's mine anyway!" smirked the all powerful one rubbing his hands with glee. "And soon she will be destroyed. The Spider Goddess will see to it. If not, her two friends. Then she can become their plaything for all eternity."*

Adam apologised.

It was exactly a week after they'd arrived in the village. Plácido was still away and there was no sign of Alejandro and the other gangsters. According to Manuel, Ramón was making good progress with antibiotics. This news had produced no response from María, positive or negative.

"María, I – I've been thinking all week how to apologise. It's just that, well – after what they threatened to do to you – the fear of you belonging to someone else – you know – in that way – I—"

The girl smiled in the face of his bumbling confession; a smile of widom, not amusement; a *Mona Lisa* smile.

"I'd rather kill myself than let anyone other than my Adam make love to me, if that's what was worrying you. Look, I knew you were kinda hung up. You'd rescued me. Saved my life. Remember? And all along I had this feeling you would. It kept me going. But sometimes—"

They were sitting together on a hammock swinging their bared feet. Adam's gaze fixed on her bright-red painted toe nails. Lela and the children had gone to bed. The boy felt the girl lift up his hand then kiss it.

"Please don't be cross if I say this. That I love you but sometimes can't understand you. It's as if—" She paused.

"Well – like there's two Adams. I love them both. But one is so much stronger. He'd never have said those things. I know it."

The boy could scarcely believe that her analysis of him was identical to his own. He slowly shook his head in agreement.

"Nope! He wouldn't. And he feels so goddamn ashamed. He'd gladly kill the other Adam for what he said."

"No more killing. Please! And I will be yours in 'that way', as you put it. I want so much to be right now – but I've taken this vow, see. To remain a virgin until – you know."

She went quiet, squeezed his hand then kissed him on the lips – long and fondly.

"Better?" she asked as her warm hand stroked his cheek.

"Until what?" the boy repeated, aroused like crazy.

"Yes!" she laughed. "Until!"

"Promised whom?"

"God."

Santa María? Pura? Is there some conspiracy here?

"We're gonna get married sooner than you think, *chico*!"

"Yeah, well – meanwhile—"

"If you love me you'll at least try to understand. It's my religion. I believe, you see. That's the difference between us."

"But those other things, María – the Golden Jaguar, the Old Woman of the Hills. They're real. I've seen them."

"Me too! Remember? I know it's happening, Adam, but it doesn't stop me believing. The reverse, in fact! Now I believe in my Faith even more strongly. And—" She kissed his hand again. "It'll happen soon! I promise. I feel it here, as Papa Pedro used to say."

"You know – all this Mayan business. Their old civilisation was so – so awesome! I saw an ancient Mayan painting of Xibalba, the Place of Fear – in that book – it's their kinda purgatory where dead people go – and I can't get out of my mind the picture of a little dog who'd died and was smiling because he'd been brought back to life. Just imagine if we could bring Papa Pedro back to life!"

"I believe he went straight to heaven," María said emphatically, carressing Adam's cheek with the back of her hand. "Not that Xibalba place! I believe that because he was such a kind man. But I know there are strange things happening – like the Golden Jaguar. And d'you know why the Golden Jaguar has turned good?"

She grinned.

"Because he has to protect Princess Arima?"

María laughed then shook her head.

"No! Because Adam Winters is truly good and kind and wears the Golden Jaguar bracelets."

A sudden change in María's expression revealed she'd just thought of something. The boy knew that face so well.

"Maybe you could—" she began, "but no! Don't you dare take them off!"

The girl playfully tousled her boyfriend's hair, laughed and kissed him some more. They kissed again – and again – and again – until Adam felt he'd have to stop for María's safety. How he yearned for her body to be his to fondle and feel and possess every square inch of – but the respect he had for the girl would always be stronger than his desire. They quietly bid each other "goodnight" after one last and lengthy kiss.

"By the way," María whispered. With her back to her boyfriend, she'd halted to pull at the curtain separating her sleeping area from his. "Who *was* Princess Arima?"

Adam shrugged his shoulders.

"Haven't a clue," he answered. "Just that the Old Woman of the Hills and the Golden Jaguar seem to think she's you."

And Santa María?

Before Adam finally drifted off to sleep, more questions whirled in his mind: why did María say 'who was' rather than 'who is' Princess Arima? And was it not María rather than the bracelets who bound the Golden Jaguar to his will?

María was up early the following morning. She was to take the children to mass in the 'chapel': a long hut in which a print of *La nuestra Señora de Guadalupe* hung above a brown, carved wooden crucifix. Carla and Pepe bubbled with excitement. The younger girl insisted María wear her red dress since she liked it so much, but before they were allowed to leave for chapel María had to wait until the child had run all round the village to find a red flower for the older girl's hair. Carla returned waving a brilliant red tropical flower, although by the time this had been slotted above María's left ear it had lost most of its petals.

"You know, in Hawai'i if a girl wears a flower on that side it means she's spoken for," Adam said, feasting his eyes upon his girlfriend.

"Well – she is!" the girl informed him.

Oh my God, if only I could believe that!

Whilst María and the children were at chapel, and Lela was busy with the washing outside, Adam walked unseen to the edge of the *plaza*. After checking that no one was watching, he slipped quietly into the forest. He reached the spot where he'd last seen the Golden Jaguar. For a few tense moments there seemed to be no sign of the beast. Then a rustling in the undergrowth behind him caused to turn: the jaguar, as magnificent as ever, crouched a few yards away, watching and waiting. Adam came up close – slowly, for, although he was now its master, the boy remained wary. He glanced at the godly animal's large paws, their claws retracted and hidden from view. The creature appeared almost cuddly.

Adam squatted and held up both wrists to reveal the bracelets. The jaguar glanced briefly at these then looked into Adam's eyes as if he no longer had any interest in the bracelets. The coal-black eyes stared at the boy, seeking his command and there was a yearning in them the boy could not fathom. For a few moments he had a crazy notion they were seeking some other dimension that only María could enter because of who she was. Their vertical red flames suddenly flickered fiercely and he banished all thoughts of removing the bracelets in front of the beast. He had come back to the forest with the intention of testing what must have been in his girlfriend's mind the previous night: that he no longer needed them to subjugate the creature to his will for the love she inspired was a power far greater than anything the jaguar had yet encountered in his timeless journey through different dimensions. Perhaps, in some way, this also came from Adam – like a mirror reflecting María's love, a power infinitely stronger than that of the bracelets.

Maybe, as the girl had implied, there was no contradiction between her religious beliefs, those of the ancient Mesoamericans and mystery of the Golden Jaguar. Could the whole thing be a kind of continuum? Had those ancient peoples merely been unaware of the full force of Love, the true meaning behind María's religion. This made sense to the boy. At last he felt he was beginning to understand the complexity of his girlfriend and what others meant by her being 'special'.

Seeing the flames glow with such intensity in those dark feline eyes, Adam knew now was not the time to test his theory. The beast was troubled. He knelt, emptying his mind of all thought and allowing his soul to sink into those flames. The voice of the Golden Jaguar responded. The Nahuatl words were so clear, so natural – so terrifying:

"Beware the spider! I will be here when it happens. Come immediately!"

The words baffled Adam.

"What about the spider?" he questioned.

The Golden Jaguar merely repeated himself: "The spider! Princess Arima! Come quickly! Xibalba!"

It made no sense to Adam. Xibalba was the 'Place of Fear' where the Mayan dead ended up, but the giant cat went silent. No explanation was forthcoming. Adam left and the jaguar remained crouching – staring – listening – waiting.

For Princess Arima? For Santa María?

María returned from chapel as radiant as ever with a happy child clutching each hand. She wondered why Adam kept looking under tables, chairs, stones, books and in every corner of the hut.

"Adam, what *are* you doing?" she asked as Pepe tugged at her arm begging her to play with him.

"Are there any poisonous spiders here? In Mexico? I know the Maya had spiders in their mythology, but—"

He lifted a rug and examined the floor on all fours.

"Adam, I think we've more to worry about than spiders. Could you play with Pepe whilst I change into something suitable?"

Adam looked at her, feeling stupid. What did the beast mean? If only it could open its huge mouth and have an ordinary conversation in English instead of making Nahuatl words appear in his head.

"Adam, I need to get changed! In here! Please!"

"Oh, yeah! Cool! Come on Pepe, I'll teach you to be a famous soccer player."

María pulled the curtain to. Moments later she reappeared wearing Anna's jeans and top, rather tight-fitting for María's fuller figure. She sat down with Carla to listen to the girl's Spanish reading. Pepe hurried off to get his football and Adam followed, checking for spiders behind the door on his way out. When he returned an hour later he stooped down and was about to look under the table again, where Carla and María were seated, when the older girl spoke in English:

"It's okay, Adam! I've checked already. No spiders! Lela uses herbs in the water when she cleans around and this puts them off. Plus snakes and other biting things. It's quite safe here. Not the Hilton, but safe!" she reassured, frowning with annoyance.

Over the next few days Adam tried to forget about spiders and about the Golden Jaguar, living in hope that Plácido would soon return with the truck and take them to the nearest village or town where there'd surely be a phone connection or a police station. Each day, when the man failed to appear, he felt frustrated. Nevertheless, they settled easily into village life, María doing many of Lela's daily chores and Adam helping the men in the vegetable plots, feeding the goats, chickens and turkeys. He also took an interest in some of their craft-work.

One of the men made little animals which he carved from forest wood and painted brilliant colours. The children loved them. Carla and Pepe often played with the ones they had. Adam was interested to see how similar these were to the ancient Mayan animals. He also watched some of the women weave cloth to make colourful garments whilst others were absorbed in basketry. They all worked so hard for such little reward.

Adam and María could never say 'no' when the village children begged them to play. On their twelfth day as village guests they were dragged away for a game of soccer with a group of boys. Adam, distracted and unable to concentrate on the game, was in one team and María in the other. Because the girl was quick and agile, her team was soon easily winning. After all, she had been one of the best cheerleaders in middle grade school. They decided to call the game to a close when some of the lads in Adam's team became irritable. They'd wanted María to swap sides with

Adam but their opponents were saying "no way!" In a fit of rage one of Adam's little team-mates kicked the ball as hard as he could away from the *plaza* and into the forest before stomping off home in a sulk. The others quickly dispersed.

"I'll go fetch it," Adam announced. María waited. He took forever but finally emerged holding the ball.

"Sorry I took so long," he apologised since María appeared fed up. "Like searching for a needle in a goddamn haystack!" He tapped the ball. "This'll have cost some kid's dad a week's earnings," he said, walking on past his girlfriend to seek out the owner.

"STOP!" the girl called in alarm. Adam froze. "NO! DON'T MOVE!" she insisted when he began to turn round. He sensed her approach and felt something brush across his shoulders.

"OW!" she screamed.

Adam swivelled to see her frantically sucking at the back of her hand.

"What?" he asked. "What's the matter? Why did you shout 'ow'?"

María stopped and stared at her hand.

"It bit me. There, on the ground. Boy, it hurts."

Adam looked down. An injured spider, the size of his palm, lay waving its legs in the air. He stamped it into the earth then examined the girl's hand. This was red and swollen and he saw two tell-tale puncture holes.

"OUCH!" she cried out when he touched the spot. Adam knew she rarely complained when hurt. She must have borne bruises which affected her sitting for days after Vicente's harsh beating but said nothing.

"Adam, it's *so* sore."

Tears filled the girl's eyes.

"Quick! We must get you to Manuel. It shouldn't be swelling so fast. You need an antidote, María. Must hurry!"

They started to run towards Manuel's house at the far end of the *plaza* where Ramón was being kept. The drug baron was now more prisoner than patient and Adam knew Manuel or someone else would be there guarding him. María, normally a faster runner than Adam, slowed then halted and put her hands to her head. She swayed like an inflatable plastic figure in a strong breeze.

"Adam, I don't feel too—" the girl began in a faint voice.

Her eyes glazed over before she slumped to the ground. Adam stooped and lifted her into his arms. She felt so light. Tapping into the strength empowered by the Golden Jaguar bracelets, he was able to run at speed with her to Manuel's 'hospital'. A group of villagers watched him dash across the *plaza* carrying the girl.

"*¡ARAÑA! ARAÑA!*" he yelled.

One man hurried on ahead to forewarn Manuel whilst others ran to Adam, helping him support the girl's weight. Manuel sprinted from his house, took María and rushed back with her to a small room where she was carefully placed on top of a bed.

She came too briefly when Adam gripped her healthy hand and Manuel applied a tourniquet around the bitten arm, the whole of which had become grotesquely swollen. The man put his mouth over the fang marks on the girl's hand, sucked hard then spat out onto the ground. He did this a few times. Adam could tell from María's eyes it was intensely painful, but she no longer had the strength to cry out.

"She'll be all right, won't she? Tell me she's gonna be okay," he begged Manuel. "She did this for me. She brushed it off my shoulder with her hand. She – she knows I'm dead scared of spiders."

María's mouth opened. The girl looked at Adam and she tried to speak, but there was no sound. Only a slight movement of the lips. Her eyes turned hazy then blank as if she was no longer there. She went still. Adam shook her arm.

"MARÍA!" he cried out. "FOR GOD'S SAKE SPEAK TO ME!"

The boy looked frantically up at Manuel who gently lowered the girl's hand.

"DO SOMETHING!" he shouted. "SHE'S STOPPED BREATHING!"

"I can do no more, Adam. Besides, we've no anti-venom," the man replied quietly.

He turned to speak to his friend who stood behind him.

"Fetch Agustín," he said. "For the last rights." Agustín, raised by Jesuits, acted as the village priest.

"No you bloody don't!" protested Adam.

"Adam, she's dead! Have respect."

Manuel placed a soothing hand on the boy's shoulder.

"No she bloody isn't!" insisted Adam, lifting María's body up against his. Agustín appeared in the doorway.

"Adam!" Manuel persisted. "Let Agustín be with her. Please! The last rights are important for us Catholics."

Adam looked at Agustín, at Manuel, and then back at Agustín:

"DON'T YOU DARE TOUCH HER!"

He pushed Manuel away so violently the man fell backwards. After lifting the dead girl up – and she felt weightless – he brushed past a confused Agustín and ran towards the forest with María in his arms. Villagers chased after him but he was too fast. They stopped, stood and watched as the boy disappeared into the undergrowth.

Chapter 10: The Forest Without Time

*"**Perhaps—**" began the ex-priest peering down, "—perhaps there's more to that boy than I thought. But your plan can never work."*

"Not my plan. Fate's. But I'm ready and I think I'll rather enjoy showing you up this time," teased the old man. "I feel it here," he added, patting his chest. He winked at the priest before taking his leave.

Adam was forced to slow down as he pushed his way through the dense jungle growth in the direction of where he'd last seen the Golden Jaguar of the Sun. He raised the dead girl's face to his and kissed her soft cheek. It was still warm.

"No, María!" he whispered. "Manuel's wrong! You can't leave me. Not now!"

He stopped. This was surely the place. His darting eyes searched the undergrowth. Nothing! He began to panic. Had he lost all sense of direction? Things around him appeared changed. Then, to one side, the face of the Golden Jaguar parted the foliage, his eyes burning like balls of gold and crimson fire. Adam had never seen them glow so vividly, the black confined to faint rims encircling two fiery globes. The beast leapt from the undergrowth and stood in front of the boy, speaking in Nahuatl inside his head:

"Up on my back! Quick!"

Adam, hugging María's limp, lifeless body, sat astride the great back of the crouching beast and gripped the hard-muscled flanks between his knees. The creature shot forwards. The boy closed his eyes, for it seemed they were heading straight for a large tree covered with hairy bark, but they skimmed past the tree and sped on into the forest, gathering speed. The Golden Jaguar ran faster and faster until with each bound he covered a distance as great as the length of a soccer pitch; faster and faster whilst the green blur of the forest flashed by. Adam held the animal tightly between both legs, all the time pressing his face lovingly against his dead girlfriend's and repeatedly kissing her.

"Adam?"

Alarmed, Adam raised his head. He stared at María. She turned her face to look up at him.

Heaven be praised, she's alive! Or is she? Am I also dead?

"Adam—" she repeated softly. "*Please* hold me tight."

"You'll be okay, María. They were wrong, you know."

"Who were?"

"The men in the village. Manuel and the others. You're gonna be fine!"

"What village?"

"Lela's – and her children's. *That* village."

"Oh!"

"Here, put your arms around my neck, María."

The girl did as he said. Adam noticed nothing wrong with her right hand and arm. No, redness, no swelling – no spider bite.

"Adam, why do you keep calling me by that strange name?"

"That's who you are. María!"

"What about Arima?"

"I think she's become María. That's you."

"María? I do like the name. María – María!" she repeated to herself, smiling. "Those men in black cloaks – will they come back?"

"No, María, they'll never come back."

"And the spider? Was there a spider too?" María tensed. She looked frightened.

"We'll stop the spider from hurting you. The Golden Jaguar will help us do that."

The girl relaxed then smiled.

"Yes. The Golden Jaguar. But *please* hold me tight," she begged.

Adam held her firmly, again placing his face against her smooth cheek. The girl's flowing hair streamed in the wind like the slender threads of an exotic water-plant in the current of a fast-flowing river. Black silken strands frivolously flicked across his face as they sped through *The Forest Without Time*. After a while – and in such a timeless place that could mean minutes, days or even years – the creature slowed to a gentle canter. His bounds became shorter and Adam was able to make out the shapes of things in the blur of the forest. There were tall trees, tangles of fronded bushes and the occasional splash of vivid colour from forest flowers: crimson, pink, purple and yellow. They were still in a forest yet one that was totally alien. The trees were from another world – giant, pre-historic tree-ferns as tall as redwoods. A dragon-fly the size of large swan buzzed past like a model aircraft. María clung to Adam even more tightly.

"Where are we?" she asked.

"I honestly don't know," the boy replied. "But the Old Woman of the Hills talked about *The Forest Without Time*. She said it's where the Golden Jaguar lives, María."

María giggled.

"It sounds so funny when you call me by that name but I do like it. Does 'María' suit me?"

"Suits you just fine. María! There you go!"

The girl grinned and Adam kissed her forehead again.

"Adam, who *is* the Old Woman of the Hills?"

"She's the one who knows everything," the boy replied. "And I mean *every*thing!"

"Oh!"

María, still smiling, closed her eyes and nestled her cheek against Adam's chest. The Golden Jaguar slowed to a walking pace then halted. They were in a large clearing and Adam heard the murmuring of running water.

"Here!" spoke the Golden Jaguar inside Adam's head. "You can get down now."

"Can you stand by yourself?" Adam asked María.

"Why d'you ask?" she queried. "Shouldn't I be able to?" María appeared truly puzzled by his question. An inner voice had warned him not to tell her she was dead, if 'dead' was the right word. Here she seemed so totally alive.

But this place is without time. Her arm may look fine but it's already happened back there. Here, in this timeless place, it hasn't happened. She's dead and she's alive. That's why we're in the Forest Without Time – in a different dimension. To make sure she survives when it happens. When we return.

María leapt to the ground with the grace and agility as might be expected from an ex-cheerleader and a gymnast who'd been highly commended after her first gymnastics exam.

"See!" she exclaimed, stretching out her arms. "I'm just fine."

She had to put out her hand to help her somewhat clumsier boyfriend dismount.

"Oh my! This is so weird!" she exclaimed, gazing at the forest. In the boy's head Nahuatl words appeared. He checked these out with the Golden Jaguar:

"So you'll wait here whilst Princess Arima – María, that is – and I take a path along by the river to see the old man? What old man?"

The girl turned and looked in astonishment at him.

"Why, you speak my language too!" she exclaimed excitedly. "You never told me you could do that!"

"Your language? Well – it's only because I'm wearing these bracelets."

"Yeah, I noticed those," she added. "Kinda scary!"

"Depends who's wearing them," reassured Adam. "Look, we must do what the Golden Jaguar says. The river's over there. I can hear it. We've gotta find the path, see an old man, whoever and wherever he may be, then return. And what's so strange is there doesn't seem to be any hurry about things. As though – well – as though time doesn't even exist. Funny that, isn't it, María?"

"Do please keep calling me María. I like it so much better than Arima. And I love this language we're speaking. What is it, Adam?"

"It's English. And you're pretty good at it! Your mama says you never stop talking in either English or Spanish! And I never want you to stop!"

"Spanish?"

"*¡Sí! ¡Español!*"

"*¿Español tambien?*" queried María.

"*Sí*, but I prefer English, please," laughed Adam.

"*¡Vale!*" agreed the girl, giggling.

She followed Adam as they passed through an undergrowth of bizarre, exotic plants with leaves like up-turned umbrellas and large, brilliant blue flowers. Soon they reached a fast-flowing stream. Ahead was a high waterfall, and a wide path bordered the stream to the fall where it zig-zagged up a cliff-face before disappearing from view at the top. Following the path, Adam kept hold of María's hand.

"Why are we here?" the girl asked, frowning.

Adam knew he mustn't tell her she'd died. He could never tell her that. Anyway, he truly didn't believe it. Nevertheless, that was why they were in this alien place.

"María, back there – in the little village with Lela and her two children – we'll have to stop you from being harmed by a poisonous spider," he said. "I'm not sure how we're gonna do this but the Golden Jaguar knows. He'll help us – always he'll protect you."

144

She put an arm around Adam's waist, holding him close whilst they continued to walk beside the fast-flowing stream.

"Adam, how did we meet?" María asked. "I really can't remember! I feel like I've known you forever." She looked embarrassed by her apparent loss of memory. "I only know that – that I love you."

"At junior high – middle grade school – in Houston, Texas. Same class. You were the goddamn prettiest girl in class. Couldn't stop looking at you. Fell in love with you and—"

"Nope! I remember now. *I* fell in love with *you* first," María butted in. "There was a big guy called Sharp."

"Spike!" corrected Adam. Something prickled inside him.

"Spike? Dunno. Maybe! I hoped if I agreed to let him date me then you might perhaps get jealous and ask me out. I was just so sad when I thought you'd *never* ask me. I remember now standing in a corridor looking at a notice board—"

"A notice about that singing contest? I remember too!"

"Perhaps! I do love to sing. Yeah, well I was standing there and you, Adam, came and stood beside me and I said to myself 'please, Adam, say something. Please ask me out'. Then that big hunk of a guy Spike appeared and you disappeared."

"María, if only I'd known! I was crazy about you. Plus there was that old guy who had an antiques shop in Houston. Remember him?"

"Papa Pedro?" suggested María.

"Hey!" exclaimed Adam. "You do remember! Well, he told me never to give up trying to win your love."

"Antiques shop? But he was more than that, surely? I thought he was a priest. And Juanita and Chloe? Who are they?"

"Spot on! Our kid sisters."

"And Chloe – she has a red guitar?"

"Almost," laughed Adam. "Santiago's guitar. We've laid it to rest here in Mexico. Did that together. With an old lady called Conchita." Adam looked thoughtful. "Kinda blessed by the Old Woman of the Hills, it was."

"Old Woman of the Hills, huh? But, you know I said to myself 'about time!' when you finally did ask me round to your place. Tell me – did I slap that Spike guy real hard?" the girl asked, grinning.

"He deserved it!

"Adam, did you really die in New York? They tried to kill you at that party, didn't they?"

Did I die? Was I some place else? In a dimension beyond death?

Adam felt confused.

"You remember that too?" He showed the girl the Golden Jaguar bracelets encircling his wrists. "One of these saved me, I think. You gave it to me. For my birthday. And yeah! There was a party. Everything went blank, but—"

He stopped short. The girl was dead yet wasn't. Had they both died and been brought back to life in New York because of the bracelets? After all, the police had told his mother he was dead. And what really did happen to María in hospital in New York? Nobody had properly explained it to him. Brain dead and no one prepared to admit it, the doctors scared they'd get sued or something?

"I only gave you one bracelet. I'm sure of it. And now you've gotten two. But Adam, that temple—?" A shadow clouded María's face.

"The temple was later. After they kidnapped you in Mexico City and took you to a hideout in the jungle and threatened to—"

"No!" interrupted the girl. "This was different. Before! A different temple! Much, *much* bigger and—" She shuddered and held Adam closer. "I never imagined I could be so

146

frightened. Urgh! Those men in black cloaks! They were gonna kill me. Cut out my heart! And they smelt awful!"

"It's coming back to you bit by bit, María, but it's bound to be a bit muddled. The temple wasn't that huge and the men wore kinda greenish camouflage flak. And it was *me* they were gonna kill. They had guns. Plus they were evil. Must've made it seem like they were cloaked in black, I guess."

María shook her head, convinced there was something else.

"You adore Chloe and Juanita! Your other brothers and sisters too. If only we could send them post-cards from here," Adam half-joked. "Just to let 'em know – let everyone know you're okay!"

"Am I? Then why are you fussing so?"

The boy grunted something and the girl gave him a doubtful glance as they reached the foot of the thundering waterfall.

"You go in front," Adam urged. "I'll be right behind you. I know you don't like heights!"

"Neither do you. You were more scared than me at the top of the Empire State."

"Wow! Soon you'll remember more than me."

Adam followed María up the steep path to the top of the fall, at which point it broadened into an unpaved road. There were even houses up there in the middle of the primeval forest. In fact, on the higher ground the forest had transformed into more of a lush, well-trained garden of brightly-coloured shrubs and small trees. It was exquisitely beautiful and the houses along the street ahead were like houses back home in Texas from a few decades back. There were even mail-boxes at the ends of the driveways.

"Perhaps we'll be able to send post-cards home after all," suggested Adam.

They walked on past the first houses as the boy read out the names on the mail-boxes: familiar-looking American names. He halted and took hold of María's arm. Because of one name. He blinked, but the name didn't change: *Pedro González.*

"This can't be! Papa Pedro? Here?"

He looked at María. She shrugged her shoulders.

"Adam, what happened to my lovely doll? The one you got me from Papa Pedro's."

"That too? Don't worry! Tía Bea's looking after her. You know, your doll, she kinda helped me find you in the jungle, María. But Papa—?"

"Please never stop calling me 'María'."

"Nope! I'll never do that."

Adam led her up to the door and rang the bell. Despite expectation, he was still dumbfounded when Papa Pedro actually appeared in the doorway.

"Well, hi there, my ole pal!" the man said beaming from ear to ear. "What kept y'all, huh? Was gettin' kinda lonely jus' waitin' here hummin' one of María's songs in my head!"

"You knew we were coming, Papa Pedro?"

"Knew and arranged, Adam! Wow, María, you look lovelier than ever." He glanced again at Adam. "Is that possible, Adam? Could María *ever* look lovelier, or is it I ain't seen y'all for so long? Hey, here's me yakkin' on leavin' you kids jus' standin'! Come on in, both of ya!"

Adam and María entered the house. It was like any house back home in Harris County might have once looked only it had a curiously timeless atmosphere. There was a strange mix of décor and furniture from different eras: some old colonial pieces, Victorian chairs, nineteen seventies sofa and armchairs and a sixties-style, formica-topped table. Nothing seemed to match anything else.

"You know me an' my antiques, Adam!" explained Papa Pedro offering the sofa to Adam and María whilst he sank into one of the seventies armchairs. "Couldn't resist all this stuff even though I won't be here for long."

"Why are you here, Papa Pedro? Are you the old man we're supposed to meet? It's great to see you but I just don't understand."

"Adam, they let me come. Asked me, in fact. 'Course, I was delighted. I knew they weren't ready for María. It isn't her time. Not before—" He paused. "She's kinda special for them, see. One day you'll find out why. They said somethin' went wrong back there an' I should try to help fix it for you."

"They?" asked Adam and María in unison.

"Because of me?" added María, worried. "Is it that spider business?"

"Does she know?" Papa Pedro asked, looking at Adam. Adam shook his head.

"Hey, you guys! Know what?" María demanded.

"Not now, María, not now!" The old man leaned towards Adam. "Listen," he continued softly, "you gotta get this right. That girl's more important back there than you could ever guess. The Old Woman of the Hills, she's gonna send you off to get what she'll use to make what you need. It's the only thing that might work. An' when you get back there with what she makes from that stuff, be prepared, son. Ain't no other way to save the girl. No other way to make certain she doesn't — you know—"

He paused then glanced at María.

"Jus' rub it into the back of her hand. Rub it in quick an' rub it in hard. All of it. Do that, son, an' it might work. But gettin' hold of what the Old Woman needs ain't gonna be much fun. No sir, won't be no joy ride gettin' it. But—"

"Save me?" María interrupted weakly. "I don't get it. Save me from what?"

Papa Pedro looked away, evasive. He tapped his broad chest with the flat of his hand.

"You'll do it, Adam. I feel it here." He leaned back in his chair and seemed to study the boy awhile. "Real proud to have a young friend like you I was in them days. And I know I done right about you up there."

Up where?

"We miss you terribly back in Houston, Papa Pedro."

María, unusually pale, nodded agreement.

"Not half as much as I miss you two, I'll bet! But listen, the big cat—"

"The Golden Jaguar?"

"Yeah, him! Stay with him, Adam. He's gonna take you places, show you things. Now when you see the Old Woman of the Hills—"

"The same one who blessed Santiago's red guitar?"

"Very same, Adam! When you see her, you jus' listen to her every word. See, she'll be tellin' you what to do about the Great Spider Goddess."

Adam looked anxiously at María. Knowing how much he hated spiders she patted the back of his hand.

"It's okay! Spiders aren't that bad. You know, Juanita gotten bit by one once and she was fine," reassured the girl.

"The Great Spider Goddess is kinda different, María," continued Papa Pedro. He paused then closed his eyes. "She – she's like the size of this house. Now I know this ain't a big house but it sure is one hellova size for a spider! An' from her fangs flows the venom that gets into all those creepy little eight-legged critters that run around back there. I'll give you a glass tube with a stopper to put that venom in when you get it. An' make sure you don't go spillin' none cos you ain't never wanna go back to her in a hurry, I can tell ya! No sir! Won't wanna see her again!"

"How am I gonna get the venom from her, Papa Pedro?" asked Adam, several shades paler than María.

"You'll do it, Adam. Trust me! An' trust the Old Woman. She'll use that spider juice to make – erm—"

The old fellow paused whilst he tried to think of the right word.

"Antivenom?" suggested Adam.

"*¡Sí! El antiveneno.*"

"You still speak Spanish?"

"Best language in the—" The old man paused. "—in the world," he added in a whisper.

"Is all of this necessary?" asked María. "Adam really detests spiders."

Papa Pedro nodded.

"*¡Sí!* Well, I mus' be gettin' back now," he said, rising from the armchair. He peered around, as if to make sure no one else was listening to what he was about to say. "An' tell Conchita that José and Santiago are doin' real good," he added in a soft voice.

He winked at Adam as they headed for the door. Adam turned to address the old man:

"Papa Pedro?"

"*¿Sí?*"

"Papa Pedro, I've a confession to make. I let you down. I killed an unarmed man. How can I ever—?"

"No, Adam, you didn't. You couldn't. An' that anger, jus' then it was right. See, the Golden Jaguar, he kinda changed after encounterin' a certain young Adam Winters in Tenochtitlan. For centuries they used him to guard those temples during sacrificial ceremonies for the Sun God. Created by the Sun God's messenger, your friend, he was."

"My friend?"

"That's for later, pal. But inside Adam Winters he found somethin' far more powerful than all those old gods. The power of love a boy gotten from a certain very special girl, an' that changed him forever like it changed the boy. Ya know, even if someone else was to wear them bracelets, I do believe he'd still answer your call, Adam. He'll never stop protectin' María. He knows about her bein' special now.

Because of your friends from Iowa. Anyways, the love between you guys is so strong it's become a part of him too. No, Adam. He killed that man. He did that because he had to. Not through anger. There was no other way. Vicente knew you couldn't kill. He was stupid but he was also cunnin'. Jus' waitin' for his chance to test you an' get María for himself an' for Ramón. He had to die, Adam, an' the big cat knew that."

"Thanks, Papa Pedro. You always did make me feel better. Will I ever—?"

"Dunno, Adam, dunno! Maybe some place else. Beyond the reach of time and space, huh? Maybe when you an' her have gotten – oh, but that's another world. They call her by a different name there, too. But you'll do this, for sure. Jus' one thing more, though."

He took Adam's arm and whispered in the boy's ear:

"Don't tell her. Not now, not later. Jus' pretend it never happened. See, it wasn't supposed to. Not like this. One day I guess you'll know who that girl you call María really is."

Adam frowned.

"My girlfriend! That's who she is! Guess that's all she'll ever be for me unless—"

María glanced anxiously back at them after opening the front door. A warm smile altered the old man's lips.

"Uh-huh! Jus' your girlfriend for the time bein'. *¡Adiós mis amigos!*"

Reluctantly, Adam and María bid their old friend goodbye and the door closed behind them. When they reached the head of the waterfall, Adam turned, expecting Papa Pedro to still be standing in the doorway, waving. Instead there was only forest. No street, no houses, no Papa Pedro. Even the path was gone, as if swallowed up by *The Forest Without Time*. He looked at the stoppered glass tube in his hand, the only proof that their meeting with Papa Pedro hadn't been a figment of his imagination, then zippered this into the back pocket of his jeans. For the moment the small glass tube was, apart from María, the most important thing in the whole—

And his thoughts hovered around the word 'world'. His world was some place else – another state of existence – another corner of the multiverse – another dimension?

As they took the path back down beside the waterfall, María gripped Adam's hand and looked up at him.

"Adam, what *is* it you're not supposed to tell me?" she asked.

"María, trust me. That's *all* I can say."

She squeezed his hand.

"I'll always do that. You know I will."

At the foot of the waterfall they followed the path by the stream before returning to the clearing and to the Golden Jaguar crouched exactly where they had left him. The beast's eyes glowed strongly but without the fierce intensity of earlier on.

Still hope then?

This time María sat sideways in front of Adam who encircled her waist with both arms before pressing into the animal's flanks with his knees. The jaguar rose up and set off, quickly gaining speed until they were virtually flying through *The Forest Without Time*.

María loved it!

"Better than the rides at the shows back in Houston!" she called out, but Adam, thinking about that spider the size of a house, was feeling somewhat less elated.

After a period of time (*time? what is time in this place?*) the beast slowed to a walking pace and Adam had a better view of the weird forest. Colourful, kite-sized butterflies fluttered in and out of a clump of giant bamboo; a swarm of huge, furry bees whirred past like a squadron of mini-helicopters and in the mud of a steaming pool, to the side of the track, a large, slow-moving, purple, frog-like creature with a long tail splashed around making a squelchy, plopping noise. There were other sounds in the forest too – sounds suggesting that far larger animals lurked there. Adam caught a glimpse of the head of a vast reptile looking suspiciously like *Tyrannosaurus Rex*. With the Golden Jaguar to protect them, Adam had no fear of such monsters for the beast was Lord of this timeless forest. Nevertheless he did worry about the house-sized spider. He could not visualize how he'd extract venom from its giant fangs.

The jaguar stopped further on – far enough for them not to be recycled as *T. Rex* food.

"I'll wait here," the Golden Jaguar told Adam in Nahuatl thought speech. "Along this path you'll see what should be, and perhaps what will be, if you follow the advice of the Old Woman of the Hills."

The great cat crouched low, allowing the kids to dismount, awaiting their return whilst Adam took María by the hand along another forest path.

The forest brightened and the trees and foliage became sparse. Soon they were walking past mown lawns between the trees and shrubs, and the trees were like ordinary trees back home. He saw a house ahead – a large house with a wooden deck – a Texan ranch house. There was a swing in the yard at the back. Adam and María stopped at the edge of the forest and looked on as a small girl swung herself to and fro, singing. Oh, how sweetly she sang! A boy, a little older than the girl, was kicking a ball around. The girl stopped singing and smiled coyly at her parents who sat on a bench with their backs to Adam and María. Her black hair was long and sleek, like her mother's, and she had the prettiest little face Adam had ever seen in a child.

"Bravo, bravo!" exclaimed the man, clapping his hands. The girl jumped happily from the swing and ran towards her parents. The woman rose up and ran to meet her daughter. She hugged and kissed the child. When she turned, carrying the girl, to rejoin her husband, Adam recognised his girlfriend, María, as he might expect her to look like in a few years' time. María-the-girl standing beside him stared, frozen in wonder. Tears glistened her eyes.

"That's us, Adam! *Us!*" she whispered.

Adam had never before seen her so deeply moved. She appeared about to run on ahead, desperate to speak with the María of the future, and doubtless her future self would have been equally happy to chatter away to her past self, when Adam grabbed her arm and held her back.

"María, no!" he cautioned. "I don't think you should. It might be – well, perhaps wrong. I dunno. The Golden Jaguar, he just wanted us to see what should be, but whether it will be depends on us – on me. I don't think he intends us to step into the future, much as I'd love to avoid certain things between now and then."

Curse that Spider Goddess as big as a house! But she's the only one who can save María.

The boy turned to leave.

"Adam, wait! Please! I'd love to know what our children's names are gonna be," the girl insisted, wide-eyed. She looked at Adam. "Shall we call our children Carla and Pepe – that is if we – you know – one day—?"

She stopped when the man on the bench – Adam of the future – called out:

"Pepe!" he beckoned to his son, taking something out of his pocket. "Here! Come and see what I've got for you."

The woman laughed.

"Adam, you're always spoiling them!" she complained.

The little boy left his soccer ball, ran to his father and climbed eagerly onto the man's lap. Adam was unable to clearly make out the object in the man's hand.

"Has Carla got one too?" the child asked.

The future Adam Winters took something from his other pocket and grinned at the little girl sitting on his wife's lap. He gave her the object and she bounced up and down with excitement, waving it in the air. The thing glittered gold in the sunlight, large in the child's small hand. Adam now saw what it was: a bracelet of the Golden Jaguar of the Sun.

Adam put his arm around his girlfriend when she sobbed. She turned from the scene and began to walk away. The boy followed and neither looked back.

"Please tell me it's gonna happen."

"Yes, María. It will." Adam patted his chest like Papa Pedro, for the vision had given him strength. "I feel it here! Quick, he'll be waiting for us!"

María smiled through her tears as they walked back along the forest path arm-in-arm.

"You know, judging by their – I mean *our* ages – that must have been after two thousand and seventeen!" she observed.

"Cool, María! Yeah, well those religious freaks ain't that clever at working stuff out."

"And another thing, Mr Adam Winters!" María said, drying her eyes with the back of her hand. "I'm gonna have to put you on a diet some day. Did you see the size of that guy? Even bigger than Jorge!"

Adam laughed. He felt cheered that the girl could remember so much of her life. This had to be a good thing for perhaps she was being prepared for a return to that other world.

Soon they were back astride the jaguar, shooting past peculiar trees and prehistoric ferns, their speed increasing until, as before, the forest became a streaming blur. After what seemed an age, although in the timeless forest might have only been a few seconds, the Golden Jaguar came to an abrupt halt. He stopped so suddenly they had to cling on to stop themselves from falling. María slipped elegantly down the animal's flank whilst Adam clumsily tumbled off. He saw why the beast had halted. Ahead, the forest ceased and beyond a path curled up the barren mountainside: the same path up which he and Alejandro had scrambled in another dimension to seek out the Old Woman of the Hills.

He turned to check with the Golden Jaguar:

"This is where she lives, right? The Old Woman of the Hills? I came here with Alejandro."

"Listen to her carefully," the beast urged in Nahuatl.

Adam followed María up the near vertical slope, intent upon not letting the girl out of his sight. The cave came into view, its entrance surrounded by gifts and parcels of food. He only wished he had something for her this time, but seeing all that food caused him to wonder why he felt neither thirst nor hunger. And he'd had no desire to use the bathroom since leaving Lela's village. These things puzzled him.

"Hey María!" he called out to the girl. "Do you feel hungry or need the bathroom?"

She stopped and turned. "No! Why?" she called back.

"Well, neither do I. Funny, huh?"

María shrugged her shoulders and walked on. Panting, they reached the ledge in front of the cave. María flicked her hair from her face as she stared at the cave entrance.

"This it?" she asked.

"Yeah! Last time she came to meet me. Pretty dark inside. She's a place deep in the cave where she kinda lives. Bit brighter there. Because of a skylight."

Leading the girl by the hand, Adam took her inside the cave.

"Spooky!" she whispered, squeezing Adam's hand as she peered into the blackness.

"Don't be scared," he reassured. "You know, she's got lovely eyes. I mean, not lovely like yours. Just kind."

"Don't I have kind eyes?" the girl protested.

"Of course you do," laughed Adam. "Yours are gorgeous *and* kind. Hers are only kind!"

"Oh!" she said, happier. She stumbled on a jutting rock in the dark and Adam hand shot out to steady her.

"*¡HOLA!*" called Adam.

"HELLO!" María shouted in Nahuatl. Adam wondered why she now used that language. They called out again together, in Nahuatl, and soon a figure appeared out of the gloom. She stood a few feet ahead of them, bent forwards on her stick, embracing them with her friendly smile.

"Adam!" María gasped. "I know this woman. Perhaps from when I was little and we lived in Mexico. Not sure why, but I know her."

"Arima! Come here, my precious princess!" the Old Woman beckoned in Nahuatl. "Oh, how you've grown! You're quite a woman now."

María stepped forwards and the Old Woman hugged her.

"So he rescued you again! From the temple at Chiculhuán. He's worthy of a princess, that one. But come, my children. We must talk. We can't let what shouldn't happen, happen!"

She turned and walked slowly back into the darkness, the teenagers following close behind.

"Adam, what *is* it that 'shouldn't happen'? Why don't you tell me? I know it's to do with a spider."

"Shhh!"

Adam held a finger to his lips and they walked on. Soon a familiar shaft of light brightened the way ahead and moments later they were in the sky-lit cavern. They joined the Old Woman at the table. The girl's gaze fixed upon the walls daubed with brightly coloured birds and beasts and ancient elaborately-dressed figures.

"Oh my, they're so awesome!" she said in English.

"You have the glass tube?" the Old Woman asked Adam. She seemed less peculiar this time – none of the incomprehensible muttering of his previous visits.

Golden Jaguar of the Sun

"Yeah!" replied Adam.

"Listen very carefully," began the Old Woman, and together Adam and María listened. "From here the Golden Jaguar will take you to a bridge. He'll wait for you on this side of it for you must cross without him. Don't look over the edge. If you do you'll see nothing – no ground, no space – nothing! This is because there is only emptiness when crossing over the ninth dimension. Besides, I know the Princess is afraid of heights."

She glanced at María.

"Adam too!" the girl insisted.

"The Golden Jaguar can't come with you because that bridge leads to Xibalba. Here the Golden Jaguar is like a god of the timeless forest but in Xibalba there are many, many forces. Some the Golden Jaguar might overcome but others would destroy him. It's the Golden Jaguar who must bring you back to me then on to the village in the jungle where it must be prevented from happening. In Xibalba you'll find the Hero Twins, Hunahpu and Xbalanque. In your world they're also the sun and the moon, but in Xibalba, where it rains all the time, they could appear as anyone or anything. What they look like depends on you, Adam, and only *they* can help you against the terrifying gods and creatures that make Xibalba the 'Place of Fear'. Beware of One Monkey. He's both evil and mischievous. Avoid Zotz, the killer bat, and, Adam, on no account be tempted by the fearsome Lords of Xibalba, One Death and Seven Death, to engage in the Ball Game if challenged. You'd surely lose, and your head would be used for the next contestant's game. Do not believe them if they tell you only the Ball Game will give María back her—" The Old Woman checked herself. "Adam, your one purpose is to find the Great Spider Goddess. You must deceive her. Use that brain of yours. That hat—"

The Old Woman pointed to a brimmed hat on the floor beside her. On its top was a large painted eye. Like the eye of

159

the Golden Jaguar, it had a central red slit which glowed in the dim light. Apart from that eye, the hat was jet black.

"Wear the hat and challenge the spider but tell her not to put out the eye on the top of your head. Say you need this eye to see her with and to destroy it straightaway would give her little sport. Being evil, she'll wish to strike it with her poisoned fangs. Be ready! It'll be like someone hitting you on the head with a large hammer. But see—"

The Old Woman picked up the hat and handed it to Adam. It was heavier than the weights Sam Royal had him train with.

"It's the girl's only hope! Turn it over," she instructed.

Adam examined the underside of the hat: a helmet of beaten gold. He felt the top – tough yet springy like thick rubber.

"The metal is the metal of the Sun God, your protector and the creator of the Golden Jaguar. The Great Spider Goddess's fangs can't penetrate it. Inside, between the rubber and the gold, is a vacuum as empty as the vacuum of space beyond the universe. It'll suck out all her venom and most of her Life-Force as well. She'll become powerless. If she were to strike again then she'd be sucked into the vacuum. But she won't. She'll have felt its strength. She'll curl up and wait till she recovers – if she ever does. That'll give you and Princess Arima time to escape."

"María?" suggested the girl. "I do prefer María. Adam always calls me that."

The Old Woman beamed agreement:

"¡Si! Pura. La Santa María!"

Adam's head span, but with his mega-gigabyte memory plus a passion for mythology, he stored it all in his brain for later use. The Old Woman saw them to the cave entrance, embraced the girl again, and wished Adam luck.

"God be with you both!" she called from the cave as they started down the steep path.

God? Which one? wondered Adam when she disappeared from view. Did she also believe in one god? María's God? The God of Love. And why *'Santa María'*? He felt bewildered and vowed to ask her when – or rather *if* – they returned.

Back on the Golden Jaguar, the words of the Old Woman and Papa Pedro jumped around in the boy's mind like agitated particles following the Big Bang. He felt the warmth of his girlfriend up against his body (*how can she be truly dead with warmth like that?*) and recalled the scene in the yard of a Texan house of a future that might never happen. Now he welcomed the challenge of obtaining venom from that Great Spider Goddess for nothing could be worse than losing María forever.

Approaching bullet speed, they shot through *The Forest Without Time* soon to emerge from the green of the trees to a bleak, barren, lifeless landscape of grey. Ahead was a dark wall of mountain. As the Golden Jaguar rushed headlong at the mountain, Adam closed his eyes, expecting fatal impact. Instead, everything went black after the beast entered a gash in the rock, and continued like this until they emerged on the other side. He halted at the edge of a bottomless chasm from where Adam made out a towering arch – the beginning of a narrow suspension bridge which disappeared into a swirling, grey mist. This was the bridge over which they would have to pass; the bridge to Xibalba, the 'Place of Fear' whence no dead soul is meant to return.

Chapter 11: Xibalba, Place of Fear

Tezcatlipoca whispered in wind-speak across the empty chasm to the Lords of Xibalba:

"Destroy the troublesome boy," he ordered. "Then you can have the girl – forever! She could even be your bridge back to the world of Man."

As Adam stared at the archway under which he and María would have to pass onto the bridge to Xibalba, a cooling, wet wind chilled his face. The bridge was supported by two great cables that swept down from the top of the arch and there was something chillingly final about the cold, colourless emptiness into which it faded.

Adam turned to face the Golden Jaguar. The fire in the beast's eyes burned like the magma of a volcano. Restless, the giant cat began to pace up and down. The jaguar realised Princess Arima would have to cross over to Xibalba and that since she was 'dead' she should not return. He so wished to follow her, to protect her from the evils she would encounter there, but there were powers in that Place of Fear far stronger than him. And yet there was the boy – the one for whom the princess's love had subsumed the beast's own primordial power; the boy to whom the beast was now beholden in lieu of the Great Sun God but whose youth blinded him from his true enemy: himself.

The jaguar knew there was a power in that love that might possibly overcome One Death and Seven Death, the Lords of Xibalba, for he'd learned something very special about this girl. He would await her return for all eternity if necessary, for nothing else mattered – only the love the girl felt for the boy. Threat to that love had stoked the fire in his eyes so fiercely they could be seen from afar: twinned beacons of longing in a place more desolate than the most distant reaches of the multiverse.

But was the boy ready?

Having bidden the Golden Jaguar farewell, Adam took María's hand and led her underneath the high archway and onto the bridge. Terror filled the girl's eyes. He sensed her trying to hold back and feared she already knew she was dead and that the place on the other side of this bridge was a land from which dead souls do not return.

"It's okay, María," Adam said softly, kissing her forehead. "You'll be fine. We're gonna win, the two of us. Remember? Carla and Pepe? The two children? *Our* children?"

Special? Was it Carla or Pepe who would turn out to be special? Were they what this was all about? Had María been chosen for something way beyond the understanding of the ancient gods?

An uneasy smile appeared on María's drawn face as they walked on into the mist. When Adam turned to look back, all he could see were the eyes of the Golden Jaguar. Ahead was a silent, grey void, and below, nothing. Adam held on to María whilst steadying himself with the hand-rail. The bridge bounced with each step. To bounce on a narrow bridge spanning such a void should have sent the most intrepid of souls scuttling back to the safety of the edge of the chasm, but not Adam. He was resolute. He *would* save his girlfriend. They *would* have a life together.

Gently coaxing her forward, he slow-stepped his way towards Xibalba. When the other arch first appeared, silhouetted through the ghostly grey haze, Adam felt almost relieved that ahead was the place where he'd perhaps get what was needed to give the girl back her life. As they inched forwards a dark shape appeared out of the mist: a motionless figure. Closer, he saw the figure was made of stone, but it was the face that caused Adam to turn round and cover María's eyes with his hand. A young man, frozen in fear during an obvious attempt to escape from Xibalba, his expression showed indescribable horror. Still shielding his girlfriend's eyes, and trying not to look at the nightmare image, Adam pushed past the man.

"Who *was* that?" asked the girl as they passed under the arch of the bridge and on to Xibalba.

"A statue," replied Adam. "Just a statue, María, and not a very good one. Rubbish compared with Rodin!"

The mist cleared, replaced by a fine, freezing drizzle. Ahead lay a vast and strange-looking land. They shivered as they stood at the top of a high dome-shaped hill covered with what appeared to be vivid blood-red flowers. It was as if a blood-soaked carpet had been dragged over the slopes and stretched to join a limitless plain below. There, the blood carpet merged with myriads of yellow and blue flowers and in the far distance protruded a range of jagged grey mountains like a set of ancient discarded dentures. A wide river, the same rich, blood-red as the hill, flowed from the mountains across the blue-yellow plain and seemed to disappear into the ground where the red of the hill touched the colours of the plain.

Their faces were now wet with non-stop rain draining out of the deep grey, sodden sky. It was so different from what Adam had imagined. Somehow he'd envisaged a land that was dull and featureless with caverns and rocks where foul gods might lurk. Instead, Xibalba was colourful, almost beautiful despite the rain, and yet there was something menacing and horribly evil about the place. Its garish colours seemed more of a mask behind which sinister forces threatened to suck out his soul, destroy his courage and take María away forever.

Golden Jaguar of the Sun

He scanned the wide, yellow and blue rain-soaked plain, for he'd no idea in which direction they should start walking to find the lair of the Great Spider Goddess. Just beyond the nearest edge of this was a cluster of stone buildings, possibly a tiny village. He checked that the Old Woman's hat with the eye was set firmly upon his head, the glass tube safe in his jeans pocket, then, holding the girl's hand, descended the blood-red hill (red stones, not flowers) towards the buildings. When within a hundred yards of these, they stopped.

There were people in between the buildings, static like the figure on the bridge. Cautiously, they walked on. Adam called out. It wasn't in Nahuatl that he spoke and certainly not English or Spanish. The language sounded similar to the language spoken in Lela's village. Mayan? Could he now speak in the tongue of the ancient Maya people?

"Funny, I understood that too!" said María. "But why aren't those guys moving, Adam? Are they—?" The girl seemed reluctant to use the word 'dead'. "Are they sick?" she asked.

Closer, it became apparent that these people had also been transformed into statues of stone, frozen in positions indicating that whatever happened had been extremely quick. One woman had a foot raised off the ground as if something had prevented her from taking another step towards safety. As with the figure on the bridge, their final moments must have been awful for their lifeless faces were darkened by fear. Adam hugged María and told her not to look at them before they headed for the largest building.

Some sort of temple, the boy reckoned, perhaps built to appease the evil deities of this freaky place. They passed a petrified young man, taking care not to knock him over for Adam felt sure the figure would have shattered into a thousand fragments had it fallen. There was a glass-like fragility about these figures – the fragility of tortured souls.

Inside the building were two stone tables and several stone benches. One of the tables was decorated with a map. Adam pointed to this.

"We're in luck," he announced. "This has to be a map of Xibalba. Look! There's the hill."

He indicated a large red hump at the top and from there the beginnings of a bridge leading to the edge of the stone table. The map was colourful. Yellow and blue for the plain, the river was blood-red, the jagged mountains greyish with chocolate brown hills and other things painted beyond the mountains. Images of fierce creatures decorated it too, plus there were Mayan people in ancient dress. All four corners were inscribed with ancient Mayan bubble glyphs. The words he seemed to understand, but together they made no sense. 'Cycle of creation', 'death', 'earth' and 'blood giver' was all he could make out. Then, whilst studying the stylized animals, he saw her.

"There!" he exclaimed. "Eight legs, two things sticking out from her ugly head. Fangs, I guess. That's gotta be the Great Spider Goddess. In those brown hills on the other side of the jagged mountains. We'll make it, María – I know we will!"

Ever impatient, he could barely wait to challenge the huge arachnid.

"Well, I'll bet you one thing. Bet she never came top of class like my Adam Winters always does!" She put her arm lovingly around the boy. "I believe in you, Adam. Always have, always will! You'll outwit her!"

An eerie, high-pitched whine, impossible to locate, needled their ear-drums.

"Stay put!" Adam warned. "I'll check outside."

He was about to leave the building when a deafening shriek stopped him. He turned to see the outline of a bat, carved into a flagstone, rear up behind María. A trap! This was a 'temple' where Zotz could ensnare newcomers who'd

just died; Zotz, the 'killer bat' demon, drinker of Life-Force. Was the red river created by Zotz from the spiritual blood of his victims?

"Out of here, María! Quick!"

"But you just said—" the girl protested as Adam yanked her by the arm out of the stone building. Inside, the black shadow had risen from the floor to hover above the map like a gigantic, flapping black umbrella. Once outside, they ran to the side of the building as first one then another furled-up bat wing emerged through the open doorway, followed by the huge, black, hairy body of Zotz. The creature was the size of a horse. They covered their ears to block out the penetrating shriek whilst pressed against the wall, praying the thing wouldn't find them. The boy lipread María's whispered words:

"What *is* that noise?" her lips asked.

"Sonar," Adam mouthed.

"What?"

With a finger, he wrote the letters S-O-N-A-R on the palm of his hand. She shrugged her shoulders. He pointed in the direction of the sound, pointed to his eyes then waved his hand in front of them, indicating that bats are virtually blind and need sonar to locate their prey.

"*¡Sí! Comprendo*," whispered María, both hands cupping her ears.

The shrieking stopped, replaced by a sound like a boat sail flapping in the wind. Then silence.

"I don't like this, María," whispered Adam, holding the girl's body up against his. "Not one little bit."

Adam squinted at the dim, drizzle-laden clouds. At first rain obscured the boy's vision but soon his worst fears were confirmed. A huge black shape swept across the grey Xibalban sky like a Halloween nightmare and the shrill shrieks started up again. Zotz was seeking them out.

The monster bat darted about in zig-zag fashion as it searched for its latest prey: two teens from Texas. Suddenly it turned to face them with outstretched wings the span of a small aircraft. They'd been discovered. Adam feared his eardrums might burst when Zotz's sonar pinned María and himself against the building.

This is it, he thought. *Over so soon!*

Great wings beat up and down and the dark outline of the giant bat rapidly grew out of the wet haze. With María hiding behind him, the boy shielded his face with clenched fists. The bat's outspread wings shut out all light. Adam was wondering where Zotz would sink its teeth to suck out his Life-Force before turning him and his girlfriend into stone statues, when the creature let out a harsh scream. The light and the rain returned. He felt a rush of wind on his face as the bat flew off and away, still screaming; screams of terror that were so different from the awful, prey-seeking sonar shriek. In no time the bat was a receding black dot in the leaden sky, heading for the mountain range. The boy and the girl looked at each other then uncovered their ears.

"Close one, Adam!"

Someone spoke in English. A man's voice. Adam looked up. He recognised the voice and it came from the roof. A familiar, smiling face appeared – a face with a wild red beard, unmistakably that of Art Weissenbach their friend from Des Moines, Iowa, whom they'd met in San Antonio and who'd visited Adam in hospital in New York with his jovial wife, Jeannie. Art leapt from the building and came over to shake the boy's hand. He gave María a kiss on the cheek.

"Why, you held up the bracelets up just in time, son!"

Adam glanced at the Golden Jaguar bracelets then looked at Art.

"But – I don't understand, Art. What are you doing here?"

"Well – you called me, Adam! Sure wasn't too soon, either. Wouldn't want each of my two favourite young people turned into one of them, now, would I?" Art pointed to the ground carpeted with yellow and blue flowers. "Yellow for girls and blue for boys!"

"Art, this makes no sense. I've no idea what you're talking about."

"Look over there, guys," Art said, pointing.

"JEANNIE!" María yelled with delight. In front of the stone building was parked a vintage red Austin Healey. A plump, middle-aged blonde sat in the front passenger's seat. She waved, got out of the vehicle and ran towards them.

Art continued:

"Yes and no, María! See, that is Jeannie an' it ain't Jeannie. Like I'm Art an' I ain't Art! Or perhaps the guy you thought you knew back there wasn't what he seemed."

Smiling, Jeannie gave María and Adam gentle hugs then stood back to look them.

"Oh my!" she said. "You both look so grown up!"

"I'll come clean with you, Adam," said Art. "Here we're Art an' Jeannie but back where you two come from you see us as different. In the sky? Servants of the gods? Sun an' moon? In this place there ain't no sun nor moon. You may have noticed. All cloud. Our real names are Hunahpu and Xbalanque, but that's a kinda mouthful for you kids. Bit like Arthur Weissenbach! So jus' call us Art an' Jeannie!"

Adam's eyes widened.

"The Hero Twins of the Mayan legends?"

"More like the 'terrible twins' as our Ma, Blood Moon, would've said. But here we can only appear in disguise. Best disguise, Adam, comes from you. Inside your head. Had to search a while, an' that's what took time. We found these guys, Art an' Jeannie, in there. Realised you both got on fine with Art an' Jeannie back in San Antonio, though you never found out who they really are, huh? They too are kinda messengers. María's God? Anyways, we all had a little discussion about it an' here we are. Ourselves still, of course, kinda merged together. But please call us Art an' Jeannie cos that's who we are now. Because of who they are, you see?"

Adam didn't see.

"But you said I called you, Art. How come?"

"The bracelets, Adam. On your wrists. See what's on 'em? My old master's face and that of my pal, the Golden Jaguar. I—" Art leant forwards and whispered in Adam's ear: "I made him! The Golden Jaguar of the Sun." He stood back with pride glinting his eyes. "Not bad, huh?"

"You mean, when I held my wrists up to hide my face from Zotz, that's when I called you?"

"Sure thing!"

"And in that brief second or two you entered my head and looked around for someone to turn into, had a discussion with—?"

Adam looked at Jeannie who grinned and nodded.

"Great being a girl for a change!" she said.

"—then together you appeared as Art and Jeannie and scared that bat thing away?" continued Adam.

"'Bout sums it up, son! See, I kinda knew you two were on your way. Golden Jaguar, he keeps me informed, see. Good, he is, in that way!"

Adam's brow furrowed. He was staring at the beautiful blue and yellow 'carpet'.

"Just now, Art, you said something about not wanting us turned into flowers."

"Ain't flowers, Adam. Look closely."

Adam got down on his knees and peered at the 'flowers'.

"Oh my God!" he exclaimed.

"Yeah, they used to call me that too. Back there in your dimension. A long time ago!" joked Art.

"María!" Adam lifted a foot as though he wasn't sure where to put it. "Art's right. These aren't flowers. They're—"

The boy paused, repeatedly lifting one foot then the other as he sought for somewhere else to stand on the spongy, rain-soaked Xibalban ground. Impossible! The colourful plain stretched to the distant mountains and on either side as far as the eye could see.

"Yeah!" Art affirmed. "They're people! Rather, were! Life-Force an' souls sucked out by Mr Giant Bat-man! Shrunk right down to tiny blobs of blue or yellow. All the redness sucked out."

"Their faces, Art! Just like those stone statues."

"Turns a few into statues, Zotz does. For amusement. But there ain't room for billions upon billions of statues so he shrinks most of 'em down to tiny blobs. They're comin' all the time, see. Folks comin' to Xibalba, hopin' to find paradise – then this, poor things. Get turned into eternal flowers for the amusement of the Lords of Xibalba! I'm jus' so pleased we came to that decision with Art an' Jeannie in time to save you kids!"

"But so goddamn quick! Searching my mind? Having a discussion? In less than two seconds?" queried Adam.

"Yeah, well where we come from time is somethin' different. Earth, she keeps her own time, right? It's one of her dimensions," Art replied. "Fourth dimension, to be correct. No need for time here in the tenth dimension. Not regular time, anyways. So, kids, how 'bout another ride in my beautiful red Austin Healey there! Done a few miles since we rode in to San Antonio with you two in the back!"

Adam smiled at María.

"Remember that?" he asked her.

"Sure thing!" she exclaimed. "I remember saying how you'd have to behave yourself in front of Papa," she chuckled. "How you'd better not let him see you kissing me!"

"Hey!" objected Adam. "You're kidding, right? I don't remember no kissing!"

The girl gave him a playful punch.

"But that's all I wanted from you on that ride. A kiss!"

María and Adam sat in the back of the red Austin Healey feeling every bit as grand as the time in San Antonio when María won first prize in the under-fifteen section of the talent contest – but this ride was somewhat spoilt by the knowledge that they had to drive over remnants of dead souls drained of 'Life-Force' towards a spider the size of a house.

"Art? That red river – is it—?" Adam began.

"Sure is, Adam!" interrupted Art as the car bumped over the yellow and blue vestiges of life back on earth. "See, Life-Force in this dimension – it looks kinda blood-red to folk like yourselves who arrive from your world. And it's all for One Death and Seven Death. Blood-thirsty guys, see. So that's where I come in. Been spoilin' for a fight with those two bullies for a long while, son. But that's for later. Meanwhile I can only take you as far as the jagged mountains. Can't go no further in this ole beauty, anyways. She ain't no good at climbin' mountains!" He glanced at Adam. "You should've had a plane instead of this vehicle in that head of yours," he joked. His expression turned serious. "No, Adam, this ain't no laughin' matter. Beyond the mountains to her lair you an' María are on your own with maybe a little help from Jeannie."

"Remember – if someone's being meanie always call for Jeannie!" responded Jeannie with a canyon-sized grin.

Adam and María glanced at each other and shrugged shoulders. Art and Jeannie never could be serious for more than a few seconds, but they were to be trusted and in this Place of Fear what else could the teens from Texas do other than trust their old friends?

For a long while the mountains ahead seemed to get no closer. The plain was so flat it felt as if they were driving over a frozen blue and yellow sea that went on forever. Then, gradually, detail appeared in the mountains: cracks, streaming gullies and ledges criss-crossing their great, wet walls revealed themselves as if an invisible artist was adding bits feature by feature. Soon their sheer rugged size was obvious. They were immense. The Rockies back home would have been dwarfed alongside the snowless peaks. But despite the endless supply of water in that terrifying place, the river of Life-Force that flowed from these barren mountains to the red hill remained red. Or was it merely an illusion of liquid? Was this a river of flowing evil extracted from Life-Force by creatures like Zotz?

When they arrived at the foot of the mountain range, Adam craned his neck to peer up at the towering, rain-streaked cliffs. He would have to conquer his fear of heights and scale them without losing the Old Woman's hat perched on his head. Minus that all would be lost and María was truly dead. He glanced at the girl. Something inside him stirred as it did when he stared into the eyes of the Golden Jaguar.

"I'll be ready, here – if you return," Art said. "Now there's one little problem up in them mountains, guys, an' you must watch out for him. See, that's where One Monkey lives. Prides himself on trickin' those that escape the fangs of Zotz. Be wary. He's meaner than a bug-eyed lizard, so you jus' remember what Jeannie said!"

Adam and María argued about who should start to climb first. María, the more agile, reckoned she'd do better following behind her boyfriend in case he should get stuck and need assistance.

"Easier me coming up to help you than trying to go back down," she insisted. There was also the question of the hat. If it were to fall from Adam's head then perhaps she'd be able to catch it.

"Pfff! If only we get could buy superglue here," Adam said, pulling the hat more firmly down over his head.

Finally the boy won, for no way would he let his girlfriend out of his sight for a split second, and so María started clambering up the sheer, glistening cliff face followed by Adam. Soon they were testing their gymnastic skills to the limit, stretching and reaching for slippery cracks and jutting rocks onto which they could grip with slime-coated hands or into which they might wedge a wet foot. Several times Adam called out to María to slow down.

"Hey, karate kid! What's holding you back?" she teased.

"It's easier for you, María! You've smaller hands and feet," was his feeble excuse. María would wait patiently on a ledge or jam herself into a crevice until Adam caught up with her.

Thus they slowly climbed up and up, at last reaching a gap between two towering buttresses of rock each of which soared towards dizzying summit peaks. The slope here was gentler and stretched from where they stood to a lofty pass between the peaks. Adam had warned María about scree, particularly if wet. Should they happen to slide down the loose stones they could find themselves launched into the void to join those bloodless yellow and blue lost souls thousands of metres beneath them. They sat together for a few moments, gazing down at the plain and across to the blood-red mound in the distance, the swirling mist and the bridge beyond, and at Art and Jeannie below, no bigger than ants. Art appeared to be enjoying himself by darting about and waving something he held in both hands whilst his and Jeannie's laughter scattered cheer into the heavy Xibalban air.

"What *is* that dude doing?" Adam asked with curiosity.

"Looks like he's playing around with a sorta club or something," replied María.

"Bit of luck he'll hit himself on the head!"

Adam turned abruptly to see who or what had spoken such cruel words. A large brown monkey tumbled down the scree, halted a few metres from them, picked up a couple of stones then chucked these at the kids.

"Hey, stop that, you filthy monkey," Adam called out as he and María shielded their faces.

"Shan't," responded the monkey who began to throw handfuls of stones. "Oh, all right!" he finally agreed, as if changing his mind. "This is boring, anyway. Let's try something a bit more fun!" Adam positioned himself between the simian and María. "Let's try—" In a flash the boy found himself staring at the ground thousands of metres below. "—This!" exclaimed One Monkey after grabbing Adam's ankles and sweeping him off a rock before turning him upside down dangled over the precipice below. There was nothing between Adam and an ant-sized Art whirling his club.

María screamed from the ledge above:

"STOP IT! JEANNIE – PLEASE HELP US!"

"Don't be so rude, you stupid girl!" objected the monkey, shaking Adam. "I'm a monkey, not a genie! Anyway, I don't like his hat. Just trying to get rid of it. One more shake should—"

The last shake was so violent Adam feared it would take his head off. He felt dizzy and sick and was on the point of passing out when he caught sight of something black and gold sailing down towards the foot of the mountain. He clutched at his head. No hat! It was on its way to the ground below. He began to retch. *What a horrible end*, he thought, his eyes tightly closed.

"What the—?" he heard One Monkey exclaim.

María was still screaming when the monkey opened its grip around the boy's ankles. Something else immediately took a firm hold of one of Adam's limp arms and he was flipped around through one hundred and eighty degrees. For a brief while the boy hung the right way up, mid-air, before being gently lowered onto the mountainside beside María.

The girl stopped screaming. Adam opened his eyes just in time to see a surprised expression on the monkey's grimacing face.

"THIS ISN'T FA – I – I – R!" the creature yelled as it got knocked off the precipice into the abyss by a nudge from the beak of the gigantic bird that had returned Adam to terra firma. In the bird's claw was the Old Woman's hat. The condor was so huge that an ostrich, by comparison, would have appeared pigeon-sized.

"Always fancied being a condor but—" The extraordinary creature looked down with puzzlement and pride at its vast body. "Do you guys think I've overdone the size thing a bit?"

Jeannie's voice! Adam chuckled.

"I'd never have made it up here in time as Jeannie. Oh, look!" Jeannie-condor said, peering over the edge of the cliff. Adam and María looked. One Monkey was a dot on the blue and yellow plain below and Art was finishing the job with his club. "Wish I could high five with you kids but I'm afraid I might knock you off with these if I tried," she added, examining one of her massive clawed feet with curiosity.

María laughed. How Adam loved to hear her laugh again. It gave him such strength. He took the hat from the giant bird and returned it to his head.

"You sure I can't buy superglue up here?" he joked.

"I've something much better," said Jeannie-condor. "Hold out your hands."

Adam cupped his hands as she made a series of odd guttural coughs that had María in fits of giggles. Jeannie-condor then cleared her throat and spat a glob of pink goo into Adam's palms. The boy stared with suspicion at the sticky stuff.

"What on earth—?" he began, but the bird ignored him:

"María, take off his hat and get him to smear this around the edge on the inside. Should help to keep it on if that happens again!"

"Again?" echoed Adam faintly.

They followed the bird's instructions and María, still giggling, patted the hat down onto her boyfriend's head.

"Thing is, you'll be able to remove it when you've gotten the venom," said Jeannie-condor. "That would've been quite a problem with superglue! Anyways, don't see many shops round here, do you?" The massive bird scanned the bleak, craggy cliffs and laughed in a 'Jeannie' kind of a way. "See guys, it's kinda fun being a condor, even if I am a bit on the large size," the bird continued. "Why don't I take you over the pass and down the other side? Then I'll wait at the top till you return. Can keep Zotz at bay and see what Art's getting up to as the same time!"

Jeannie-condor cocked her head to one side to peer over the precipice.

"Sure is steep and it wouldn't be that easy going down without a rope. I'll fly y'all back to the car when you're done with her. That is – erm – if – you know." She looked from Adam to María then back at Adam. "A deal, then?"

They nodded. The ridiculously over-sized bird gripped each firmly but gently about the waist with a massive clawed foot and in a flash they were soaring up and over the pass between the two peaks before sailing down towards the grey, lifeless ground on the other side of the range. Although Adam had every confidence in the condor's sticky glob, he still held onto his hat with both hands.

A mile or so from where the bird came in to land, a cluster of dark brown hills stood like a collection of hideous warts, the largest scarred by a gaping hollow. Red trails streaked the hillside below the edge of a jutting platform.

"That's where she lives, Adam. I only wish I could do it for you but she'd never waste her precious venom on me. I could easily destroy her, of course, but then you'd get no venom. She'd immediately turn to dust. Only one way to help your girlfriend, Adam." The giant condor glanced at María. "You're gonna have to challenge the Goddess. The spider's gotta believe you'll make a juicy meal – think she could enjoy your Life-Force after storing you a while, all neatly parcelled up in her web. A regular wine cellar of wrapped souls, her lair is! And she'll want *her* Life-Force too!"

She pointed her beak at María. Adam hugged the girl close.

"Getting two for the price of one will make the Goddess all the more eager. Do it, Adam! I'll be waiting up there for you!"

Adam looked back at the mountains, thankful that at least on this side the slope was gentler. Should they survive, the return journey would be one long uphill crawl.

"Bye!" he called before the bird lifted herself into the air on plane-sized wings and glided towards the range. María, stiff with fear, remained silent. Facing the grim hills, Adam took the girl by the hand and walked doggedly on towards the lair of the Great Spider Goddess.

The hills were unimpressive in comparison with the jagged mountains and would be easy to scale, but in other respects they were far worse; desolate and enveloped by dread, though perhaps through knowledge of who lived there. The teenagers began to climb in the rain, Adam up front. He repeatedly tapped the top of his head to ensure the Old Woman's hat was firmly in place, even lowering it for María to examine the eye so as to check it was clearly visible.

"Your head's on fire!" the girl gasped.

"Good! Like the eyes of the Golden Jaguar. Burns more fiercely when you're in the danger. Means she'll be in her lair."

Golden Jaguar of the Sun

They reached the lowermost edge of a red tongue protruding from the mouth of the Spider Goddess's lair. As Adam had guessed, the ground was stained red with spilt Life-Force. It had the same foul, putrid smell as blood. Further on, human skulls, bones and fragments of clothing were strewn about where the spider had callously pushed them from the opening of her gory dwelling-place.

"Just keep right behind me all the time, María," whispered Adam when they got to the rim of her lair. The air was thick with the stench of decay and death. Thick, silvery strands of cobweb cords encircled the entrance, glistening like cables of steel. They'd be doomed if the Spider Goddess were to trap them in her web. The boy would have to be quick but he also needed to outwit her. He prayed that even a spider the size of a house would have a diminutive brain.

"Great Spider Goddess!" Adam called out in ancient Mayan, a language in which he now felt fluent. "They tell me you're a weak and stupid goddess and that you've grown feeble because of lack of Life-Force. I want to prove them wrong. I've come to challenge you. If you dare to venture out you'll see I'm unarmed. I've only my hands with which to fight and my sole weapon is 'karate'. Where I come from that means 'empty hand', and look – I've only two of them and you've got eight legs and two fangs. If you are strong, you've nothing to fear. You'll easily defeat me. And if our fight is fair you'll not suck out the Life-Force of my soul as I'll not take yours. So if you win I go to heaven and those who sent me will fear you and pay tribute with more victims for as long as you wish. If I win, I'll spare your soul and you may live on forever in the comfort of paradise."

This was the speech Adam had planned in his head after their meeting with the Old Woman and its effect was immediate: a low growl was followed by a scraping noise as if something large, heavy and hidden from view was dragging itself across the ground. First one telegraph pole-

179

sized leg then a second and soon several appeared at the gaping entrance, feeling the space, wavering, testing, as gradually the enormous and hideous brown bulk of the Great Spider Goddess crawled out onto the stinking, red-stained litter-ground of death fronting her lair. Adam broke into a cold sweat when he saw the size of the creature's face. Her fangs were tucked back under her head and he saw only four huge discs, each made up of glass-like balls in which danced multiple reflections of him and María as the spider turned her ugly head from side to side. Adam knew about composite eyes and how accurate they were in localising prey and realised that their survival now depended on one thing alone: his brain.

The spider spoke in a deep, grating voice; a voice that knew nothing of compassion or love:

"You cheat, miserable mortal! There are two of you! I should suck out your Life-Force here and now. Hers too!"

"Great Spider Goddess," Adam continued, his head bowed to ensure the red glow of the hat's eye was reflected many times over in the creature's black glass eyes, "the other mortal doesn't challenge you. She's only here to see fair play. As neither you nor I is armed we must not touch each other's eyes. I can see how magnificent yours are, but my single eye is also important to me if we're to fight fairly. Please leave my eye intact and I'll only use my two small arms and two weak legs against your eight strong limbs. If you win a fair fight I'll be proved right and you should allow me and the other mortal to pass on into paradise."

Adam kept his head bent forwards. He knew spiders were incredibly fast when they pounced, but this one seemed to be trying to do something she wasn't used to; think and formulate a plan in that vile head of hers. Perhaps she was wary of the fire in his single 'eye'? She remained silent and still. Adam goaded her further:

"Of course, if you're afraid I quite understand. Perhaps you really are weak and feeble like they say! I'll still spare you, being fair, but those people who told me this would've been proved right."

Adam waited, crouched on all fours and making sure the only part of his head facing the Great Spider Goddess was covered by the Old Woman's hat with its burning eye. When it happened María let out a piercing scream. It must have been terrifying for the girl to watch as the giant spider sprang forwards. Adam was aware only of the shadow of the spider before she stabbed her fangs into what she felt certain was her adversary's only eye. As the Old Woman had warned the boy, it was like being hit on the head with a hammer. Although the gold molding within the hat diffused most of the blow, Adam was forced to the ground from the impact. The spider went momentarily quiet.

The pressure on the boy's head eased when the huge arachnid jerked backwards in a frantic spasm, desperately trying to escape and get back to her lair. She stumbled, crashed into the hillside beside the entrance, attempted to scramble up the slope, slid down and ended up on her hairy back, all eight legs waving feebly. Soon the legs went still apart from an occasional twitch. Her venom and much of her Life-Force had been sucked out of her. The vacuum in the hat was even stronger than the Old Woman had hoped for, and it was now so heavy with spider venom that the boy struggled to keep his face off the ground.

"Yuk!" he spluttered, his nose pressed into the red, salty earth. "María, help me off with this goddamn thing – please!"

Using all her strength, the girl managed to remove Adam's hat which she placed carefully onto the ground beside him.

"Phew," the boy exclaimed, rubbing the back of his neck and wiggling his head about. He grinned at María then removed the glass tube from his jeans pocket. The painted eye of the hat no longer glowed and there were two large holes in the centre. Each was about the diameter of Adam's thumb. He carefully tilted the hat forwards, holding the opened glass tube in place as the clear, colourless venom trickled into this from one of the holes until it was filled to the brim. Cautiously, he replaced the rubber stopper and held the tube upside down to ensure the seal was perfect. After zippering it into his jeans pocket, he stood, triumphant, and took hold of both María's hands.

"You're gonna be fine!" he promised, lifting the girl's right hand and kissing the smooth unblemished skin.

They headed for the jagged mountains and started the slow climb towards the gap between the two peaks. Adam had never before felt so strong but María began to tire. The boy easily lifted her in his arms and continued on up the long, steady slope. María's face was alive with admiration.

"How come you're so strong?" she asked. "I'm sure that Spike guy couldn't have done this!"

"Comes from you. You're the one who's strong!"

Jeannie-condor was waiting, as promised, at the high mountain pass.

"I knew it!" the bird said when she learned how Adam had extracted venom from the Great Spider Goddess. "Art'll be ecstatic. And know what? He can't wait to pit himself against those devils, One Death and Seven Death. Just leave the rest to him – but there is one thing. Don't on any account be tricked into joining in their Ball Game, Adam, however strong you feel. Being under-confident is bad enough, as you well know, but over-confidence always spells disaster!"

The giant condor took a gentle hold of each with her great claws, flapped her vast wings and lifted them high above the blue and yellow plain. From their lofty position Adam could see even further than before, but he was still unable to make out an end to that colourfully dreadful landscape. The condor circled and banked several times, like an aircraft, before landing softly beside the red Austin Healey and changing back into Jeannie.

"Wow! I did enjoy that!" Adam said.

"Me too," laughed María.

"HEY, ART!" Jeannie shouted at her husband still busy stabbing and slashing at the air with his large, stone-headed club. He'd failed to notice his wife-turned-condor was back on the ground, no longer a bird.

"That was quick!" responded Art. He strode towards them, the club resting on his broad shoulder. "I don't need to ask. You've got it, huh?"

Adam nodded as his old friend from Iowa returned the club to the trunk of the vehicle.

"In the car, you guys! Jus' one more little bit of business then it's up to yourselves and my pal the Golden Jaguar."

The boy and girl from Houston climbed into the back of the Austin Healey and Art drove towards the distant blood-red hill. This time Adam was aware of a hauntingly-disturbing sound. He'd either not noticed this on the way out to the mountains or had dismissed it as vehicle noise. It came not from the car but from the ground beneath – from that colourful carpet of drained human souls. They were screaming. Each and every one of those tiny, shrunken yellow and blue remnants of human life was screaming and the knowledge of this made Adam feel sick. He reckoned María also knew it from the way she looked at him before nestling her warm body up against his.

When they'd reached the bottom of the red hill, Art swung the car around, slowing the pace to that of a searching hedgehog as he drove along the divide between the bright yellow and blue of the plain and the garish red of the hill. He was looking for something.

"Gotta be some place along here, guys!" he said, scanning the psychedelic landscape.

There was a movement on the side of the hill ahead. Art stopped the car and Adam stared, dumbfounded, as a part of the hill separated off before moving across and placing itself in front of the car. Having taken human form, the object remained the same blood-red as the hill – hair, face, body, loin-cloth and a headdress bearing a single red feather included. The thing resembled a huge, crudely-moulded red rubber figure of an ancient Mesoamarican warrior. It stood legs apart, arms folded, hatchet-faced and scowling. Another figure emerged from the red hill, identical apart from having seven feathers stuck into its headdress. It strode forwards to stand beside its companion in the same threatening pose.

"One Death and Seven Death! Stay in the car till it's safe," warned Art before getting out and going to the back of the vehicle to retrieve his club. Holding this with both hands, he walked slowly up to the red rubber figures.

"Let us pass," Art called out. "She's not yours. They must return together to *The Forest Without Time*!"

One Death shook his head.

"The girl's not yours!" repeated Art, moving closer to the Lords of Xibalba. Seven Death held up a large red hand, warning Art to go no further.

"The girl–" he growled, pointing to María. "Ours! It was promised! Do you consider yourself more powerful than Tezcatlipoca? She's dead, you idiot."

Adam heard a stifled gasp from his girlfriend.

"Adam – that red thing – he – he said—" she began in a faint voice.

The boy hugged her close.

"Don't listen to him, María. Do *not* listen!" María began to cry. Adam stroked her hair. "Not here you aren't and you won't be when we get back either."

"That's the secret you've all been trying to hide from me, isn't it? The thing I mustn't know," she sobbed. Adam wrapped the girl's trembling body in his arms.

"María, please believe me," he said. He gently touched her face when she looked up at him, tears spilling from her wide, brown eyes. "You won't die. Papa Pedro said you weren't supposed to die and you won't – cos he was always right about everything!"

"But Adam!" the girl cried. "I am dead! Those dreams I had back there. They were all about death. I am, Adam! I'm dead, I'm dead, I am *dead*! Don't you understand?"

"You'll not have the girl!" bellowed Art edging forwards and raising his cudgel with both hands. "She's here because of love and there is no love in this place. Even if the girl were dead she'd never belong with you, Seven Death. She's too much love in her! From a different dimension, you numbskull! One you'll never know!"

"Love? Pfff!" scorned Seven Death. "And that 'thing' with her now. Is that what she died for? A pathetic little boy?"

"That boy has more power in his heart than all the gods in Xibalba put together," replied Art, moving closer. "Because of the girl! Back in Tenochtitlan her love changed my companion, the Golden Jaguar, forever. No more human sacrifices for the Not-So-Great Sun God. That love comes from the one and only true God. With her love, she's shown us it isn't the blood of man that contains the Life-Force you demons crave. That's an illusion, just like the two of you, you blood-filled, over-sized rubber toys. It's only about power for you two, isn't it? Well, in the face of the girl's love you have none!"

With that, Art swung his club three times above his head then ran forward, swiping One Death across the face. The red rubber puppet was sent reeling. It bounced a few times, recovered its stance then walked back towards Art, its arms still folded.

"This is useless, Hunahpu," sneered Seven Death. "Neither you nor Xbalanque truly belong here. You can do nothing with that club. But if what you say about the boy thing beside the girl is true it'll gladly accept our challenge to a Ball Game. If its power is greater than ours it'll win and we'll give the girl back! See how fair we are in Xibalba? Listen! Over there on the hillside is the Ball Court. You can hear the Xibalbans shouting for your 'thing' to accept our challenge."

Adam heard shouting and yelling from the side of the hill where he was now able to make out a large rectangular structure built of blood-red stone blocks.

Seven Death called out to Adam:

"Thing – you can keep the girl if you beat us in our Ball Game. Then hang on to her ghost if you must – ha-ha-ha! It's her only chance!"

Jeannie turned and whispered to the boy:

"As soon as Art attacks them with his club get out of the car and run for the bridge. You're gonna have to carry María now because she'll be so weak after hearing what Seven Death said. Just run! Don't stop. Don't look back, and on the other side jump onto the Golden Jaguar and go straight to the Old Woman. Do it! And hurry! She's getting weaker. You've no time to lose – particularly not here in the tenth dimension where time can change in a blink!"

Adam opened the car door in preparation for a dash to bridge.

"Nothing to say, Thing?" menaced Seven Death. "So much for the power of love, Hunahpu! Come on. Hand her over. The girl's ours!"

One Death and Seven Death moved forwards together, lasering María with their evil gaze. Art immediately turned into a whirling fury, his large club spinning like the blade of a huge aircraft propeller as he darted between the red rubber lords of Xibalba, sending One Death and Seven Death flying off in opposite directions.

"NOW!" yelled Jeannie.

Adam leapt from the car, gathered María up in his arms and ran with her up the blood-red slope faster than he dreamt possible. Behind them, the rumbles and crashes of the tumult of battle informed him that the two red demons were unleashing their own powers against Art and Jeannie, but he never once looked back. God, how he loved the girl! Nothing could prevent him from saving her from the awful fate those monsters had planned – a permanent Venus-like statue for their private amusement, perhaps? As he approached the brow of the hill, the arch marking the Xibalban end of the bridge appeared out of the mist. He almost flew towards this.

"Adam, I – I can't leave. I'm dead!" whispered María.

"Hold tight! I won't let you be dead. Our love is stronger than them."

Adam felt the girl's arm about his shoulder tighten as he sprinted onto the swing bridge. He knocked aside the frozen statue-man, causing it to shatter into a billion particles of shimmering death-dust and the dust merged with the bleak, dull-grey, misty drizzle. He ran on with María through the wet mist and shattered-soul dust and continued running whilst the bridge shook and bounced over that bottomless chasm: the chasm of a place known on earth as 'Hell', elsewhere as the ninth dimension. The arch at the other end of the bridge loomed out of the mist, becoming clearer all the time, and beyond that two bright points of fire penetrated the haze: the eyes of the Golden Jaguar.

Adam forced his legs to carry him and María at an athlete's pace under and beyond the arch and off the bridge. The Golden Jaguar, his eyes burning like white hot coals, bounded up to the steps leading down from the bridge. Still holding the girl, Adam straddled the beast's back and the Golden Jaguar shot forward, a godly arrow from an invisible bow, straight into the black gash scoring the dark mountain ahead.

"Adam, I feel so weak. I'm dead and can never go back home," María murmured. "Never see Mama and Papa again."

"We're going straight to the Old Woman, María. She'll make that anti-venom then we're going back to the village. We'll enter our own dimension – our world – at an earlier time. Before you get bitten. And nothing's gonna happen after the spider bites you. I'll stop it from happening with the anti-venom. Believe me, you weren't supposed to die."

He stared at the girl's deathly face as the Golden Jaguar rushed them on to the Old Woman of the Hills. There was so little time left in this timeless place, the eighth dimension.

"I love you, María. *So* much!"

The girl managed a faint smile and squeezed his hand. He cradled her gently when they came to an abrupt halt at the bottom of the steep path that led to the Old Woman's cave. Jumping down, he ran up the slope with his girlfriend in his arms, shouting out as he clambered onto the ledge in front of the cave:

"I HAVE IT! I HAVE THE SPIDER VENOM!"

The Old Woman of the Hills appeared, bent over her stick, and hobbled towards him.

"Zippered into my back pocket." he added, turning around, not wishing to let go of María. He felt the woman's searching fingers fumble in his jeans pocket before she extracted the glass tube.

"Wait here," she said before disappearing into the cave. María, her eyes now vacant, whispered so quietly that the words were barely audible: "I'm dead – I'm dead – I'm dead—"

Golden Jaguar of the Sun

Adam prayed the Old Woman wouldn't take long but he wasn't prepared for her immediate return. No sooner had her shadowy back vanished into the gloom of the cave than her wrinkled, smiling face re-emerged, the glass tube in her hand. Panic gripped Adam in its claws.

"What's wrong? Can't you make the anti-venom?"

Still smiling, the woman pushed the tube back into the boy's pocket.

"That's it. The Golden Jaguar will take you back and it'll never happen!"

Gone for just a few seconds – how could he believe her?

"But—" Adam began.

"Shhh! Using time as it is back there where you come from, I took at least two months to make it. Even tested it out on myself. It works, Adam, it really works, but do it quick and rub it in hard however much María complains. Use it all up."

As the boy left, still carrying the girl, the woman called out:

"And Adam, never ever let María know she once died. You may remember everything, but she, María, must know nothing. Just think of it as her getting another chance – because of the importance of her love for you – and because of who she is. One day you'll understand. And you ask about my God? *María's* God? The one and only true God? Her love will give you the answer. Her love, Adam, her love – because her heart comes from the eleventh dimension. Remember how you looked down from that bridge into the void of the ninth dimension? Think of its polar opposite."

They sped back through *The Forest Without Time*, back and back, until, for the final time in that alien place, the Golden Jaguar of the Sun slowed and came to a halt. Beyond was a clearing in the forest, out of which spilled the excited shouts of children, the bark of a dog. Delicious smells of cooking teased the boy's nostrils and Adam suddenly felt hungry. The girl in his arms was barely alive, but her lips moved. She was breathing. The Golden Jaguar crouched low to make it easier for Adam to slip down with his precious burden and the boy ran from the forest and out into the clearing, carrying the girl.

Chapter 12: Plácido

*"**So** he succeeded!" exclaimed the deceased cleric. "Who'd have believed it? A boy who isn't even one of us?"*

The old man frowned but he wasn't angry. After all, the ex-priest had never known the boy as he had. But he felt disturbed by what the other spirit had said.

"What do you mean by 'not one of us'?" he asked. "Who are we to either accept or reject him?"

As Adam ran into the village *plaza* María started to laugh.

"Put me down, put me down!" she giggled.

Remembering how awful she'd looked just moments earlier, Adam lowered her gently to the ground as if she were made from brittle bone china that would break into a thousand precious pieces should he drop her. She reached up and kissed him on the cheek.

"Oooh!" exclaimed a little boy just yards away. "*¡El amor!*"

Another boy standing next to him said something in Mayan, but Adam couldn't understand. He had no memory for the language of Xibalba.

"Soccer?" the first boy asked.

"Ah, soccer! *¡Sí!*" agreed Adam.

He remembered and he knew there was no other way. They would have to relive the nightmare. María appeared totally unaware of what they'd been through together in *The Forest Without Time* and, beyond that, in the Mayan Place of Fear. Adam glanced at her right hand. It was fine. The boy pointed to María.

"Her too? Soccer?" he repeated.

María laughed and shrugged her shoulders.

"Why not?" she said. "Try anything! Never played much soccer at middle school being a cheerleader. S'pose we'll have to be on opposite sides though, us being the only big guys. That should be interesting, *chico!*"

They waited in the *plaza* as the boys ran off to get their mates and a ball. Adam un-zippered the back pocket of his jeans. He'd need to act fast when it happened. A dozen eager little boys soon appeared. A few, including Pepe, spoke Spanish. Teams were formed and the game began, María on one side, Adam on the other.

Adam feared the glass tube would get broken if he was too energetic, so most of the time he just stood around. His team thought he was useless. By contrast María was brilliant and her team kept scoring goals. He tried to apologise to his team-mates and muttered in English about having an off-day because of one thing and another, but they shouted angrily back at him in Mayan. María thought the whole thing very funny.

"It's okay, Adam," she giggled from the other end of the *plaza*. "I've never fancied soccer players anyway! Prefer archaeologists!"

After María's side had scored yet another goal against Adam's team's score of zero, one of the boys on his side suggested María and Adam do a swap.

"Can't!" said Adam. "Against the rules."

He was talking different rules and it was no game where these rules were concerned. The present game would have to finish as before with Adam retracing his steps into the forest to search for the ball. This part of the 'movie re-play' could not be over-ridden.

There was a heated argument amongst the boys. The one who'd asked Adam to change sides with his girlfriend took hold of the ball, kicked it into the forest and stomped off in a temper. The others quickly dispersed.

"I'll go get it," muttered Adam and he headed into the jungle where the ball had left the *plaza*. He quickly found it but spent time checking the glass tube, ensuring he'd easily be able to remove the stopper, giving thought to where he should place his grip around María's arm to act as a tourniquet. He hated the idea of having to hurt the girl but there was no other way to save her life. On returning to the *plaza*, retracing his earlier route, he became aware of something tickling the back of his neck. He knew what it was but he kept going – to re-live the nightmare. Holding the ball, he passed by María.

"STOP!" she called out. Adam moved slightly, as if to turn and face her. "NO! DON'T MOVE!" She came up behind him and flicked something off his back.

"OW!"

Immediately Adam dropped the ball, spun round, slipped his hand into his back pocket, extracted the glass tube and removed the stopper.

"Ouch, it hurts. There on ground. It bit me."

Adam wasted no time talking or staring at the spider. He gripped his girlfriend's forearm, squeezing with all his strength, tipped some of the contents of the glass tube over the puncture holes left by the spider and rubbed it hard into the bite ensuring the fluid got pressed into those twin holes.

"OW, OW, OW!" screamed María, "What are you doing? You're hurting me! That's worse than being bitten."

She tried to pull her hand away but Adam's remained clamped like a vice around her arm as he continued to rub in the antidote. María started to cry.

"Adam, please stop! Please, *please*! You're hurting me so much. AAARGH!"

Adam didn't stop. He massaged the liquid into the wound keeping a firm hold on the girl's arm until all the contents of the tube had been used up and there was no more wetness on her hand. Only then did he dare to slowly release his grip. María was sobbing uncontrollably when villagers arrived at the scene wondering what the commotion was about. But she was alive. Adam lifted the girl's bitten hand. Although red where he'd been rubbing, there was no swelling and no redness further up the arm. He hugged her living body against his.

"Thank God you're gonna be fine, María! Just fine!"

The boy stroked the girl's sleek, black hair, kissed her several times on the forehead then once on the lips.

"Adam, why did you do that? You really hurt me. What was that stuff, anyway? I don't understand. It was only a spider bite!"

"I'm sorry, María. I really am, but I had to do it. Look! Your hand's fine!"

María wiped the tears from her eyes.

"I was afraid it would bite you. I know you hate spiders!" the girl said. "But was that necessary? I mean, Juanita got bitten once but nobody did that to her. And she was fine."

Adam gazed at the girl. The pain of an enormous and unbearable weight had been lifted off his soul. Never before had he felt so happy.

"Why are you looking at me like that?" she asked, frowning. "It did hurt, you know. I wasn't making it up."

"I know. And I'm sorry. Believe me. But do you really feel okay?"

María looked at her hand. Even the redness was beginning to fade.

"Think I'll live!"

Adam turned and stamped on the flailing spider, a miniature version of the Great Spider Goddess.

"Thank you everyone!" Adam whispered.

"Adam Winters, are you sure you're all right?" María asked. "Who on earth are you thanking?"

Golden Jaguar of the Sun

There were certain things he'd have to withhold from María. How could he possibly tell her he was thanking Papa Pedro, the Old Woman of the Hills, Art and Jeannie who were also ancient Mayan gods plus the Xibalban Hero Twins and, of course, the Golden Jaguar of the Sun?

"Oh, just thanking those kids for showing the world how bad I am at soccer," he lied. "So I don't have to suffer my girlfriend beating me again."

"Manuel? We take her to Manuel?" one of the village men asked in Spanish. It was Agustín. Adam merely gaped at him. "Shall we take María to Manuel?" the man asked again. "Spider bites can be dangerous. You probably didn't know that. Not in Texas, huh?"

The boy glanced sideways at María.

"She's okay!" he replied. "No need to bother Manuel."

"Sure!" agreed María. "I'm good. Honest I am, but thanks." Then, addressing Adam, "Hey, dunno about you but I'm starving! Feel I haven't eaten for weeks! Must've been that game of soccer!"

"Yeah, that game of soccer!" echoed Adam glancing at the jungle beyond María.

"Come on, professor!" María playfully tugged Adam along by the arm. "Not everyone's meant to be a world class soccer player! Don't take it to heart!"

"Nope!" replied Adam quietly, and together they returned to Lela's hut.

With the rich, spicy aroma of cooking wafting from the open doorway, Adam felt he must be entering heaven – particularly with a fit and lively María by his side. But he knew he'd never forget the horror of his girlfriend's death and resurrection – *The Forest Without Time*, the reunion with Papa Pedro and with Art and Jeannie, the terrors of Xibalba and the magic of the Old Woman in the Hills and the awful emptiness of the ninth dimension. These memories would remain forever indelibly etched upon his mind but María must never know she had once died and come back to life. However, one vision kept replaying in Adam's mind: that of himself, his beautiful young wife, María, and their two children. In the future, should he feel sad, or things go badly, he'd recall that image, smile to himself and feel happy again. This would sometimes help to keep that other Adam – the jealous one – at bay.

After lunch, Pepe cornered Adam for a 'man-to-man' talk. He'd been in Adam's soccer match team and told him not to feel bad since he wanted the other team to win anyway because they had María on their side.

"I wished her to win, you see!" the little boy said. "So blame me! Otherwise I'd have tried harder."

"Me too," agreed Adam, winking at Pepe. "I wished her to win as well!"

Later that afternoon, whilst María was helping Lela with the washing and Adam was listening to Carla practise reading Spanish from a book entitled *La Tortuga Traviesa*, the sleepy village was jerked to life by whooping and shouting from the *plaza* and the unmistakable noise of a diesel engine. Carla sped from the house, followed by Pepe. Lela beamed at the two teenagers.

"Plácido!" she explained. "He's back!"

They joined the throng of villagers gathered around a rusting, once white, now mud-spattered grey truck and its short, sturdy driver who was busily unloading boxes from the open back. The man stopped when he saw Lela. His jovial face lit up as he walked towards the young woman. They talked in Mayan and Lela pointed to Adam and María.

"*¡Mis Amigos!*" Plácido greeted, extending a friendly hand to Adam and to María.

Adam loved the man's face. It was straight out of an old Mayan painting – curved nose, strong cheek-bones and mysterious almond eyes. His skin was dark and pock-marked, his hair a tangled black mat and his firm arm muscles bulged out from his tatty T-shirt. He should have appeared fearsome but before the boy stood the gentlest soul imaginable.

Now that Plácido was back, Carla and Pepe appeared to have temporarily forgotten about María and Adam. They joined the other babbling, bubbling children thronged around the jovial young man, demanding to see what he'd brought back from the tourist towns.

"Later, *mis niños*," he laughed.

"See how happy they are to see Plácido again!" remarked Lela. "We all are."

"So, I'm to get no rest, huh!" announced Plácido in mock anger. "Tomorrow we must drive together to Comitán with the man whose devils killed my friend." He winked at Adam. "Tomorrow, *mis amigos*, will be the best day in Plácido's life. Adam, you're a saint, delivering that monster to us."

He patted Adam on the back. María was looking at them and the boy sensed the warmth of her pride. This made him feel awesome and banished Adam-the-Jealous to a dark recess of his brain.

"But today we celebrate, all righty?"

Plácido raised his hands in the air, and everyone went quiet. Even the children. There was a lovable charisma about the man who went on to deliver a lively speech in Mayan. Although Adam, now back in the world of the living, couldn't understand a word, he got the gist of it. Plácido repeatedly pointed to the boy and to María and everyone cheered and punched clenched fists into the air. An old woman stepped forwards, ruffled Adam's hair and kissed him on the cheek. A man at the back shouted something, followed by more cheering.

"He says you've given us back our lives! María too," Plácido explained in Spanish. Carla and Pepe ran up to María and hugged her legs as if to claim her for themselves.

"This evening we have a *fiesta* for our good friends, Adam and María. We dance, we sing – and we live," Plácido announced before returning to the job of unloading the truck. Lela interrupted him in Mayan. He turned.

"María – you sing? A famous singer here in the jungle? Incredible! I have my guitar – see! We must share it this evening, you and me!"

He went to the front of the vehicle and took out a guitar. After kissing it, he handed the instrument to María whose face lit up with the sheer heaven of holding a guitar again.

"In America you're just a famous singer. Here you'll live on as a legend," Plácido said.

The look in María's eyes when she glanced at Adam made the boy blush.

"Adam too! We sing together!" she insisted.

"*Bravo.* Even better! A double legend! But first help me unload, Adam. Children – come and see what we have in these boxes!"

It was as if he'd fired a starting pistol. A wave of yelling children engulfed the boxes, excitedly pulling out toys at which most US kids would have turned up their noses. All afternoon the children played in the *plaza* with their new toys, screaming delight, whilst the women undertook the more serious task of sorting out the essentials Plácido had brought back: rice, sugar, salt, flour and oil.

He'd also bought a dress for Lela. Adam could see how fond Plácido was of the young widow and it appeared that the man was unmarried. Nevertheless, he kept a respectful distance from the wife of his murdered friend.

María helped with culinary preparations for the feast whilst Adam wondered how they should proceed when they got to Comitán. He'd grown wary after Alejandro's trickery. Could they trust the local police? Might Ramón's influence have infiltrated their ranks? After all, Alejandro had been in the Special Drugs Unit. Adam trusted Plácido and decided to discuss the matter with him. He wasn't too surprised to learn the man also had an innate distrust of authority, both governmental and Zapatista – understandable when the village had no protection against people like Ramón and Alejandro. Besides, local services and Zapatista rebels were far too busy with other concerns.

"I tell them about the phone lines every time I go into town but they do nothing!" Plácido complained.

They agreed that before handing their prisoner over to the police they should first contact María's and Adam's folks back home. Adam would get Tío Federico to go directly to the Chief of Police in Mexico City, plus friends in government, to explain that the drugs baron was to be handed over to the police in Comitán and that the local police should be given full credit for his arrest. On this point, Adam was adamant.

"It'll encourage them to listen to you lot," Adam explained to Plácido. "Maybe their own chief will get decorated."

The boy kept quiet about the real reason for his insistence.

As a final measure, Adam decided he should also phone Sam Royal in Houston. His own family had enough on their plate and Sam would know what to do. He would make sure the DEA knew everything. No way was Álvaro going to get away with suggesting they use María as bait so Ramón could publicly rape her to hurt Adam. Sam would ensure Álvaro got his just deserts. Adam smiled to himself, thinking how boy's actions would lead to his downfall as in karate.

But the problem of Alejandro had not gone away. They'd chosen to leave the two guns behind for the villagers' protection, so the risk of driving with Ramón to Comitán with nothing but a machete and a knife was huge. Nevertherless, Plácido remained undeterred.

Golden Jaguar of the Sun

Adam put the threat of Alejandro to the back of his mind and enjoyed the *fiesta*. Besides, crouched in the forest sat his secret weapon. Before the festivities the boy disappeared off to speak with the Golden Jaguar. The glow in the beast's eyes told him that María was still in danger, so he commanded the jaguar to follow Plácido's truck the following morning. The best solution would be to flush out Alejandro in the creature's presence for it seemed unlikely the man would escape a second encounter unscathed.

The celebration party, lit by burners in the *plaza*, was the liveliest event Adam had ever experienced. There was some kind of liquor flowing but no one got drunk. They were too happy to be bothered with inebriation – plus, of course, there was dancing.

Despite his musicality, Adam had never gotten into dancing – not beyond tapping out a rhythm with his feet or swaying his body. María, on the other hand, was a brilliant dancer. After Plácido shouted '*¡La Salsa!*' his fingers started to fly over the string-board of his guitar like the legs of a frenzied spider. Adam felt stupid and embarrassed when María, laughing, pulled him up and dragged him to where the children and younger adults jigged and twirled about. As she gracefully turned and twisted her lithe body up against his, Adam started to jerk awkwardly, first to one side then the other, vaguely in time with the music and feeling painfully self-conscious. Gradually he got caught up in the energy of the rhythm and, with gentle coaxing from María's guiding hands, was soon gyrating like everyone else.

Stunning in her flaming red dress and red shoes, María swirled in perfect time with Plácido's strumming. No one could take their eyes off her but jealousy had abandoned Adam – at least for the *fiesta*. The girl wore make-up for the first time since the recording studio party in Mexico City. Not only the children but also most of the adults wanted a turn to dance along with her. No one apart from María

Nope! I'm not gonna let Adam-the-Bad out again. She's special and that's why she's worrying! Cares about everyone. Forget the other reason! Bloody forget it!

"They'll be okay," suggested the boy. "It's not that cold and there's absolutely no room inside here! Wouldn't be safe!" He paused then frowned at his girlfriend. "The other guy, sure, but why Ramón? How can you feel sorry for him? I just don't understand how you're able to forgive those monsters. And so easily. Vicente, for example. Gave him a hard slap and that was it. I just wanted to kill him in the worst way possible for what he did. Despite what Papa Pedro said about it, I—"

Adam checked himself and María stared in amusement.

"Papa Pedro? What are you talking about?" she asked.

"I meant despite what – what Papa Pedro might have said – erm – I mean the Golden Jaguar, that is if—"

María laughed.

"Adam Winters, I do believe the jungle is getting to your brilliant brain! We'd better get you out of this place pretty damn quick!"

The girl snuggled up to the boy and took hold of his hand.

"You know, that Vicente monster kinda reminded me of a fairy tale ogre," she added.

"Like Fee-Fi-Fo-Fum?"

"Yeah, and I knew my handsome prince would rescue me like in fairy stories!"

She kissed him on the cheek.

"¿Amor, eh?" Plácido grinned, turning to look at the young love-birds beside him.

"STOP!" yelled Adam.

The man slammed the brake and María screamed as the truck swerved, skidded in the mud and came to a standstill tilted precariously in a gully. Just ahead a black 4x4 blocked the road and in the gloom Adam made out the outlines of two guys with raised assault rifles. Plácido leapt from the truck, knife in hand, but dropped this when another armed man emerged from the dripping trees and pointed a gun at him. Two more gangsters appeared, one of them Alejandro. Adam felt María tremble.

"It's okay, María," he whispered. "*He's* following us in the forest. Saw him again before we left the village. He won't let any harm come to you."

Alfredo was ordered out of the back of the truck and a soaked, single-armed Ramón joined his cousin.

"ADAM!" shouted Alejandro. "Come on out! I'm not interested in these men! I just don't like what you did to my cousin. But look, I'm a kind man. You know that. Those presents I gave you, huh? So we do a deal, *mi chico*. Give me the girl and those pretty little bracelets you're wearing so I get the pussy-cat as well and these men live." María tightened her grip on Adam's arm and the boy felt angry with himself for ever doubting her love. "Oh yes, you spoke about those bracelets and the pussy-cat when you fell asleep on the plane. At first I thought you were crazy – until I saw what happened to our men. Fairy tale indeed! But if you're a real good boy and come and apologise to my cousin for what you did, then he may let you live. Plus you get to see how it's done properly – with her! So, Adam, how about it? A deal?"

Flaming eyes reappeared in Adam's mind as he opened the truck door. To Alejandro's obvious amusement, the boy bellowed at the trees in Nahuatl:

"COME NOW! PRINCESS ARIMA IS IN DANGER AGAIN. SHE NEEDS YOU!"

"I don't understand your funny American, Adam. Is that white gringo speak? Do we have a deal, then?"

A rustle in the forest caused the man to turn his head. Something large was edging forwards, preparing, its breathing measured. Movement distubed the undergrowth.

María, petrified, snuggled up close and Adam gently squeezed her hand.

"I love you," he whispered.

"You can't fool me with your games, Adam Winters! Out! The girl too! She's ours now! Mine and Ramón's!"

Adam helped his terrified girlfriend down from the cabin of the truck. Almost immediately, she was drenched by the fury of the tropical storm. Rivulets of water trickled down her face. She looked utterly wretched standing in the mud in high-heeled shoes, with her sopping, red party dress clinging to her shapely body.

"That's a good little boy. Oh, how beautiful the girl is! And still a virgin! I can tell from the anxious look in those pretty eyes. You're obviously not man enough to do the job. Don't look so worried, my lovely one. You'll soon get what you crave for. Won't she, Ramón? Two for the price of one, ay? And we'll let *el chico* watch. Right, cousin?" taunted Alejandro looking at María. But Ramón's eyes, also fixed on María, told a different story: that of a lapsed Catholic who had seen the Holy Virgin. "We'll show him how it's done, *vale*?" persisted his cousin. "But the bracelets first, *amigo*. Here, on the ground! Quick!"

Adam let go of María's hand but kept watch over her from the corner of his eye as he slowly removed the bracelets and threw them at Alejandro's feet.

"Good!" exclaimed Alejando. "You learn fast. Pity you won't have time to learn for much longer!"

Alejandro bent down to pick up the bracelets.

"NOW!" yelled Adam in Nahuatl.

With a blood-curdling snarl, the jaguar broke through the undergrowth and came to a halt between Adam and Alejandro, his rain-soaked golden coat glistening in the headlights of the 4x4. Alejandro lowered his gun and with shaking hands quickly slipped on the bracelets. The jaguar glanced briefly at the man then turned to face Adam.

"SEE, PUSSY-CAT! I HAVE THE BRACELETS. THE MAGIC BRACELETS. ME! KILL THE BOY AND I'LL HAVE THE GIRL! FORGET RAMÓN!" Alejandro screamed at the beast's rump. But the eyes of the beast burned for Adam and for the love a certain very special girl felt for the boy.

"NOW!" shrieked Alejandro. "KILL HIM! IT WAS HIS FAULT THAT RAMÓN GOT HURT!"

Adam spoke calmly to the beast:

"Do as you wish. I only know I love the Princess."

"NOW!" repeated Alejandro, frantically waving his wrists at the flicking, curling tail of the Golden Jaguar. "LOOK! YOU MUST OBEY ME, PUSSY-CAT! I'M WEARING THE PRETTY BRACELETS!"

The cat turned to face Alejandro, bared his huge yellow teeth, settled down onto his haunches and gave a low growl as he fixed the man with eyes of fire.

"Me – I – br – br – br—"

Alejandro's speech failed, and for several seconds he stood as still as a museum insect pinned to a cork-board.

Adam became aware of a commotion beside him. Another of Alejandro's bastards had grabbed María's arm. The boy was quick. When the Golden Jaguar leapt, he spun round, deflected the arm of María's assailant, snapped the gun from his hand and, as the gangster struggled to regain his balance, the boy used the man's own weight to fling him to the ground. He snatched the freed weapon and pointed it at the mud-covered dude. Sam Royal would've been proud of his pupil.

Meanwhile, the Golden Jaguar hurled his great body at Alejandro and, in mid-flight, snapped at the man's head between powerful jaws, crushing it beyond recognition. His victim would have been dead before he hit the ground. The other men panicked and fired at the beast but Adam knew how useless gun-fire was against this creature from another dimension. He grabbed María and pushed her behind the truck out of harm from ricotheting bullets whilst keeping his own weapon trained on the gangster he'd sent sprawling. Ramón, terrified beyond words, tried to make a break for the forest. Plácido was onto him in no time and held the man securely with his single arm bent high behind his back.

"STOP! THROW DOWN YOUR WEAPONS NOW!" Adam called out as the Golden Jaguar reared back and swiped at the legs of one of Alejando's men with a clawed paw. The man cried out as he slithered in the mud, clutching at his leg where massive claws had slashed through clothing and flesh. The remaining two drugsters flung their impotent weapons to the ground, put their arms in the air and edged back from the snarling animal. Alfredo picked up the guns, keeping one and handing the other to Plácido. María emerged from behind the vehicle and went to stand beside her boyfriend, holding onto him. She shivered in her thin red dress for it wasn't warm in the mountain jungle storm. Adam ordered one of the gangsters to remove his top and, after wringing it dry, covered María's shoulders with the garment then told her to wait in the truck cabin.

Plácido and his friend set to work tying the hands of *los gángsters de drogas* behind their backs with the bastards' bootlaces before bundling them into the vehicles. Their boots he kept for villagers back home. Ramón's single hand was secured to one of his feet. Meanwhile Adam walked up to the Golden Jaguar who stood triumphantly over Alejandro's bloodied body. The boy could tell the creature was relaxed, and María no longer in danger, for those black eyes showed only the merest hint of a red slash. His mind penetrated the flickering red and they spoke together in Nahuatl:

"Thank you," said Adam. "Thank your creator, the servant of Tezcatlipoca and thank the Hero Twins. Thank the Old Woman of the Hills. I understand so little. I only know that I love the girl." Adam glanced back at María just visible through the mud-spattered windscreen of the vehicle as she sat combing her long hair. "So much!" he added.

"No, we must thank you, Adam," insisted the voice of the Golden Jaguar. "You'll not remember, but long ago in a different world you two changed everything for us. With your love for the Princess and hers for you. The servant of Tezcatlipoca said "no more human sacrifices" after I, his creation, felt the power of that love – the love of the one true God. Only love like that can span our parallel worlds, enter different dimensions and change things forever. Some call that love the eleventh dimension. María might use a different word."

The eleventh dimension of the multiverse?

Adam was puzzled. He'd read all about the M-theory and its eleven dimensions in *Scientific American*, but what the jaguar was saying made little sense to him.

"María and me? Our love had that effect?"

"Just so!" replied the Golden Jaguar. "Our gods now know where this force you call love truly comes from. It comes from the feelings of one for another. All those thousands of people who were killed at Tenochtitlan, all were once loved by those close to them and yet we didn't see it. We took their life-blood for the ever-hungry forces of nature, the equivalent of Life-Force in Xibalba, but these forces are as nothing in the face of love, Adam. You and the Princess showed this to us – because of who she is – and we thank you. We now know what is good and what is bad."

"Parallel worlds?" queried Adam. "Other dimensions? What do you really mean?"

"There'll always be a past somewhere, Adam. And a future. Fifth and sixth dimensions. There'll always be other worlds for those who die, good and bad. And out there somewhere in the many universes are many, many more worlds sharing eleven dimensions. Some are identical to yours and others impossibly weird. There are links between these dimensions: dreams, my forest and the Old Woman of the Hills, those bracelets – even death. But never before has the love between two people traversed these links in quite the same way. One day you'll know why. One day something wonderful will happen because of María. A child!"

"A child?" queried Adam. "Pepe or Carla?"

"A child," repeated the beast. "And from now on it'll be your job to protect her with your love, not your jealousy. It must happen but I can only do so much. Many wait for that day. Never weaken and always believe in her. But remember, nothing is certain. Right now your friends, Art and Jeannie, The Hero Twins, the two that you might call María's 'guardian angels' here, they're busy trying to bring love back to that Place of Fear, Xibalba. For too long One Death and Seven Death have ruled, draining the Life-Force of departed souls. But who knows – maybe Xibalba may again become the paradise it once was if you let that day happen – but you must see to it that María never returns there. Plus there's another girl, Adam. Almost as special and very close to you."

"Rubbish!" exclaimed Adam, angered by the jaguar's insinuation. "María's the only one. I learned my lesson. I'll never let her down again!"

"Xibalba is where the greatest danger will always lie. María must never return there. And watch over that other girl—"

"There *is* no other girl! I promise you! But what should I do with these Golden Jaguar bracelets?"Adam asked.

He stooped to remove the bracelets from Alejandro's body.

"Only toys where I'm concerned!" answered the Golden Jaguar. "You've already seen your children play with them. But they could still serve as links for you – your love – and for that other girl. Links with other dimensions."

"The future's another dimension? A parallel world?" the boy asked, thinking of that Texan Ranch House and those two children.

"It's what you make it, Adam," came the reply.

"But that house in Texas – those kids? Did you know it was happening already in that parallel world of the future? Where we're married and have children?"

For a few moments the Golden Jaguar stared blankly at Adam.

"The future is what you make it," repeated the beast. "And never forget how special the Princess is."

He turned, stepped over the body of Alejandro and slunk silently off into the forest without looking back. Briefly, Adam was aware of a rushing sound – that of something large speeding through the undergrowth. Then all went quiet.

Plácido came up behind Adam and placed his hand on the boy's shoulder.

"There were stories from our ancestors about a huge spotless jaguar made from the gold of the ancient Sun God with eyes that burned with his fire. They said it would appear from the forest only to vanish again, but—" He shook his head and grinned at Adam. "I've never been one for fairy tales myself!" he added.

Adam laughed.

"Me neither!"

"Look," continued Plácido, "I've put María in the 4x4. Got a heater in it. We'll have her dry in no time. You get in beside her – she'll warm up even more quickly that way!" Plácido winked at Adam. "I'll drive you guys. Lela said not to let you out of my sight! We'll have to put up with three trussed animals in the back! Alfredo can follow in the truck with Ramón and the other bastard. They're pretty much bound up but you might want to dissuade them from trying to roll off the back of the truck. Perhaps they'll be more inclined to believe your fairy tales than mine!"

He winked again. Adam sauntered to the back of the truck to tell the two terrified men lying there of rumours about a large cat-like creature lurking in the forest, adding that they'd be fine so long as they stayed exactly where they were. Plácido pulled the body of Alejandro off the road and Adam ran to the 4x4. María opened the door. He climbed in and squeezed up beside the girl, putting his arm around her. She nestled her head against his shoulder.

"Thanks again," she said quietly. "My hero – always my hero!"

"There'll be no more of them, I promise," reassured Adam.

Plácido turned the vehicle around and drove off. Alfredo followed close behind in the village truck, a one-armed drugs baron and his accomplice bumping painfully up and down in the open back.

Adam and María nodded off to sleep snuggled up together. When the boy awoke some hours later, they were driving along a highway in hilly country with fields and houses flashing past. It had stopped raining. María was still asleep. He stroked her hair, now dry, and the girl stirred in her sleep.

'Special'? Of course she is! But 'parallel worlds'? What the heck did the Golden Jaguar mean? 'One day it must happen – a child' Our child? Pepe or Carla? And another girl, 'almost as special'? Nonsense! Why couldn't the beast just tell me?

Adam looked back and saw the rusty old truck trailing close behind.

"Good sleep?" asked Plácido.

"*Sí. Bueno.*"

They drove on for another hour or so before reaching Comitán. María finally awoke as they entered the outskirts of the town.

"I missed your monologue, María," teased Adam as the girl rubbed her eyes. She smiled.

"Where are we?" she asked, peering out at the busy streets.

"Comitán."

María immediately picked up her handbag from the floor of the vehicle, took out her cell phone and switched it on. She stuck up her thumb, grinning, dialled a number and put the phone to her ear. Tears welled even before the call was answered, but after a familiar voice came out of the phone they streamed down her cheeks:

"*¡Hola!*"

María sobbed so much she had difficulty speaking.

"*¡Hola! ¡Hola! ¿María? ¿Adam?*"

"*¿Tía Bea?*" sobbed the girl. "*¿Mama? ¿Mama está ahí?*"

A pause, then—

"*¡María!*"

Even Adam felt his eyes moisten as he held her close. There was audible excitement at the other end of the line.

"*¿Mama?*" María asked again, softly.

Adam heard a woman crying at the end of the phone.

"*¡Mi niña, mi niña!*"

Then the girl opened up. She spoke in Spanish so fast Adam had difficulty understanding most of what she said. He heard 'he rescued me' and 'so brave, so brave – my hero' and the names Lela and Carla and Pepe and Plácido (Plácido high-fived with Adam on hearing his name). She spoke about the *fiesta* in the village and the spider bite ('*¡nada, Mama, nada!*').

Plácido found a parking spot for the two vehicles and pulled in.

"*¡Sí, Mama, sí! – ¿Y papa? – Sí, Vale – vale* – okay, okay. – (she smoothed her red dress) – *Sí*, Lela – *sí, está muy bien, Mama – Sí, mi valiente,*" María continued, proudly patting Adam's hand.

"*¿Chocolate?*" Plácido asked Adam, offering the boy a chocolate bar he'd pulled from his pocket.

"*¡Gracias!*"

Adam broke off a piece for himself and a piece for María. Grinning, he pushed María's chocolate into her mouth whilst she was still talking. Her words came out funny and her mother sounded alarmed, asking if she was all right.

"*¡Mmm, delicioso!*" María said.

"*¿Como, María?*" the phone asked anxiously.

"*El chocolate, Mama.*"

"*¡Ah!*" exclaimed the phone before taking off again.

"*¡Sí! – ¡Vale!*" continued María.

Finally she handed the phone to Adam and wiped her tears with a floral-patterned hankie she'd pulled from her bag.

"Your Momma," she explained. "Still in Mexico City."

Adam's heart jumped with excitement on hearing his mother's voice.

"Adam?"

"*¡Sí!* I mean, yes, Mom. I'm fine. We're okay – María's all right. Honest, we are both okay. Look, tell Tío Federico to call the police – like now! Tell him to speak to no one less than the Chief of Police in Mexico City – yeah, Mom – yeah – and his friends in government – yeah – I think so. The head of this racket is about to be handed over to the local police in Comitán – yeah, that's C-O-M-I-T-A-N. – Yeah – straightaway – and some of his gangsters – yeah, drug gangsters – yeah, immediately. Need to break up the whole goddamn show. I'm gonna call Sam – yeah, karate Sam. He'll get onto the DEA. – No, Mom, it isn't – no – yeah. –

We'll call again from the police station in a few minutes. Federico oughta speak with the local police. Arrange to get María back home as soon as possible – what's that? Straight to Houston?"

María shook her head. She obviously had the same thought in her mind as Adam: Anna.

"No, Mom, Mexico City – Ciao! Love you – and Dad – and Chloe! Special big hug for little Chloe!"

Special? Another girl? Chloe?

Afterwards, he made a quick call to Sam who knew nothing about the kidnapping. Adam was relieved. Obviously there'd been a blanket over the whole affair. The media had been kept in the dark, but no longer. Sam agreed to do exactly as Adam suggested.

The boy turned off María's cell phone. He and the girl hurriedly hugged before getting out of the car. A group of street kids had gathered around the vehicles. One spotted an armed Alfredo squatting in the back of the truck guarding Ramón and his fellow gangster.

"Who's in charge amongst you?" asked Plácido as the urchins craned their necks to get a better view of the ruffians strapped into the back of the 4x4. The eldest stepped forward.

"One hundred *pesos* if those animals are still here when we get back!" Plácido promised the boy.

Adam could have sworn he saw dollar signs flash in the lad's bright eyes. When they returned half an hour later, accompanied by four armed policemen, the boy was still dutifully watching the occupants of Alejandro's vehicle like a hawk. Plácido said something to one of the officers who reached into his pocket and pulled out a couple of money-notes for the grubby urchin who vanished in the blink of an eye.

"Here we have to say goodbye!" announced Plácido. "How can we ever repay you and your girlfriend, Adam?"

"No need," the boy replied. "Your kindness was something we'll never forget. And we'll send you a copy of our album when it comes out."

Plácido looked embarrassed.

"We – erm – don't have a CD player in the village."

"I'll send you one," laughed Adam. "With lots of batteries!"

"Oh, by the way, they've promised to get the solar panel fixed and the phone line restored," added Plácido. "Manuel has a phone. You can reach Lela through him. And—" Plácido glanced at the most senior of the officers. "And they say I can have my picture included in the press photo of them arresting Ramón. Just imagine – the DEA had already spoken with the police by the time we got to the police station! And another thing. They say we can keep the 4x4 when the forensic boys have finished with it. Meantime they'll put us up in a real hotel! Four star. Alfredo's gonna have ten showers a day, aren't you Alfredo?"

Alfredo, who spoke no Spanish, grinned and nodded.

The first thing the police found when they opened the trunk of the 4x4 was the attaché case full of Tío Federico's money. However, Adam and María had something far more important than money on their minds.

"Plácido, tell Lela we'll get Anna back whatever it takes!" Adam said.

After fond embraces with Plácido and Alfredo, Adam and María were taken by a police vehicle to Tuxtla-Gutiérrez where a small plane was ready to return them to Mexico City. After the final leg of their journey, a tearful María ran into her mother's arms at a military airfield outside Mexico City whilst Adam was kissed, hugged and made a fuss of by Ann Winters.

"Real proud of you, Adam. *Real* proud," she said.

Funny, that's just what Papa Pedro said...

Chapter 14: Anna

"Point is," said the old man, "belonging ain't what counts. It's who you are that matters down there. And the girl, she knows better than the boy himself who he really is."

Tío Federico was naturally delighted the kids had retrieved the money but this was as nothing compared with the family's joy at seeing María again, unharmed.

"Only because of Adam," the girl insisted a thousand times over.

Neither she nor Adam mentioned the help they'd had from the mysterious Golden Jaguar, and no one other than Adam knew about María dying and coming back to life. There was, however, one thing about that nightmare that Adam never could understand, and there was only one person who might have been able to answer his question: Papa Pedro. The question was this: how was it the villagers made no mention of María's death and resurrection after his and María's return from the *Forest Without Time*? Had they chosen not to do so for some reason? Or had time changed? Was it possible that a future that had already happened had been erased and the present relived in a way that would alter the future so drastically? Like re-recording over a DVD? Had another dimension overwritten the fourth dimension?

'Love is not love which alters when it alteration findeth...'

One of the few lines of poetry that had stuck in Adam's brain. But how could love itself be a dimension? Adam turned this over many times in his mind yet still could not puzzle it out.

"You're looking very thoughtful," María would say whenever he struggled to understand how playing with time had erased her death.

Golden Jaguar of the Sun

"Am I?" he would reply. "Just – erm – just thinking about something, I guess."

To which María would say, pointedly:

"Well, just so long as that's not another girl you're thinking about!"

At which he would take her in his arms and kiss her over and over and over again.

Another girl 'almost as special'? No way – unless – little Chloe? Could it be? No! Too young!

Gradually he thought less about what happened in the remote Chiapas village but he never did forget those other words of the Golden Jaguar: *the future is what you make it.*

They had a few days left in Mexico City before flying back to Houston and there was one thing left to do. Thankfully Jorge had flown down to help his father after María's kidnapping, and Jorge's help would prove to be invaluable in this final operation: Anna's rescue.

Jorge succeeded in putting pressure on the authorities to act fast. The US media were abuzz with the capture and break-up of one the fastest growing drug cartels spanning South America, Mexico and the USA, and photographs of the captured Ramón and of his jungle hideout at Chiculhuán appeared on the front pages of all national newspapers. The world awaited with baited breath the release of those young women held prisoner by Ramón in his penthouse suite in Cali. It was thanks to Jorge that one of these, Anna from the Chiapas jungle, was promptly escorted back to Mexico City. Adam and María, together with Jorge, met the woman at the airport.

Anna, like most of the Mayan people, was short and dark-complexioned with striking features similar to Plácido's. To Adam she wasn't beautiful in the same way as María who had that awesome blend of Spanish and Native American beauty to give the girl her ravishing looks, but there was something fascinating about the woman's face that

219

held his attention. In that face Adam saw all the suffering of her people yet there was also nobility there despite outward poverty, timidity and wariness. Adam could understand why Jorge was immediately taken with her.

"D'you think she knows?" María asked her boyfriend when they first spotted the diminutive figure being escorted by plain clothes officers into the arrivals area.

Jorge thanked the police for all they'd done to secure Anna's speedy return to Mexico. They took her to an airport café for refreshments and a chance to talk. It turned out that Anna spoke very little Spanish beyond '*sí*', '*no*' and '*gracias*'. She obviously hadn't a clue who Adam and María and Jorge were, or why they had an interest in her affairs. Nevertheless, she warmed to María and kept smiling at the girl, but Adam sensed she only wanted to get back to her husband in the Chiapas and put her ordeal behind her. They used a mix of Spanish and sign language in an attempt to explain to Anna that they would take her home with them and she looked worried. She kept close to María all the time, refusing to leave the girl's side. Jorge phoned his parents from the airport and asked them to urgently find someone conversant in Mayan.

When they arrived back with an increasingly distraught Anna, they were relieved to discover Tío Federico had managed to track down a woman in the Cultural Studies Department of the University who was fluent in Tzeltal Mayan. Her name was Merissa.

Merissa was one of those people with a rare ability to put anyone at ease. It fell upon her and María to break the news to Anna as they sat around the kitchen table drinking hot chocolate. Adam remained in the background pretending to read, although he listened to every word, even when Merissa spoke in Tzeltal. As the tragedy unfolded, Adam wished someone could have done for Anna what the Golden Jaguar and the Old Woman in the Hills had done for him: bring her beloved back from the dead. Adam had never before seen anyone so traumatized as poor Anna on learning of her husband's suicide. To witness the grief etched upon her deeply expressive Mayan face was heartbreaking. María, too, was in tears when she took hold of one of Anna's hands to comfort the woman.

"He was such a good man," Anna said through Merissa. "Everyone loved him. I was so happy when he married me. I reckoned I was the luckiest woman in the world. And he was all I thought about in that awful place (Ramón's penthouse in Cali) but never once did I ask God whether he too suffered."

María, Anna and Merissa sat together for at least two hours. Adam was allowed to join them after Anna learned he'd been with María in her village and that he also knew the people of her village of whom María spoke: Lela and her children, Carla and Pepe, Plácido, Alfredo, Manuel and Agustín. When she learned of Ramón's capture, his injury and his imprisonment, she showed little emotion. She shrugged her shoulders as if it was of little importance now that her husband was dead.

Adam knew there'd never be a good time to suggest to Anna his plan, about which María had been most unhappy, but he felt now rather than later would be better. Merissa explained to Anna, on Adam's behalf, that the boy planned to show the Old Woman of the Hills something of Anna's husband that Lela had given him for this very purpose – a small knife that the man had used for carving animal figurines that Plácido would take with him to sell along with other hand-crafted goods from the village. Anna gently stroked the knife, touching the stubby wooden handle in a way that suggested to the boy that this brought back memories of her husband. Although it pained Adam to see Anna so upset, he hoped the sad little item might serve a purpose.

"I think my plan might just help her," Adam tentatively suggested after he and María had left the grieving Anna to talk on her own with Merissa. "It really would mean a lot to Anna to at least know her husband's all right now and at peace."

"How do you know that?" María asked tetchily.

"He was obviously a good man. He must've loved Anna very much. I know she's Catholic and she'll believe in heaven and all that, but these Mayans also have other beliefs. Hidden, like. The Old Woman of the Hills really does have amazing powers, María. If it wasn't for her, you – I mean I..." Adam seemed to stumble over his choice of words. "I wouldn't have found out where they'd taken you."

María looked at him in a funny way.

"There really is something you're hiding from me, isn't there?" she asked.

"I believe the Old Woman can put Anna in contact with her dead husband if she holds that little carving knife. Just like she knew exactly where you were by holding your doll."

"Adam!"

"What?"

"You didn't answer my question!"

"I – no – María, don't ask me that. Please don't! Trust me, but don't ever ask me that again. I love you – and that's all."

"And I'm not supposed to know that?" María looked amused.

"Just don't ask me again," Adam replied quietly.

She didn't, but for her it was like having a secret about a secret – one she must never know. And María's knowledge that there was some sort of a secret in a strange sort of a way excited the girl. There were occasions when Adam worried that her memory of what had happened might return – like when she said, out of the blue, "I'm so happy that Papa Pedro's old friend José and his son, Santiago, are fine," and another time, "I wonder how Art and Jeannie are doing back there. You know. Fighting those big red rubber things."

Thankfully María didn't show any inclination to want to accompany Adam and Jorge when they took Anna to the cave of the Old Woman of the Hills. He'd feared meeting up with the woman might have brought it all back to her, particularly if the old lady were to go into one of her peculiar moods and call the girl 'Princess Arima'.

Conchita kindly agreed to come instead of María. Jorge remained formal yet courteous towards Anna, and always made certain that the other woman was present in her company. Seeing Conchita again gave Adam the opportunity to reassure the old lady about her late husband and Santiago. The way he put it, he said that Papa Pedro came to him in a dream and told him José and their son were just fine. He felt he wasn't actually lying since somehow it did all seem like a dream, and the woman looked so happy after hearing about Adam's "dream". Conchita was the ideal person to accompany Anna to the Old Woman of the Hills. Not only did her presence put the girl at ease, but Adam would have had great difficulty directing Jorge since he'd only been there once before in this dimension – in a car driven by that fiend Alejandro. His other visits to her cave on the bleak hillside had been in parallel worlds.

They arrived in the late morning. Conchita stayed in the car for she would never have made the hill on foot, but Anna now had full trust in both Adam and Jorge. She followed them up the steep path to the familiar cave entrance. This time Adam brought gifts: a box of chocolates and some corn, which he left with the other presents piled outside the cave. After entering, the boy felt a hand gently come to rest on his back and soon they were swallowed up by the darkness. He felt pleased that Anna trusted him enough to use him as a support whilst they crept further into the cave. The boy wondered whether the young woman was afraid of the dark for he felt her hand tremble. Jorge followed in the rear.

After they'd gone a short distance, Adam stopped. He called out. Although still wearing the Golden Jaguar bracelets, he used Spanish. Inexplicably, he was unable to remember any Mayan or Nahuatl and feared this might affect his communication with the Old Woman. His fear was unfounded.

"*¡Hola Adam, Anna y Jorge!*" the Old Woman said as soon her face appeared from out of the darkness. "*¿La Princesa Arima, donde está? ¿La Santa María?*"

She knew who Anna and Jorge were without Adam having to introduce them, but her first concern had been to make sure María was well. She smiled and nodded when Adam explained the girl was fine and he sensed she fully understood why he hadn't brought María with him.

"*¿Y Anna? ¿Ella no habla espagnol?*"

She went up to the young woman and touched her arm. Immediately she started conversing with Anna in Tzeltal. Anna was delighted. She turned and looked at Jorge. He knew what she needed and took the small knife from his pocket. He gave this to Anna who passed it on to the Old Woman. Holding the knife, she closed her eyes and, leaning on her stick, rocked to and fro for a minute or two. Then she opened her eyes, smiled at Anna and beckoned to the young woman to go with her further on into the cave – alone. Anna looked anxiously at Adam and at Jorge but together they nodded reassurance. Using sign language, Jorge indicated he and Adam would wait for her at the entrance to the cave.

It wasn't long before Anna re-emerged with the Old Woman. Adam was fully aware that time inside the cave belonged to a different dimension to time as he knew it – as if the cave was an outpost of *The Forest Without Time*. Anna looked upset and Adam regretted not having María with them to comfort her. The Old Woman had one arm around the girl and was speaking in Tzeltal. Anna nodded repeatedly without saying anything. Then the Old Woman gave her a hug and stood watching from the ledge in front of the cave as the three made their way back down the path to Jorge's car. How strange, thought Adam, that the last time he came down that very same path he was carrying María in his arms frantic to reach the Golden Jaguar and Anna's Chiapas village in time to save his girlfriend's life – or, more accurately, to prevent her death that had already happened.

Back in the car, Jorge phoned home, asking for Merissa to come round urgently however busy she might be. Meanwhile Adam felt thoroughly stupid for having taken Anna to the Old Woman. The poor woman seemed unable to stop crying. María would be livid.

Merissa was an angel. She cancelled her afternoon tutorials so she could come round to the López house and find out why Anna was so distraught. Adam felt mighty sheepish when he saw how upset María was to see Anna upset. Although the girl said nothing, her silence was enough to inform him that taking Anna to the cave had been a dumb thing to do. His girlfriend would never criticise him in public, or willingly make him feel uncomfortable, but nevertheless he went around heavy with guilt.

Anna was taken by Merissa into the sitting room where they could talk alone whilst Adam sat in the kitchen twiddling his thumbs and wishing he'd listened to María. Meanwhile his girlfriend disappeared upstairs to her bedroom on the pretext of packing her bag for the return trip to Houston the following day – a sure sign that she was none too pleased. Or so he feared. Ann Winters had gone out for the day with Tía Bea to the *Museo de Antropología* whilst Carmen López sat talking with María in her room.

"Adam!"

Adam looked up. Merissa stood at the door.

"Adam, could you come in please. Anna wants to say something. I think María and her mother should come too."

Adam's heart sank. He was to be humiliated in front of María just as used to happen at middle school when she was the girlfriend of that hunk of a bully, 'Spike' Klaus O'Driscoll.

"MARÍA!" he shouted from the bottom of the stairs.

"¿SÍ?" the girl called back.

"It's Anna. Merissa says she wants to speak with all of us. Your mama as well."

María appeared, followed by Carmen. She wasn't exactly scowling, but Adam could tell the girl was far from happy. Carmen aswell. Both only managed the weakest of smiles. They all went into the sitting room and sat hunched awkwardly together on the sofa opposite Anna and Merissa. Anna seemed so pitifully small next to the larger woman, but she'd stopped crying and she grinned at Adam as Merissa spoke:

"Anna wants to thank you so much for helping her, Adam. Before seeing the Old Woman of the Hills she felt there was no hope. She simply didn't know what to do. After speaking with her husband in that cave, it's all so different. He's helped her as only he could."

Merissa paused and looked at Anna.

"¡Gracias, Adam, gracias, gracias!" Anna said over and over.

"Anna wants to keep the baby." María gasped. "She told him she knows it's his baby. He was so happy and that made Anna feel good. Her husband told her to be stronger than he was however hard it might be to care for the child on her own. He said he understood why she didn't wish to return to their village without him. They both want the same thing. For his child to get a better chance in life."

Merissa looked at Adam.

"Anna was crying because she's sad the child will never know what a good man her husband was."

María also focused on Adam and differently from a few moments before; a look of pride as if Adam was her 'good man'.

"Another thing," continued Merissa. "I'm sure we could find Anna somewhere to stay here in Mexico City. For the time being she'd be welcome in my home and in due course I think I could persuade the University to find her a job in my department."

She glanced at Anna.

"She's a very bright girl, you know. I can tell from talking with her. But she must learn Spanish. She asks whether you, María would teach her. If you have the time?"

María appeared disappointed.

"I really wish I could," she replied, "but we live in Houston, you see. We leave tomorrow. I'm so sorry, Anna."

"You as well? I thought only Adam was – you know – American."

She was clearly puzzled that this Mexican girl in Mexico City lived in America. No one had enlightened her as to the complexity of the López family.

Adam noticed María whisper something to her mother as Merissa was explaining this to Anna. He could tell from María's expression she'd come up with an idea and the boy knew only too well how impossible it was for anyone to ignore her ideas. Once the girl got something into her head it nearly always happened.

"Wait!" María exclaimed, interrupting Merissa. "Mama says she could come and stay with us in Houston. At least until she's fluent in Spanish. Then she could learn English as well. Perhaps she could study a bit too and come back and get a really good job at the University here. When the baby's a bit older."

The opportunity of once again helping to look after a little baby in their house back in Houston was, for María, too great a chance to let slip by. Anna produced more tears as she listened to Merissa repeat in Tzeltal what María had just said – tears of joy.

"And your husband?" Merissa asked Carmen López. "Will he agree to this?"

"We women always win our battles without a fight!" Carmen joked. "Sure he'll agree. If his favourite daughter wants it, he'll agree!"

"Oh Mama!" objected María.

On the plane, María couldn't stop talking about the baby; where it would sleep and what they would need to get. Adam learned everything there was to know about babies on that flight back to Houston. How to wind them, the importance of responding when they start to cry, where to change a diaper in shopping malls, and so forth and so forth. He sat back happily and let her talk on. He hardly said a word throughout the flight but he could not stop smiling as he looked at his girlfriend and listened to her monologue. He prayed she would never again stop talking as happened in the Chiapas jungle; never whilst he remained alive.

Chapter 15: Forbidden Memories

*"**All** over?" repeated Tezcatlipoca. "Nonsense! It's only just begun. The boy has so many weaknesses we're bound to win. And his weaknesses will become the weaknesses of the Golden Jaguar. Once that happens we can't lose!"*

"Mom, what do you think of the names 'Carla' or 'Pepe' for a baby?" Adam asked when Ann Winters came into his room to say 'goodnight' on the eve of their return to Houston.

The boy's mom sat on the edge of his bed. She'd had little time to speak with him on her own whilst staying at María's uncle and aunt's place in Mexico City since Adam had shared a room with Camilo and Javier, the talking champions of Mexico.

"Are they the names that Anna's chosen for her baby – depending on whether it's a boy or a girl?" she asked.

"No. They're the names María wants for hers." replied Adam casually, glancing up from his book about the Maya people.

"Adam?"

Ann Winters' face was contorted with horror.

"She isn't – you haven't – I mean they didn't—?" For a few moments she sat speechless. Adam frowned then laughed.

"Oh no, Mom! You got me wrong," he said to her great relief. "She isn't, I haven't and no one touched her at Chiculhuán. This is for the future. As long as two thousand and seventeen doesn't stop us. Those little kids in the village where we stayed, Carla and Pepe, they were mad about María. Wouldn't let her out of their sight. They were kinda cute and, well – she likes the names. She wonders what I thought of them. For when we have our own kids, Mom. Don't worry!"

"What is it about two thousand and seventeen, then?" Ann asked, grinning with relief.

"You don't know?" the boy queried, lifting Alejandro's book up for his mother to see the front cover. "Some thought that the ancient Maya believed the present cycle of life on Earth would end in 2012. They obviously misinterpreted the glyphs. Now a whacko bunch of religious dudes has changed that date to January 2017. So this'll give me a good excuse to marry María before then – like pretty goddamn soon, huh?"

"Adam, you're only fifteen! Far too young to be talking like this!"

"Am I? Some cultures allow it." Adam shrugged his shoulders. There'd never be another girl for him, whatever the Golden Jaguar had implied. So why wait? Surely there was someone in the dimension in which he now found himself who could make this happen? "Guess I'll have to wait. It's the way she feels about it, anyways. Kids at school are having sex all the time, you know. Boast about it. But they don't seem to stay together for the sex alone. Not for long. Boy moves on to another girl, girl dumps boy for another dude—" Adam paused. "It's not like that for us. María's quite—"

"Her religion?"

"Yeah! And I respect that. We've never really had religion in this house, have we?"

"Do you miss it, Adam? Have we failed you by not taking you to church? Your father's a complete agnostic – well, guess you could call him an atheist. Me, I just don't know."

"Mom, we live in Bible Belt country! You can't 'not know'!"

Ann raised her eyebrows.

"You teasing me, Adam Winters?"

"Yep! Sure am!"

They both laughed.

"Think I'm like you, Mom. Or at least, was. Kinda not sure now. Feel different, I guess. Might go to mass with María on Sundays just to see – if you're okay with that. If I get bored I'll have María López to stare at."

"That'll be fine, Adam," Ann Winters said before kissing her son good-night. On leaving the room she turned to speak: "And those would be great names for your children – one day but not yet!"

After Adam's return to school, what happened in Mexico soon became a fading memory. Normality replaced chaos and the volume of work saw to it that the boy had no time to dwell on events that no sane person would believe. Inside, though, Adam felt changed for good. To his great relief there was no mention at school of Ramón and no talk of María's kidnapping. Like the girl's death, these were forbidden memories. He was thankful his and María's families had, at his request, said nothing to anyone about the events and this also helped him in his struggle to forget María's death.

The bravery award and previous publicity had done them no favors, for he was certain that being put in the spotlight had caused Ramón to set his sights on him. Ramón was only one of many drug operators who would see him as a threat if they knew he'd had a hand in the drug baron's downfall; worse still, they could target María again. Complete silence was essential. After his experience with Álvaro and Alejandro, Adam would trust no one other than María, Sam Royal and the Winters and López families.

Sam was terrific and Adam had absolute faith in him. The man had told the police and the DEA that he'd had a tip-off from Mexico about Alejandro's cousin. Needless to say, Álvaro did not reappear at school and no one missed him.

Sam actually enjoyed the whole exercise and thanked Adam as much as the boy thanked him.

"See, I'm getting kinda bored doing an office job all day long," the man told Adam. "Police work would suit me just fine. Could make more use of my karate as a police officer than in the oil business. Just have to convince the good lady!"

Adam's chief worry was little Chloe. She felt strongly that Adam should get another bravery award and more front page cover in the newspapers, but somehow did manage to stay in on the secret when told that spreading word about what he'd done could get both Adam and María killed. So she spent two whole evenings creating her own cardboard bravery award certificate for her brother, decorating this with elaborate designs in gold and red. She also made a mock *Houston Chronicle* with painstakingly, hand-printed pages expounding the bravery of Adam Winters for fighting off a hundred armed drug villains bare-handed and rescuing a 'damsel in distress'.

"Yeah!" said Adam, laughing when he read her childish effort. "Pretty much sums it up, Chloe!"

He kept her *Houston Chronicle* and bravery award safely in his bedside cabinet. Chloe promised not to tell her best friend, young Lorna, three houses away, which big brother thought truly remarkable. Lorna, who worshipped Adam, was privy to almost all Chloe's thoughts.

Only one person mentioned Álvaro on their first day back at school and that was Fernando. He took Adam aside and told him things that were quite upsetting but at least everything now fell into place. Álvaro had lied to Fernando and other Hispanics in their class. He'd told them that Adam had treated María abominably and that María only went out with him because Adam's Dad had a hold over Miguel López for some unknown reason that he, Álvaro, was determined to find out for María's sake because, as Álvaro put it, María "couldn't stand Adam Winters". Fernando first realised Álvaro wasn't telling the truth when María slapped him hard in public and he hoped Adam would understand why he and his buddies had beaten him up that evening. Adam said he bore no grudges and they became reasonably good friends, although Adam remained wary for he knew that Fernando was still madly keen on María.

"It shows," María whispered to Adam during a math class one morning.

"What?"

"The baby," she replied.

Adam raised a finger to his lips when the teacher glared in their direction.

So there was Anna to occupy their minds as well. Jorge had stayed on in Mexico City until her passport and other documents came through, and the two arrived in Houston about a week after school had restarted. At first, Anna looked totally lost – a small Mayan village woman in a great American metropolis – but she adapted quickly. María proved to be an inspiring and patient teacher of Spanish but Jorge was continually offering to take her place, saying how difficult it must be for María with her school work. María got the message and soon Jorge took over all the teaching. A 'Spanish lesson' could also mean Jorge taking Anna to the zoo or to a museum. The woman began to waitress in Jorge's restaurant, purportedly to improve on her Spanish but soon Jorge and Anna were rarely out of each other's company.

Not one of Adam and María's classmates knew anything of what happened to them in Mexico following the record label party, and no one associated the Mayan woman staying in the López household with María's visit to Mexico, but the whole school was abuzz with excitement about the new album. The media had even visited and spoken with the principal, the girl's music teacher and with several of the students, asking about the two musical prodigies. That was the sort of publicity Adam hoped for and, boy, did they get it! Not a single gangster or drug pusher was mentioned in connection with young Adam Winters. The album was out in Mexico two weeks after they returned to Houston and María had endless phone calls about it from family, friends, and friends of family and friends of friends back in Mexico. Everyone loved the tracks, their school was delighted with the positive publicity, and Adam was so caught up in everything he consigned to the back of his mind the terrifying happenings in the Chiapas jungle. María, too, helped to divert his attention with constant talk of the new life growing inside Anna.

Then, one evening, Jorge came round in a highly excitable state to the Winters' home. Adam and María were supposedly 'singing' together in his room although Ann Winters thought it had gone rather quiet up there. Of course she trusted her son with the girl whom she'd come to think off almost as a second daughter. She never normally interfered when María was alone with Adam. However, on hearing the news from Jorge she was so keen to tell them straightaway that she bounded upstairs and burst into Adam's room – forgetting to knock first.

Chapter 16: The Wedding and the Painting

*"**She's** ready," announced the old man.*

"Of couse she is," replied the one-time priest. "That's why you went down to the Forest. To help the boy."

"Not María!" said the old man. "The other girl. And I do believe she's old enough."

"Other girl? You never said about another girl."

"We don't need to say things here. We just know."

"Oh, I am sorry," Ann apologised, quickly looking the other way as Adam and María disentangled themselves from a passionate embrace on the bed.

"Mom!" exclaimed Adam. "What the—?"

Ann couldn't wait.

"They're getting married!"

"Uh?" Adam queried blankly, forgetting his annoyance at being interrupted whilst kissing María. "Anna and Jorge getting married?"

"Yes! Next week. Jorge's come round to tell us himself. He's downstairs."

"Wow!" cried María, bubbling with excitement as she sprang up from the bed. "Jorge getting married? Jorge? And next week? I can't believe it!"

The girl gave Adam a quick hug then rushed downstairs to see Jorge. Adam remained seated on his bed, grinning, and Ann came and sat beside him.

"Hey, Adam, I'm so sorry I burst in like that."

"Never mind, Mom. Was just thinking, won't be seeing much of María till after the wedding now. She'll want to be involved in just about everything. You know, Jorge's always been a kinda hero-figure for her since she was little."

"Oh, I think Adam Winters is her hero now!" beamed Ann.

"Yeah, but Jorge's different. He's kind of – well, he's just so nice. I guess that's it!"

"And Adam Winters? Isn't he nice too?" Ann joked.

"Jorge's the sorta guy you can go to with any problem and he'll do everything he can to help," he explained.

"I know what you mean," said Ann. "He really was so kind to Papa Pedro during his last six months."

Papa Pedro? Yeah, thought Adam! *Papa Pedro would have been over the moon about the news. Moon? Jeannie? Should they invite Art and Jeannie? So much to think about and so little time.*

He could hear María jabbering excitedly in Spanish downstairs. As with most Hispanics when in full-tilt conversation mode, it was more of a performance: the stance of her body and the hand gesticulations every bit as important as the speech.

How dull an all-American, non-Hispanic, white girlfriend would be!

"Adam!" exclaimed Jorge when the boy joined him and María in the living room. "Just had to come round and tell you both in person. If it wasn't for my beautiful cousin and her fortunate boyfriend I'd never have met Anna. She's the most wonderful woman imaginable. I would've waited a lot longer, she's still that upset, but it's for the baby. He'll need a father and she understands this. She said her husband who died told her it must happen – that she should marry someone else soon. He wanted her to do the right thing for his baby. We'll make it work. I know we will. And of course she'll have time and space to herself. I'll always respect that. Merissa's helped a lot over the phone too."

"You and Anna will bring the baby round, won't you, Jorge?" María asked anxiously in English. "Like a lot of the time?"

The girl looked worried, afraid she might now have little chance of playing with Anna's baby.

"Cousin, Anna adores you! I reckon you're gonna get your fill of babies! Hope that won't stop you wanting your own in the future!"

He glanced knowingly at Adam who felt his face redden.

"No way!" said María. "Jorge, promise you won't call the baby 'Carla' or 'Pepe', right?"

"Why not? Don't you like those names?"

María bit her lower lip and glanced in Adam's direction. By now the boy was a deep shade of lobster.

"Guess she fancies using those names for her own kids some day," explained Ann, helping the girl out of her embarrassment.

"I'm sure Anna will have thought of Mayan names already but we'll avoid Carla or Pepe when it comes to Spanish names," reassured Jorge.

María was disappointed to hear it wasn't to be a huge, grand wedding with half the world invited, but she fully understood when Jorge explained how, in the circumstances, this would have been inappropriate.

"A small affair," he explained. "Family only." He turned to Ann Winters. "Which, of course, includes all the Winters," he added giving a small bow and winking at Adam.

Excludes Art and Jeannie, thought Adam. *But I'll tell them when we send a CD of our new album.*

"The reception will be at the restaurant. Anna wants to arrange for a few Mayan dishes. Bit different from what we usually serve. And—"

Jorge's eyes twinkled as he reached for something in his pocket.

"What?" María questioned, her face aglow. She knew her cousin well enough to guess what he had hidden there.

"Great music! Nothing but the best!"

Jorge pulled out a CD with a cover picture of a beautiful Mexican girl in a red dress wearing a ruby and pearl necklace.

"Our album!" María shrieked, rushing forward and grabbing the CD. She jumped up and down with excitement. "Look! *Our* album!" she exclaimed waving it in front of Adam. "Yours and mine! Do I look all right in the picture?"

"Can't see. You're waving it about so!"

She handed him the CD.

"Could make a fortune on that photo alone," Adam said, but the other Adam felt angered on seeing the necklace.

"My father got it the day before yesterday. Had a few sent by Fedex," explained Jorge. "You two are gonna be millionaires, you know! Just had to play it over and over at the restaurant before coming here. All our clients were asking where they could get the disc. I've already ordered a batch from Mexico. Should arrive before your US launch!"

After Jorge and María left to brave the ferment of the López household, the Winters family sat and listened to '*Lo Siento Dentro di Mí*' many times over.

"Did María really write all those songs herself?" asked an incredulous Johnny Winters.

"Sure thing, Dad!" Adam replied.

Johnny smiled in disbelief.

"She's a genius," Chloe insisted, "so it's not hard for her."

"Guess you're right, Chloe. A genius!" agreed Adam.

Chloe always seemed to hit the nail on the head in her childish sort of a way. As a singer-songwriter María was nothing short of a genius and it hadn't been hard for her. Music just flowed from the girl. There was so much feeling in her songs that both Ann and Chloe were soon reduced to tears.

During the week before the wedding, Adam applied himself wholeheartedly to school work, also creating for himself a mountain of additional extracurricular reading. His interest in Mesoamerican culture had taken a new turn in that he now read about the present day Maya and he told

María he'd be better off doing anthropology than archaeology.

"Better the living than the dead, huh?" she suggested. "Hey, why are you looking at me like that, Adam Winters?"

It was the sheer joy of seeing her alive that shone back at her in Adam's smile.

"Very much better the living, Señorita María López!"

But Chloe had difficulty in forgetting she'd nearly lost her beloved brother for good over the Christmas recess. Of all the family, she was the most traumatized by what happened. That neither she nor any other family member should tell even their closest friends about Adam's involvement in bringing a big time drugs baron to justice made it doubly difficult for a child always intent on informing the whole world about everything her awesome elder brother did. Adam was barely beginning to understand how awful the affair must have been for his sister, and although she only knew a fraction of what really happened in that Mexican jungle, she obviously sensed there was far more to the story than Adam had told them.

Funny how younger kids somehow see more deeply into things, the boy thought. But Chloe was a truly remarkable little person as her brother was about to discover – from the painting.

At first Adam was stunned speechless but later he understood how it helped his sister come to terms with what troubled her. He was also thankful, since the painting made it easier for him to close the book on those events in the Chiapas jungle, as if the painted image might take over from his memory and allow the boy to seal up the past.

"Adam, I'm gonna do a painting for you," Chloe said that weekend before the wedding.

"Great, Chloe! Horses? Birds?" he queried.

Chloe was an unusually talented artist-in-the-making, particularly skilful at drawing animals. A large horse of hers hung on Adam's bedroom wall.

"Nope," she answered. "It's gonna be you. You and María."

Chloe spent all day at the kitchen table bent over a large sheet of paper with her paint-pots spread out before her. She was meticulous about detail and would bring her face close to the paper, usually with the tip of her tongue between her lips to aid concentration. Adam often feared she'd end up with a green or blue patch at the end of her nose or tongue. That particular day her concentration was even more intense than usual and everyone crept quietly about the house so as not to disturb her. Adam knew from past experience not to look at the painting until finished otherwise his sister would most certainly have become upset. Only the completed creation could be seen by others.

There was a knock on Adam's bedroom door late in the afternoon. It was Chloe. She did indeed have a blob of green paint on her nose and rainbows of other colours decorated her hands and arms.

"You can look at it now," she said. "It's rubbish but you can look anyway."

"Chloe, no way could a painting of yours be rubbish," affirmed Adam, putting down a book about Native North American culture. "I could never draw or paint like you do."

True!

He slipped downstairs for a quick look at Chloe's latest artistic effort, wondering what he and María would look like. He was simply not prepared for what he saw lying on the kitchen table.

"I do hope you like it!"

Adam was too shocked to say whether he liked it or not.

"Is it okay?"

Golden Jaguar of the Sun

The boy's little sister seemed desperately concerned that her artistic achievement should meet with his approval but he could only stare in confused disbelief.

Chloe had painted them in a jungle. That, of course, was not surprising. She knew about the temple and Ramón and the drug gangsters, and they were all there in the picture. María had been beautifully painted in her red dress, holding hands with the painted Adam. But it was the other things the girl had included that caused Adam's jaw to drop.

"What's this?" Adam asked after a while, pointing to the image of a large feline.

"Oh, I think it's a jaguar. They do have them in the jungle, don't they?"

"Yes, Chloe, but they have black spots – usually. Or they're totally black."

"I'm sure this one doesn't have spots," the child said confidently.

She'd painted it almost entirely with gold paint and it glistened in the kitchen light. That was one thing. But the eyes? How could Chloe ever have guessed about the eyes of the Golden Jaguar? Adam stared at the large cat's coal-black eyes and their vertical slits of red. He almost expected to see the fire in those eyes burn holes in the paper. His own eyes moved from a steep-stepped pyramid temple, which Chloe had depicted with remarkable accuracy, to a painted forest. There was a hill with a cave. A path led up to the cave and in front of the cave was the figure of a bent old woman leaning upon a crooked stick. At the other end of the picture a man and a woman sat on a bench and a small girl swung on a swing. Then the boy's gaze fixed upon the horizon beyond the forest. A high bridge spanned a space where Chloe had put no paint at all. And at the far end of the bridge was an eerily beautiful place with a red hill and a bleak blue and yellow plain that stretched away to a wall of jagged, snowless mountain peaks. In the top left corner of the painting Chloe had painted a spider.

Adam looked again at the images of himself and of María. His sister had put a small golden crown on María's head.

"This?" asked Adam, pointing to the crown.

"I wanted her to be a princess," Chloe replied. "I wish I could be like María one day. Like a princess."

"Just be yourself, Chloe. We all love you as you are."

"But I'll never become famous like you and María!"

"Chloe, the future is what you make it," Adam said, repeating the words of the Golden Jaguar.

Then he remembered those other words of the Golden Jaguar: "—*there is another girl almost as special as María. A girl very close to you.*" It had to be Chloe. There was no need to implicate a rival to María – impossible, anyway.

Adam sellotaped the painting over Chloe's horse then stood gazing at it for a very long time. His story, his princess who had died and had been brought back to life – their love.

María never saw the painting. Whenever she came round there was only Chloe's horse on the wall, for the other painting would be hidden underneath it, the boy's concealed memory remaining an unspoken secret between Adam and Chloe. And whilst he tried to understand the depthless goodness and love in his girlfriend, and struggled to fathom the mystery of his little sister, he realised there was one person whom he knew less than any other member of his family or circle of friends: himself.

Although the wedding was to be a small affair by Texan Mexican standards, María still managed to fill all her free time with wedding-related business. Adam saw less of the girl than he would have wished for during that week, but he understood. After all, for a woman what could be more important than a forthcoming wedding, however small? Adam and María had hoped that someone from Anna's village might have made it to the wedding, particularly Lela or Plácido, but logistically this proved impossible. However, they did manage to talk to Manuel over the phone, for the telephone line had been promptly repaired, as promised, and it was arranged that Jorge and Anna would make a phone call to the village, after the wedding, at a predetermined time. Anna would speak to her mother, to Lela and other friends. Also, Adam learned from Jorge that the couple planned to visit the little village in the Chiapas jungle at the first opportunity when Jorge's work allowed. Knowing this encouraged Adam to discuss his and María's plan with Jorge:

"Jorge, you're probably gonna be right about María and me making a whole bunch of money from the new album," he said. "María's already raked in a small fortune from her first album. They're gonna release that in Europe, Australia and Japan. Possibly China, too. See, we both want to do more for Anna's village. We owe it to them. So please find out what they need and we'll pay for it. And tell them—" The boy paused then grinned. "Say we'll come down and cut their telephone wires if they won't accept our money!"

"I'll do what I can," chuckled Jorge, "but it seems they're a proud people. Guess Anna could persuade them, though."

"And another thing," Adam continued. "We'd like to pay for Manuel to go to med school. Become a real doctor. Dad's been looking into this and making contacts for us. There are some off-shore med schools in the Caribbean. Cuba's famous for making doctors as well as ballet dancers! Manuel deserves a break."

"Adam, I do believe you've gotten infected by my little cousin's generosity!"

Infected? She's done more than infect me – more like changed me totally! Yeah, the bad old Adam's well and truly dead.

He hoped.

María, Juanita and Chloe were to be the three bridesmaids and María was constantly in the company of the little girls. Carmen López was making the bridesmaid dresses and worked flat out to have them ready in time. On María's insistence, they were to be pink for the girl thought that was the right colour for the occasion.

"Of course, Anna and I don't get a choice in the matter!" joked Carmen.

"But Mama, the bridesmaid's dresses have to be pink," María protested. "Any other colour would be wrong, wouldn't it, Adam?" she added, turning to her boyfriend for moral support.

"Why – erm – yes – well – um – pink. Definitely pink!"

"See!" María said to her mother. "Adam knows about these things. He knows so much, my boyfriend does!"

Adam turned a vivid shade of pink himself and left the women to argue the point, but, as he predicted, the bridesmaids' dresses were pink.

Ann Winters, being a beautician, was to supervise the make-up and repeated what she'd said before when getting María made up for the San Antonio talent show: how could she possibly make the girl more beautiful?

The wedding day turned out to be one of those clear, sunny winter days, cool by Houston standards but perfect for the occasion. Jorge's parents, the twins and Ana-María flew in from Mexico City the night before. Ana-María stayed with the Winters since the López home was as much bursting with people as with excitement. Adam reckoned the buzz of the wedding was, in a way, helping Anna with her grief; helping her to move forwards and think about a future with her baby and Jorge. Jorge knew he could never replace Anna's husband in her heart. He was as sensible as he was kind and only wanted to help, in whatever way he could, the woman whom he now loved.

Golden Jaguar of the Sun

María, bursting with happiness, looked stunning. All through the ceremony, and afterwards at the reception, Adam could not stop staring at her. *Right about the pink too*, he thought. Somehow it did seem to be the correct colour, for seeing her in pink half-reminded him of another wedding in a different dimension.

Someone started to play the CD of '*Lo Siento Dentro di Mí*': María's songs, with Adam's voice weaving like a thread around his girlfriend's as their lives had done since that first kiss. Adam sat alone and listened whilst everyone else stood around chattering in Spanish or in English. He listened to the haunting music that told of sadness and of happiness and he looked at the girl whose beauty, innocence, vitality and sheer joy of being alive had transformed him, turning the boy into a man – and he remembered how all of that had, for a timeless and terrifying period, been lost.

"Thank you," he whispered again to the Golden Jaguar. "Thank you" to the Old Woman of the Hills, to Art and Jeannie (who really were they?), and "thank you" to his deceased friend Papa Pedro. Perhaps one day he would understand why the girl was so 'special', as they all kept on telling him, but for now just being her boyfriend seemed special enough. He looked at María again and again until he realised for the first time it was her happiness that made him feel so good. He knew this was real love, to feel happy through the girl. The rest – the nightmares, her kidnapping and death – these things belonged to both past and present parallel worlds that should never again impinge on their lives.

He thought.

Until he went to the rest room for a pee. When he opened door he halted, for there stood Art Weissenbach. For a few moments, Adam merely stared at the man.

"You?"

Art nodded.

"Yeah! Me!"

"But – does Maria know? Who invited you? And what about Jeannie?"

"Jeannie? Let's just say she's trying to contain things. Till I return."

"The haulage business, you mean? You've been invited to the wedding, right? María wanted it kept a secret from me, I guess."

"Don't know nothin' about a wedding, son. Just came to deliver a warnin'. See, they both kinda felt something when María was there. The thing about who she is. You've gotta know this. They want her. Plus they once came from the world of man – from your dimension."

"But who – I mean you are the *real* Art, aren't you?"

Art laughed.

"Only ever been one of me," he said.

"But – in Xibalba – all that business about finding Art and Jeannie in my head? And the two Hero Twins becoming them – that is, you – to protect us from Zotz?"

"All true. Just think multiple realities. Like María and Princess Arima and – well the eleventh dimension too. If they allow it to happen."

"The Lords of Xibalba?"

Art nodded.

"They threaten to cross over. Never thought that could happen, and maybe it can't, but seems like they've found a new strength. Not just Life-Force. Comes from María and – if they get stronger and win the girl there will be no special child. Well – not as it's supposed to happen. Not yours. Could turn out to be the very opposite. A child of their dimension would destroy your world."

Just when Adam was beginning to feel all that business in the Chiapas had finally been consigned to his past it seemed as if his happiness would now take its place.

"You mean a child of María and – and one of them? The Lords of Xibalba?"

The jealous Adam fought to be free, to say "I told you so" then punch Art for suggesting such a thing.

"Only if you let it happen. My fear, Adam, is that you're not ready for the merging."

"The merging?"

"Yourself. The love you have from María and the beast I created."

"You mean – I turn into a giant goddamn cat?"

"No – I didn't say that. The merging! You'll find out pretty soon. And both of you will be tested to your limits, for only then can you finally be strong enough to overcome the evil Lords of Xibalba. See, I learned they've grown stronger. The other girl you love—"

"I've said it before and I'll say it again! There *is* no other girl. Chrissy in New York – she was nothing. I didn't even like her as a person. Only her legs!"

Art slowly shook his head.

"A very special girl! Listen to her. And watch over her as well as María! She may seem strong but she's also vulnerable and – and *very* young."

Of course, Adam had always known.

"Little Chloe, right?"

"I have to go, Adam. Do as she says."

"Wait – let me talk to my sister. Please."

Opening the rest room door, Adam looked for Chloe in the crowded restaurant but couldn't see her.

"I'll go find her. Ask her whether—" he began, but when he turned round Art was gone...

The story continues in 'The Merging' due out 2016...

Golden Jaguar of the Sun

Why did the ancient Anasazi Puebloans so abruptly leave their comfortable homes in the magnificent Mesa Verde canyons of Colorado in the thirteenth century?

What connection did they have with the forebears of the ancient Aztecs?

Because of Chloe, Adam's extraordinary little sister, Adam and María discover first hand the terrifying answers to these questions and learn from an ancient prophesy about the threat that Coyote Spirit poses for Leaping Jaguar and White Deer... and for the world.

But will Adam be closer to finding out who his girlfriend really is?

Ackowledgements: I am grateful to my wife and family for their patience and support, to friends and to fellow writers who have given me advice and encouragement and to the Native (First Nation) Peoples of North America whose communion with Nature inspired me, and from which the world has yet much to learn.

The Author

After Oliver Eade woke up one night with a ghost story in his head, he took to writing short stories, several winning prizes. During a visit to his Chinese wife's mother country in 2006, he became interested in Chinese mythology, thus inspiring his first middle grade readers' novel, *Moon Rabbit*. A winner of the Writers' and Artists' 2007 New Novel Competition and long-listed for the Waterstone's Children's Book Prize, 2008, this was followed by a sequel, *Monkey King's Revenge*, plus five other novels, one of which is also for young adults and another, set in ancient China, for adults.

Although not confined to any particular genre or style, Oliver feels most comfortable in that magical space between reality and fantasy; the space into and out of which children slip so easily in their play; the place of dreams, myths and legends and deeply ingrained in diverse cultures across the globe; the magical realism of Latin American writers like Gabriel García Márquez and Isabel Allende in her young adult trilogy.

The *Beast to God* trilogy was inspired by Native North American and Mesoamerican beliefs. Oliver lived and worked in Vermont, USA, for a year and his son and two half-Spanish eldest granddaughters live in Houston, Texas.

Website: www.olivereade.co.uk
Blogs:
http://olivereade.blogspot.co.uk/
http://runawaywheeliebin.blogspot.co.uk/
http://childrenaswriters.blogspot.co.uk/

Contact: olivereade@googlemail.com

Novels by Oliver Eade, most also available as e-books:

For middle grade readers:
Moon Rabbit: Stevie Scott from Peebles, Scotland befriends Maisie Wu, a new classmate from China, when she when she gets teased for being different. Early one morning he takes her to the river to see some ducklings, she falls in, can't swim and he dives in to rescue her. They emerge in mythological China and have to undertake a perilous mission before they can get back Peebles. A fun introduction to mythical Chinese beasts and legends.
Monkey King's Revenge: Sequel to *Moon Rabbit* (available as print book only).
The Rainbow Animal: Rachel takes her pet hamster for a birthday ride on a strange-looking animal at a local mall carousel only to end up embroiled in a paint war between the funny little Colorwallies and Dullabillies.
The Kelpie's Eyes: Two Scottish sisters are caught up in a battle to save one of them from the evil intentions of the Kelpie on the other side of a Scottish Borders waterfall, the Grey Mare's Tail. A tale of sisterly rivalry and love.

For young adults:
The Terminus: Oliver's debut young adult novel in which he returns to the city where he was brought up, a city now changed beyond recognition from the drab post-Word War

II era and which, in a post-apocalyptic world, gives Mankind a second chance: London.

For adults:

A Single Petal: A widowed village teacher in Tang Dynasty China links the death of his merchant friend with the disappearance of local Miao girls, endangering himself and his daughter as he digs more deeply into the mystery.

Lost Whispers: A collection of short stories inspired by travels across the globe.

Plays:

The Gap: Staged in Scotland 2012, a one act surreal comedy about a dysfunctional Peacehaven family split apart when the earth divides into two along the Greenwich Meridian. Short-listed for the *Rowan Tree One Act Play competition, 2009.*

Pool Britannia: Full-length farce about British ex-pats sharing a condominium pool with locals in Turkey. Short-listed for the Sussex *Playwrights' 80th Anniversary Competition, 2014.*

Give the Dog a Bone and ***The Other Nathan:*** One act black comedies, both long-listed for the *British Theatre Challenge, 2015.*

Other Mauve Square books:

For young readers:

Shadows from the Past series by Wendy Leighton-Porter. '*...Wendy has written a fantastic series of books (Shadows from the Past) filled with mystery, suspense, and adventure.*'

Firestorm Rising & ***Demons of the Dark*** by John Clewarth '*...Children learn that there are far more terrifying things in the universe than they ever learned at school, as a terrifying monster is awakened from a long hot sleep.*'

For adults:
Crying Through the Wind by Iona Carroll. '*...Sensitively written novel of love, intrigue and hidden family secrets set in post-war Ireland... one of those books you can't put down from the very first paragraph...*'
Familiar Yet Far by Iona Carroll. Second novel in *The Story of Oisin Kelly* trilogy follows the young Irishman in *Crying Through the Wind* from Ireland and Edinburgh to Australia where the author was born and broght up.
The Manhattan Deception, The Minerva System, Seven Stars and ***Bomber Boys*** by Simon Leighton-Porter. '*...Fast paced thriller with a plot which twists and turns.*' 'I loved it...' 'As soon as I picked this book up I knew I wouldn't be able to put it down...'

Lightning Source UK Ltd.
Milton Keynes UK
UKOW06f0044091015

260123UK00001B/3/P

9 781909 411357